21世纪英语专业系列教材

Linguistics:
An Elementary Course Book (Second Edition)

语言学基础教程
（第二版）

苗兴伟　◎主编
胡壮麟　◎主审

图书在版编目 (CIP) 数据

语言学基础教程 / 苗兴伟主编 .—2 版 .—北京：北京大学出版社，2018.7
（21 世纪英语专业系列教材）
ISBN 978-7-301-29658-5

Ⅰ．①语… Ⅱ．①苗… Ⅲ．①英语—语言学—高等学校—教材 Ⅳ．① H31

中国版本图书馆 CIP 数据核字 (2018) 第 136327 号

书　名	语言学基础教程（第二版） YUYANXUE JICHU JIAOCHENG（DI ER BAN）
著作责任者	苗兴伟　主编
责任编辑	刘文静
标准书号	ISBN 978-7-301-29658-5
出版发行	北京大学出版社
地　址	北京市海淀区成府路 205 号　100871
网　址	http://www.pup.cn　　新浪微博：@ 北京大学出版社
电子邮箱	编辑部 pupwaiwen@pup.cn　　总编室 zpup@pup.cn
电　话	邮购部 010-62752015　发行部 010-62750672　编辑部 010-62754382
印刷者	河北滦县鑫华书刊印刷厂
经销者	新华书店
	720 毫米 ×1020 毫米　16 开本　17 印张　300 千字 2010 年 7 月第 1 版 2018 年 7 月第 2 版　2024 年 11 月第 5 次印刷
定　价	58.00 元

未经许可，不得以任何方式复制或抄袭本书之部分或全部内容。
版权所有，侵权必究
举报电话：010-62752024　电子邮箱：fd@pup.cn
图书如有印装质量问题，请与出版部联系，电话：010-62756370

第二版前言

《语言学基础教程》自2010年出版以来,得到了语言学学习者和教师的广泛认可。当然,教材中也有一些问题和不足。在多次印刷中,我们曾经对教材中的个别细节做了适当修改。为使学生能够更为系统地掌握语言学知识,使《语言学基础教程》更好地服务于英语类专业的人才培养,我们决定对本书进行修订。在教材的使用过程中,我们也获得了许多教师和学生的反馈,为本次的修订工作提供了有用的信息。我们在认真梳理反馈的同时,对教材中存在的问题进行了分析,并于2017年底开始了《语言学基础教程》的修订工作。

在修订过程中,除了修改了语言表达方面的细节问题,重点对第六章、第七章和第十三章的内容做了修订。第六章主要增加了对理论的解释,以帮助学生更好地把握语用学的理论。第七章增加了批评话语分析的内容,以反映语篇分析的最新发展和前沿。第十三章增加了"语法化和词汇化"一节,目的使学生了解语法化和词汇化及其背后的认知机制。为使学生巩固所学知识并进一步学习有关知识,拓展语言学学习和研究的空间,每章增加了"深入阅读"(further reading)书单。其他方面的修订就不一一介绍了,希望修订后的《语言学基础教程》能以全新的面目出现在大家的面前,更好地满足广大的语言学教师、学生和爱好者的需要。我们真诚地期待读者的鼓励和反馈,希望《语言学基础教程》在大家的帮助下不断成长。

参加修订本书各章的人员为:

第一章	严世清	苏州大学
第二章	董宏乐	复旦大学
第三章	李 力	厦门大学
第四章	刘世铸	山东大学
第五章	苗兴伟	北京师范大学
第六章	陈新仁	南京大学
第七章	常晨光	中山大学
第八章	向明友	对外经济贸易大学
第九章	陈毅平	暨南大学
第十章	苏立昌	南开大学

第十一章	朱　晔	浙江大学
第十二章	刘振前	山东大学
第十三章	文　旭	西南大学
第十四章	崔　刚	清华大学

感谢北京大学胡壮麟教授对本书的关心和鼓励，特别是在第一版的编写和出版过程中，胡壮麟教授为我们出谋划策，并对初稿提出了非常详细的修改意见，保证了本书的质量。感谢北京大学出版社外语部领导张冰女士和责任编辑刘文静女士对修订工作的大力支持和帮助。

热忱欢迎专家同行和读者一如既往地对本教材不吝赐教。

编者

2018 年 5 月 29 日

第一版前言

随着高等教育事业的发展和社会对高层次人才的需求的日益增长,本科生教材的正规化和系统化的必要性越来越明显。语言学知识在高等教育乃至整个社会发展中的作用已不言而喻。为使学生能够系统地掌握语言学知识,满足高校培养创新型、应用型人才的需要,我们应北京大学出版社的邀请编写了《语言学基础教程》(中、英文版)。

本教材的使用者主要为全国各高校英语专业的本科生。在内容方面,体现本科阶段课堂教学的特点,在提供基本知识的同时,更注重教材的科学性、系统性、实用性和时代性。在编写过程中,我们力求"化难为简",尽量做到概念清晰,既要保证知识的系统性,又要避免术语的堆砌。本教材在传授基本知识与概念的同时,通过丰富的实例提供了有关语言分析和描述的基本方法,同时强调语言学与其他学科的联系,以便适应创新型人才培养的需要。为使学生巩固所学知识并进一步学习有关知识,每一章后都有练习题,并列出了"深入阅读"书单。全书共有十四章,教师可以根据教学大纲的课时安排和课堂教学的需要,合理地安排教学。

《语言学基础教程》的作者是来自全国13所211工程大学的知名中青年学者,都是教学第一线的英语教师,具有丰富的语言学研究和教学经验。参加本书编写的人员为:

第一章	严世清	苏州大学
第二章	董宏乐	复旦大学
第三章	李 力	厦门大学
第四章	程晓堂	北京师范大学
	刘世铸	山东大学
第五章	苗兴伟	北京师范大学
	彭宣维	北京师范大学
第六章	陈新仁	南京大学
第七章	常晨光	中山大学
第八章	向明友	对外经济贸易大学
	赵学德	浙江理工大学

第九章	陈毅平	暨南大学
第十章	苏立昌	南开大学
第十一章	朱　晔	浙江大学
第十二章	刘振前	山东大学
第十三章	文　旭	西南大学
第十四章	崔　刚	清华大学

感谢北京大学胡壮麟教授在百忙之中担任本书的主审并为之作序。胡壮麟教授主编过多部语言学教材，为我国的语言学教学事业做出了巨大贡献。本书的作者也都是在胡教授的教材的引领下步入语言学殿堂的。在此我们谨以此书向胡壮麟教授表示敬意，并衷心地感谢他为本书的编写提出的宝贵建议。

我们还要衷心地感谢同济大学马秋武教授和浙江大学许力生教授对本书的关注和厚爱。感谢北京大学出版社刘强先生和宇航出版社姜军先生对本书的关心和支持。

由于编写人员来自不同的院校，每人分工写一部分，因而各章在写作风格和难易程度方面难免有不尽一致之处。虽然我们在统稿过程中进行了反复的修改和调整，谬误或疏漏在所难免。书中不当之处，恳请专家同行和读者批评指正。

编者

2009 年 10 月 16 日

第一版序

　　北京大学出版社外语部的领导和编者策划出版供英语专业学生使用的各种教材系列取得重大成就，受到高校英语专业教师的热烈欢迎，被列入教育部精品教材，但在这套系列中缺了有关英语语言学课程的教材，美中不足。我虽然编过《语言学教程》等多种教材，已无法归入这套系列，因此这个问题迟迟未能解决。与此同时，山东大学外国语学院副院长苗兴伟教授跃跃欲试，自愿张罗此事，我对此早有所闻，乐观其成。

　　此后，苗兴伟教授充分发挥了他的组织才能，拉起了一支庞大的编写队伍，并希望我在书成后写个序，我答应了。2009年7月份在北京清华大学主办的第36届国际系统功能语言学会议上，我从兴伟手中拿到书稿后，才发现我还要担任"主审"的任务。这时我才意识到自己犯了自不量力的错误。一则本人退休多年，已入老弱病残之列，掌握新知识有限，二则本书的作者均是我国学术界中生代的领军人物，不是教授博士，就是院长主任；三则我给不同出版社友情打工多年，尚未脱手的任务众多，加之国内外这个会议那个会议未见有尽头之日，时间上赔不起。

　　这样，所谓"主审"是仓促上阵的，虚有其名。恳求读者不要把"主审"二字看得太重，而是把我看作一个学习本教材的第一批学生。除了在眼所能及的范围内提出一些印刷错误外，我的学习心得报告如下：首先，本教材各章作者均是有关学科的佼佼者，功底扎实，保证了教材的学术性；第二，本教材作者有第一线教学的丰富经验，做到了论述深入浅出，适合本科生的需要；第三，本教材注意到有关学科在本世纪的最新进展，具有充分的时代性。

　　国庆和中秋长假，使我得以把大部分时间投入此项任务，借花献佛，以表我对北京大学出版社外语部和各位作者的钦佩之情，更表我对祖国六十华诞的无限喜悦！

胡壮麟
北京大学蓝旗营
2009年10月9日

CONTENTS

Chapter 1　Language and Linguistics ·················· (1)
1.1　What is Language ·················· (1)
1.2　The Design Features of Language ·················· (3)
1.3　The Origin of Language ·················· (4)
1.4　What is Linguistics ·················· (5)
1.5　The Scope of Linguistics ·················· (7)
1.6　A Brief History of Linguistics ·················· (9)
　　1.6.1　Saussure as the Father of Modern Linguistics ·················· (9)
　　1.6.2　American Structuralism ·················· (10)
　　1.6.3　Generative Linguistics ·················· (11)
　　1.6.4　Functional Linguistics ·················· (12)

Chapter 2　Phonetics and Phonology: The Sounds and Sound Patterns of Language ·················· (14)
2.1　Introduction ·················· (14)
2.2　Phonetics ·················· (14)
　　2.2.1　Speech Organs ·················· (15)
　　2.2.2　Consonants ·················· (16)
　　2.2.3　Vowels ·················· (18)
　　2.2.4　Transcription of Speech Sounds ·················· (20)
2.3　Phonology ·················· (21)
　　2.3.1　Phoneme ·················· (21)
　　2.3.2　Phone and Allophone ·················· (22)
　　2.3.3　Phonotactics ·················· (22)
　　2.3.4　Prosodic Features: Stress, Tone and Intonation ·················· (25)
　　2.3.5　Co-articulation Effects ·················· (26)

2.4　Summary …………………………………………… (27)

Chapter 3　Morphology: The Word Structure of
**　　　　　 Language** ……………………………………… (30)
3.1　Introduction ………………………………………… (30)
3.2　The Words of Language …………………………… (30)
3.3　The Structure of Words …………………………… (31)
3.4　Morpheme, Morph and Allomorph ……………… (32)
3.5　Classification of Morphemes ……………………… (33)
　　3.5.1　Free Morphemes and Bound Morphemes …… (33)
　　3.5.2　Roots and Affixes ……………………………… (33)
　　3.5.3　Inflectional Morphemes and Derivational
　　　　　 Morphemes …………………………………… (33)
3.6　Word Formation Processes ………………………… (34)
　　3.6.1　Derivation ……………………………………… (35)
　　3.6.2　Compounding ………………………………… (36)
　　3.6.3　Conversion …………………………………… (38)
　　3.6.4　Blending ……………………………………… (39)
　　3.6.5　Backformation ………………………………… (39)
　　3.6.6　Abbreviation or Shortening ………………… (39)
3.7　Summary …………………………………………… (40)

Chapter 4　Syntax: The Sentence Structure of Language …… (42)
4.1　Introduction ………………………………………… (42)
4.2　Sentence Structure ………………………………… (43)
　　4.2.1　Definition of Sentence ………………………… (43)
　　4.2.2　The Linear Structure of Sentence …………… (43)
　　4.2.3　The Hierarchical Structure of Sentence ……… (44)
4.3　The Traditional Approach ………………………… (44)
4.4　The Structural Approach …………………………… (46)
　　4.4.1　Immediate Constituent Analysis …………… (46)
　　4.4.2　Endocentric and Exocentric Constructions …… (47)
4.5　The Transformational-generative Approach ……… (48)
　　4.5.1　The TG Model of Grammar ………………… (48)

  4.5.2 Syntactic Structure ……………………… (50)
  4.5.3 Movement ………………………………… (57)
4.6 The Functional Approach ……………………… (62)
  4.6.1 Functions of Language ………………… (62)
  4.6.2 Functional Analysis of Syntactic Structure …… (64)
4.7 Summary ……………………………………… (65)

Chapter 5 Semantics: The Meaning of Language ……… (68)

5.1 Introduction …………………………………… (68)
5.2 Approaches to Meaning ……………………… (68)
5.3 Sense and Reference ………………………… (70)
5.4 Word Meaning ………………………………… (71)
  5.4.1 Grammatical Meaning and Lexical
     Meaning ………………………………… (71)
  5.4.2 Classification of Lexical Meaning ………… (71)
  5.4.3 Sense Relations ………………………… (74)
  5.4.4 Semantic Field ………………………… (79)
5.5 Sentence Meaning ……………………………… (79)
  5.5.1 Definition of Sentence Meaning ………… (79)
  5.5.2 Semantic Relations at the Sentential
     Level …………………………………… (80)
5.6 Ambiguity ……………………………………… (82)
5.7 Semantic Analysis …………………………… (83)
  5.7.1 Componential Analysis ………………… (83)
  5.7.2 Predication Analysis …………………… (84)

Chapter 6 Pragmatics: The Use of Language in Context …… (89)

6.1 Introduction …………………………………… (89)
6.2 Pragmatics as a New Branch of Linguistics ……… (89)
  6.2.1 Defining Pragmatics …………………… (89)
  6.2.2 Syntax, Semantics and Pragmatics ……… (92)
6.3 Speech Act Theory …………………………… (93)
  6.3.1 Constatives and Performatives ………… (93)
  6.3.2 Locution, Illocution, and Perlocution …… (94)

  6.3.3 Felicity Conditions ……………………… (95)

  6.3.4 Classification of Speech Acts ………… (96)

6.4 Theory of Conversational Implicature ………… (97)

  6.4.1 The Notion of Implicature ……………… (97)

  6.4.2 Cooperative Principle and Its Maxims …… (99)

  6.4.3 Flouting the Maxims …………………… (100)

6.5 Politeness Principle ………………………………… (101)

  6.5.1 Politeness: The Principle and the Maxims … (101)

  6.5.2 Clashes Between the Maxims ……………… (102)

6.6 Summary …………………………………………… (103)

Chapter 7 Discourse Analysis: Language Above the Sentence ……………………………………… (106)

7.1 Introduction ………………………………………… (106)

7.2 What is Discourse Analysis ……………………… (106)

7.3 Cohesion …………………………………………… (107)

  7.3.1 Reference …………………………………… (107)

  7.3.2 Substitution ………………………………… (109)

  7.3.3 Ellipsis ……………………………………… (109)

  7.3.4 Conjunction ………………………………… (110)

  7.3.5 Lexical Cohesion …………………………… (111)

7.4 Coherence ………………………………………… (112)

7.5 The Structure of Discourse ……………………… (114)

  7.5.1 Thematic Structure and Information Structure ……………………………………… (115)

  7.5.2 The Structure of Conversations ………… (119)

  7.5.3 Patterns in Written Discourse …………… (121)

7.6 Critical Discourse Analysis ……………………… (122)

7.7 Conclusion ………………………………………… (124)

Chapter 8 Historical Linguistics: Language through Time ………………………………… (127)

8.1 Introduction ………………………………………… (127)

8.2 When Language Changes ………………………… (127)

8.3 How Language Changes ……… (129)
    8.3.1 Phonological Change ……… (129)
    8.3.2 Lexical Change ……… (130)
    8.3.3 Grammatical Change ……… (133)
8.4 Why Language Changes ……… (135)
    8.4.1 External Causes ……… (135)
    8.4.2 Internal Causes ……… (135)
8.5 Summary ……… (136)

Chapter 9 Stylistics: Language and Literature ……… (138)
9.1 Introduction ……… (138)
9.2 Important Views on Style ……… (138)
    9.2.1 Style as Deviation ……… (139)
    9.2.2 Style as Choice ……… (139)
    9.2.3 Style as Foregrounding ……… (140)
9.3 Stylistic Analysis ……… (140)
    9.3.1 Phonological Analysis ……… (140)
    9.3.2 Graphological Analysis ……… (143)
    9.3.3 Lexical Analysis ……… (144)
    9.3.4 Syntactic Analysis ……… (145)
    9.3.5 Semantic Analysis ……… (147)
    9.3.6 Pragmatic Analysis ……… (150)

Chapter 10 Sociolinguistics: Language and Society ……… (158)
10.1 Introduction ……… (158)
10.2 The Relations Between Language and Society ……… (158)
10.3 Speech Community and Speech Variety ……… (160)
10.4 Dialect ……… (162)
    10.4.1 Regional Dialect ……… (162)
    10.4.2 Social Dialect ……… (163)
    10.4.3 Standard Dialect ……… (166)
10.5 Register ……… (166)
10.6 Language Contact and Contact Languages ……… (167)
    10.6.1 Lingua Franca ……… (167)

　　　　10.6.2　Pidgin ··· (168)
　　　　10.6.3　Creole ·· (168)
　　10.7　Choosing a Code ·· (168)
　　　　10.7.1　Diglossia ·· (169)
　　　　10.7.2　Bilingualism ·· (169)
　　　　10.7.3　Code-switching ······································ (170)

**Chapter 11　Intercultural Communication:
　　　　　　Language and Culture** ·································· (172)
　　11.1　Introduction ··· (172)
　　11.2　Definitions of Culture ······································· (172)
　　11.3　The Relationship Between Language and
　　　　　Culture ··· (173)
　　11.4　Naming the World Through Language ············· (174)
　　　　11.4.1　Color Terms ··· (174)
　　　　11.4.2　Kinship Terms ······································ (175)
　　　　11.4.3　Culture-loaded Words ······························ (176)
　　11.5　Communicative Patterns Across Cultures ········ (177)
　　　　11.5.1　Address Forms ····································· (177)
　　　　11.5.2　Greetings ··· (178)
　　　　11.5.3　Giving and Accepting Compliments ········ (179)
　　　　11.5.4　High Context Versus Low Context ········ (180)
　　11.6　Language and Thought: Sapir-Whorf
　　　　　Hypothesis ··· (181)
　　11.7　Intercultural Communication ·························· (183)
　　　　11.7.1　Intercultural Communication as a Field of
　　　　　　　Research ··· (183)
　　　　11.7.2　Conquering Obstacles in Intercultural
　　　　　　　Communication ······································ (183)
　　　　11.7.3　Value Dimensions ·································· (184)
　　11.8　Summary ·· (186)

Chapter 12 Psycholinguistics: Language and Psychology (188)
12.1 Introduction (188)
12.2 Language and the Brain: The Biological Foundations of Language (188)
    12.2.1 Cerebral Lateralization and Language Functions (188)
    12.2.2 Evidence of Lateralization (189)
12.3 Language Comprehension (189)
    12.3.1 Human Information Processing System (190)
    12.3.2 The Mental Lexicon (191)
    12.3.3 Sentence Comprehension (193)
    12.3.4 Discourse Comprehension (195)
12.4 Language Production (196)
12.5 Language Acquisition (198)
    12.5.1 First Language, Second Language and Foreign Language (198)
    12.5.2 First Language Acquisition (199)
    12.5.3 Second Language Acquisition (201)

Chapter 13 Cognitive Linguistics: Language and Cognition (206)
13.1 Introduction (206)
13.2 Categories and Categorization (206)
13.3 Conceptual Metaphors (208)
13.4 Conceptual Metonymies (210)
13.5 Image Schemas (211)
13.6 Iconicity (213)
    13.6.1 Iconicity of Order (213)
    13.6.2 Iconicity of Distance (214)
    13.6.3 Iconicity of Complexity (214)
13.7 Grammaticalization and Lexicalization (215)

Chapter 14　Applied Linguistics: Language Teaching and Learning ………… (218)
14.1　Introduction ………… (218)
14.2　How is Language Learned? ………… (218)
　14.2.1　Behaviorism ………… (218)
　14.2.2　The Innateness Hypothesis: Universal Grammar ………… (219)
　14.2.3　Interlanguage Theory ………… (220)
　14.2.4　The Input Hypothesis ………… (221)
　14.2.5　The Output Hypothesis ………… (221)
14.3　Individual Differences in Language Learning ………… (222)
　14.3.1　Language Aptitude ………… (222)
　14.3.2　Learning Style ………… (222)
　14.3.3　Motivation ………… (223)
　14.3.4　Anxiety ………… (224)
　14.3.5　Learning Strategies ………… (224)
14.4　Approaches and Methods in Foreign Language Teaching ………… (225)
　14.4.1　The Grammar-Translation Method ………… (225)
　14.4.2　The Direct Method ………… (226)
　14.4.3　The Audiolingual Method ………… (227)
　14.4.4　The Communicative Approach ………… (227)
　14.4.5　The Task-based Approach ………… (229)
14.5　Language Testing ………… (229)
　14.5.1　Types of Test ………… (230)
　14.5.2　Qualities of a Good Test ………… (231)

References ………… (234)
Glossary ………… (242)

Chapter 1

Language and Linguistics

1.1 What is Language

Language is something that we use almost every day, but we will feel at a loss when asked to define what language is. A most common definition of language might be: Language is a means of human communication. The merit of this definition consists in its brevity and popularity among users of language, yet it does not necessarily follow that it is an adequate definition. For example, it points out only the instrumental aspect of language and does not actually tell us what language is. Suppose someone has never seen a train and asks you what a train is. Do you think he or she will be satisfied with a simple answer like "a train is a means of transportation"? Furthermore, the term human communication also needs further explanation, because communication can happen in various forms, such as gestures, pictures, smoke signals, traffic lights, noises in the throat, or even occasionally secret codes, but none of them can be regarded as language.

The above-mentioned definition of language is not exhaustive in many other aspects as well.

First of all, we have been talking about "language", rather than "a language", "the languages" or "languages". In other words, we use the word "language" in the singular form without the definite or indefinite article, but the word can certainly be used in other forms. We can talk about languages, because there are several thousand kinds of languages in the world, although the total number of world languages has been decreasing since the twentieth century. Thus, the language we use or learn is only a language shared by a certain number of people.

Second, we can also use the word "language" to refer to some special features of language use by an individual or people in a certain period of history, such as Shakespearean language or nineteenth century language. Indeed, some radical linguists even argue that everyone's use of language is unique or that language is changing all the time, which might create obstacles to communication. That explains why a teacher sometimes may not understand the jargons used among students.

There are many other uses of the word "language". The *Webster's Dictionary* (*Third Edition*) *provides* 13 annotations of the word and perhaps this list is still not yet exhaustive. It can be argued that the dictionary definition of a word is not academic enough, but the situation is even more complicated among linguists, who tend to provide definitions of language from their own theoretical perspectives. Or to put it the other way round, the way a linguist defines language indicates the theoretical perspective that the linguist takes. The following definitions of language are quoted from John Lyons' (1981: 3—7) *Language and Linguistics*:

- According to Sapir (1921), "language is a purely human and non-instinctive method of communicating ideas, emotions and desires by means of voluntarily produced symbols."
- According to Blochand Trager (1942), "a language is a system of arbitrary vocal symbols by means of which a social group co-operates."
- Hall (1968) defines language as "the institution whereby humans communicate and interact with each other by means of habitually used oral-auditory symbols."
- Chomsky (1957) points out that a language is "a set (finite or infinite) of sentences, each finite in length and constructed out of a finite set of elements."

The list of definitions of language can be continued, but we can detect from the above definitions the common aspects of language that linguists generally agree upon and a summary of these common aspects can serve as a definition of language of our own. To begin with, language is a system, which means that language consists of a finite set of interrelated elements that can be combined according to rules. Second, language is a system of vocal symbols, which suggests that spoken forms are more cardinal to a language than written forms. Illiterate people can communicate with others at ease even though they do not know how to read and write. Third, communication is an important aspect of the function of language though language can also be said to perform other functions. If we look at language from the angle of the relationship between people, we can argue that language is a means of human interaction. If we look into the psychological aspect of language, we will see language as a kind of knowledge that language speakers share. Fourth, the language we study in linguistics is human language in general, although other forms of communication can also be touched upon and may shed new light on human linguistic communication. Fifth, language is arbitrary in the sense that the relation between speech sounds (form) and the ideas the sounds convey (meaning) is arbitrary.

To sum up, language can be defined as a system of arbitrary vocal symbols used for human communication and interaction.

1.2 The Design Features of Language

The structural linguist C. F. Hockett (1958) proposed a set of key properties of human language, which are said to be the **design features** that distinguish human language from the system of communication in any other species, such as bees' dancing, birds' singing and even music. Hockett identified 13 features, and later linguists differ from each other as to the number, name and perhaps importance of these features. However, most linguists would recognize the following features as most important, that is, arbitrariness, duality, productivity, displacement and cultural transmission.

Arbitrariness, as a property of language, means that there is no intrinsic relation between sound and meaning. In Saussure's terms, arbitrariness refers to the arbitrariness of the relation between sound image and concept. As Hudson (1984: 19) puts it, there is no reason why we attach the meaning "animal with a grunt and a curly tail" to the sequence of sounds *p-i-g* other than the (perfectly good) reason that this is what we found others doing in our particular community when we arrived on the scene, so we are simply following their example. What Juliet says in Shakespeare's *Romeo and Juliet* makes a lot of sense: "What's in a name? That which we call a rose by any other name would smell as sweet." From this quotation we can say that what matters is what something is, not what or how it is called. This reveals the truth about the arbitrariness of language. Arbitrariness can also be illustrated by cross-linguistic evidence: different sounds are used to signify the same object in different languages. To put it the other way round, the same meaning is represented by different sounds in different languages.

Duality is the property of having two levels of structure or patterning. At the primary, higher level, language is analyzed in terms of combinations of meaningful units (such as morphemes or words); at the secondary, lower level, language is composed of a sequence of segments (phonological units) which do not have any intrinsic meaning but combine to form units of meaning. For instance, in the sentence *He goes to school*, at the first higher level, the sentence consists of meaningful units, *he*, *go*, *-es* (a morpheme indicating third person singular number), *to*, *school*. At the lower level, these meaningful units are made up of phonological units, /h/, /iː/, /g/, /əʊ/, etc. As individual sounds, these units do not have any meaning in themselves. Therefore, duality is also termed double articulation. The articulation of words or other meaningful units is the primary articulation, that of phonological units within words the secondary articulation. Duality is a design feature that enables language to be productive, because language users can use or produce a large number of forms by combining a relatively small number of lower-level elements in a variety of different ways.

Productivity, also termed **creativity**, refers to the creative capacity of language users to produce and understand an infinitely large number of sentences, including sentences they have never used or heard before. Productivity is one of the distinctive features of human language because it allows novel combinations of elements and thus contrasts with the "unproductive" communication systems of animals.

Displacement means that human beings can talk about objects or events which do not belong to the immediate setting in space and time. This is a very normal property of communication in human beings, rarely demonstrated in other species. As Bertrand Russell once said, no matter how eloquently a dog may bark, he cannot tell you that his parents were poor but honest. Human language can be used to talk about real or imagined matters in the past, present, or future. We can write science fictions, tell fairy tales, handle generalizations and abstractions, and even lie and deceive by means of language. This is the chief reason why linguists tend to believe that language is a more distinctive feature of human species than any other features like the use of tools or the size of brain, etc.

Cultural transmission means the transmission of language from one generation to the next through members of a society as opposed to genetic inheritance. In other words, the details of the linguistic system must be learned anew by each speaker. Though the capacity for language in the human being has a genetic basis, the particular language one learns is a cultural fact rather than a genetic one.

1.3 The Origin of Language

Although interest in the origin of language dates back to antiquity, we are still far from knowing when and how language arose. There are three well-known theories concerning the origin of language: the divine-origin theory, the invention theory and the evolution theory.

The divine-origin theory suggests that language is God's gift to mankind. According to *Genesis* of the Bible, God created Adam and gave him the power to name all things. Similar stories can be found in many religions of the world about a divine source who endows humans with language.

The invention theory maintains that language is a human invention. This theory is manifested in the five theories summarized by the Danish linguist Otto Jespersen (1922) with the following names:

- **The bow-wow theory**: Language originated by the imitation of natural sounds such as animal calls. The evidence for this theory is the existence of onomatopoeic words in language.
- **The pooh-pooh theory**: Language arose from instinctive cries of emotion, such as pain, anger, pleasure, fear and surprise. This theory can be supported by the interjections in language.
- **The ding-dong theory**: Language arose out of people's responses to the things around them by sounds. The original sounds people made were supposedly in harmony with the world around them. This can be explained by **sound symbolism**, which is the phenomenon that vocal sounds suggest meaning. One frequently cited example is the "gl-" words for shiny things: *glisten, gleam, glint, glare, glam, glimmer, glaze, glass, glitz, gloss, glory, glow, and glitter*. Similar to the ding-dong theory, the **oral-gesture theory** suggests that language is an oral mirror of physical gestures through the movement of the tongue, lips and other vocal organs. One possible example is the oral gesture (movement of the tongue) in a "goodbye" message as a vocal mimicry of the physical gesture (waving of the hand or arm).
- **The yo-he-ho theory**: Language developed out of the rhythmical grunts of humans working together. Examples supporting this theory are the prosodic features, especially of rhythm in language.
- **The la-la theory**: Language derived from sounds associated with the romantic aspect of life, such as song, love, art and poetry.

The evolution theory maintains that language developed in the course of the evolution of the human species. The development of language is closely related to the evolutionary development of the speech organs, especially the oral cavity and the pharyngeal cavity. For example, the shapes of human teeth, lips and the tongue evolved in such a way that enables humans to produce a variety of speech sounds. However, some people think that the major evolutionary step in the development of language relates to evolutionary changes in the brain (Fromkin & Rodman, 1983: 28). As Yule (1996/2000: 5) puts it, there is an evolutionary connection between the tool-using and language-using abilities of humans, as both are related to the development of the human brain and are largely confined to the left hemisphere of the brain for most humans. The evolution theory seems to provide a better explanation for the origin of language than the divine-origin theory and the invention theory.

1.4 What is Linguistics

Linguistics is often defined as the science of language or as the scientific study of language. However, people constantly challenge the possibility of rendering linguistics scientific, because it is first and foremost the study of language by means of language and thus people have every reason to suspect whether linguistic theories are simply the result of linguists' play on words. Furthermore, linguistics clearly belongs to the humanities and social sciences, which are obviously different from disciplines like physics, chemistry or biology, whose scientific status is unquestioned.

Linguistics is a science because linguists share the goal of scientific enquiry, which is objective understanding. The primary aim of linguistics is to understand the nature of language and of languages. Linguists attempt to construct theories of language, and to apply theoretical considerations to a description or analysis of language or languages. Objectivity is the most important principle of the scientific method. In order to obtain objectivity in linguistic study, linguists should see and describe a language as it is, not as what they think it ought to be. Language is something that we tend to take for granted, something with which we are familiar from childhood in a practical and unquestioning manner. As a result, there are some biases that we assume to be truth but are actually unjustifiable. For example, people tend to believe that their own language is the easiest to learn, but scientific study shows that learning a foreign language is equally difficult or easy if you like, though there are rare cases of individuals who seem to be talented for learning new languages. Another deep-rooted bias is that only the standard variety is the pure or correct form of a language, such as the kind of English spoken by BBC and VOA announcers or the kind of Mandarin Chinese spoken by CCTV news broadcasters.

Linguistics is scientific in its methodology. It is concerned with observing facts about language, setting up hypotheses, testing their validity and accepting or rejecting them accordingly. To avoid biases of the kinds mentioned above, modern linguists differ from traditional grammarians in adopting empirical rather than speculative or intuitive approaches in their study. Here follows the first distinction between modern linguistics and **traditional grammar**. That is, linguistics is descriptive rather than prescriptive. That is, linguists try to make statements which are testable, and take language as it is rather than say how it should be. The empirical approach to language that linguists adopt usually consists of four stages: data collection (usually in the form of a corpus), tentative rule construction, tentative rule examination and rule finalization. Unlike the traditional grammarians, linguists do not believe that there is any absolute standard of correctness concerning language use which school teachers should view as their duty to maintain. Instead, linguists prefer to be observers or recorders of facts.

The second contrast between modern linguistics and traditional grammar is that linguistics regards spoken rather than written language as primary. Traditional grammar tends to emphasize the importance of written language and the writings or styles of classical writers are considered the most prestigious (if not the best) form of language that learners should imitate. Linguists, however, give priority to spoken language, though written language is also part of linguistic research.

Thirdly, linguistics differs from traditional grammar in that it does not force languages into a Latin-based framework. In the past, Latin was considered the language that provided a universal grammar for all languages and other languages were forced to fit into Latin patterns and categories, especially its case system and tense divisions of past, present and future.

It must be emphasized, however, that linguistics, like any other discipline, builds on the past, not only by challenging and refuting traditional doctrines but also by developing and reformulating them. When criticizing traditional grammar for being unscientific, linguists do not deny altogether the contributions of traditional grammar to the development of modern linguistics. A balanced view on traditional grammar, therefore, is needed in order to track down the continuity of Western linguistic theories from the earliest times to the present day (See Chapter 4 for a detailed discussion of traditional grammar).

1.5 The Scope of Linguistics

Language has been studied from different points of view. As a result, different dimensions of linguistics can be distinguished according to the point of view that is adopted or the special emphasis that is laid on certain aspects of language. Thus, the distinctions in the field of linguistic studies can provide a window on the scope of language.

The first distinction to be made is between general and descriptive linguistics. **General linguistics** deals with language, aiming at developing a theory that describes the rules of human language in general. **Descriptive linguistics**, on the other hand, is the study of particular languages, attempting to construct models that describe the rules of individual languages like Chinese, English and Russian. However, it should be made clear that general linguistics and descriptive linguistics are by no means unrelated. Instead, each depends on the other explicitly or implicitly. For example, general linguistics provides descriptive linguistics with a general framework in which a particular language can be studied.

The second distinction to be drawn is between **diachronic linguistics** and **synchronic linguistics**. The former is the study of language change, such as the changes in grammar from Old English to Modern English; the latter is the study of a language existing in a "state" at one particular point in time, regardless of its historical change, for example, the grammar of Old English or Modern English. In the nineteenth century, linguists were chiefly concerned with investigating the historical development of particular languages and formulating hypotheses about language change. Such an approach to the historical development of language was termed diachronic description of language by the Swiss linguist Ferdinand de Saussure, who argued that priority should be given to the synchronic description of language, that is, the study of language as it is at some particular point in time.

The third distinction is between **theoretical linguistics** and **applied linguistics**. According to Lyons (1981: 35), "theoretical linguistics studies language and languages with a view to constructing a theory of their structure and functions and without regard to any practical applications that the investigation of language and languages might have, whereas applied linguistics has as its concerns the application of the concepts and findings of linguistics to a variety of practical tasks, including language-teaching." Two points are especially worthy of note here. First, the distinction between theoretical linguistics and applied linguistics does not entail that there is no theoretical concerns in applied linguistics at all. Instead, hypothesis formulation and confirmation are also of vital importance to applied linguistics. Secondly, in talking about the distinction between theoretical linguistics and applied linguistics, people generally neglect the distinction between theoretical linguistics and general linguistics. As illustrated by Lyons (1981: 35), "the goal of theoretical linguistics is the formulation of a satisfactory theory of the structure of language in general."

General linguistics attempts to establish a workable theory of language at all levels. On the basis of the stratification of language and the corresponding foci of study, we can further divide general linguistics into several sub-branches, that is, phonetics, phonology, morphology, syntax, semantics. These areas are traditionally said to form the core of linguistics, because they deal with the mostly formally structured aspects of language. Although the primary object of description for linguists is the structure of language, many linguists study this in relation to its functions and in relation to social and cultural factors. As a result, pragmatics has come to be regarded as a branch of study in general linguistics.

In contrast with the core of linguistics, there are also branches of linguistics often called **macrolinguistics** where there is an interdisciplinary and applied orientation. Linguists have drawn on recent discoveries or developments from other areas of study and come up with enlightening views on language. This leads to the emergence of studies like psycholinguistics, sociolinguistics, cognitive linguistics, anthropological linguistics, computational linguistics, forensic linguistics, applied linguistics, and so on. Studies in all these aspects contribute from different perspectives to the edifice of linguistics as a whole.

1.6 A Brief History of Linguistics

Linguistics dates back to more than 2000 years ago and scholars from different civilizations have all contributed to the study of language. For example, linguistics is termed Xiaoxue (The Primary Learning) in ancient China and perhaps Xunzi is the first philosopher in the world who pointed out the arbitrary relationship between Name (名) and Object(实). In the Indian culture, the grammarian Pānini dealt with rules of word formation in the Indian language systematically, in the form of a set of 4000 aphoristic statements, in the era between 5th and 7th centuries B. C. The Western linguistic tradition can be traced back to ancient Greek times around 500 B. C. Serious considerations of linguistic issues can be found in the writings of Plato and Aristotle. Modern linguistics evolves from the Western tradition of linguistic study, which is greatly influenced by the pioneering work of the Swiss linguist Ferdinand de Saussure.

1.6.1 Saussure as the Father of Modern Linguistics

Saussure is considered the father of modern linguistics because the book under his name *Course in General Linguistics* is the first systematic elaboration on linguistic theory. Published in 1916, three years after Saussure's death, the book was actually a collection of the notes taken by his students during his lectures. Saussure's central ideas were expressed in the form of pairs of concepts called **dichotomy**: diachronic versus synchronic, langue versus parole, signifiant versus signifié, and syntagmatic versus paradigmatic.

We have mentioned above the distinction between **diachronic** and **synchronic** approaches to language. The former sees language as a continually changing medium; the latter views it as a living whole, existing in a "state" at a particular moment in time. Saussure's ideas were revolutionary in this aspect because he called for the priority of synchronic study of language, which was opposed to the nineteenth century historical linguistic tradition. According to Saussure, it is always necessary to carry out synchronic work: Before we can say how a language changed from State X to State Y, we should know something about X and Y.

Langue and **parole** are recognized by Saussure as two important aspects of language. Langue is the totality of a language or the abstract language system shared by all the members of a speech community, while parole is the realization of langue in actual use, that is, the concrete act of speaking at a particular time and in a specific situation.

Signifiant and **signifié** are the two aspects of meaning in a linguistic sign. Signifiant (signifier) refers to the thing that signifies, and signifié (signified) is the thing or concept signified. The relationship between them is seen by Saussure as arbitrary.

Syntagmatic and **paradigmatic relations** are employed by Saussure to describe the relationships between linguistic signs. When the signs are seen as a linear sequence, the relationship between them is syntagmatic. A paradigmatic (or "associative") relation is a relation between a linguistic sign in an utterance and other signs in the language. These two dimensions of structures can be applied to phonology, vocabulary, or any other aspect of language, rendering the conception of language as a vast network of interrelated structures and mutually defining entities, a linguistic system.

1.6.2 American Structuralism

The American linguistic tradition chiefly originated from the American anthropologists' concern to establish adequate description of the American Indian languages and cultures on the brink of extinction. Since the American Indian languages presented drastically different kinds of structure from the European languages, and there were practically no written records to rely on, anthropologists had to develop some efficient and systematic procedures to provide a careful account of the speech patterns of the living languages. Among these anthropologists were scholars like Franz Boas and Edward Sapir, who were pioneering structural linguists as well.

American structuralism flourished from the 1920s to the late 1950s. The structural approach to language description and analysis was synthesized in the book *Language* (1933) by Leonard Bloomfield. This book dominated linguistic thinking for over 20 years and led to progress not only in the studies of phonetics, phonology, morphology and syntax of the American Indian languages but also in the descriptive studies of grammar and phonology of the English language. The Bloomfieldian approach was termed structuralism chiefly because it employed techniques to identify and classify features of linguistic structure, especially the analysis of sentences into constituent parts.

However, the influence of American structuralism diminished in the 1950s, especially after Noam Chomsky put forward the notions of generative linguistics as a reaction against structuralism.

Chapter 1
Language and Linguistics

1.6.3 Generative Linguistics

In 1957, the publication of Noam Chomsky's *Syntactic Structures* inaugurated the linguistic revolution known as **generative grammar**. Chomsky might have intended the book as a challenge to the structuralist tradition in America but the impact of this book has gone beyond its era and later proved to be a milestone in the history of modern linguistics.

Chomsky's theory on language is termed generative grammar or generative linguistics because it attempts to describe a native speaker's tacit grammatical knowledge by a system of rules that can generate the well-formed, or grammatical, sentences of a language while excluding all the ungrammatical, or impossible, sentences. The basic tenets of the Chomskyan view on language in the early days are expressed in a set of terms or hypotheses he proposed, including the dichotomy between competence and performance, universal grammar, deep structure and surface structure, and transformational rules.

To Chomsky, linguistics should discover the mental realities underlying the way people use language and thus he proposed the distinction between **competence** and **performance**. Competence refers to an ideal speaker's knowledge of his language as manifest in his ability to produce and understand a theoretically infinite number of sentences. Performance refers to the actual use of the language by individuals in speech and writing. Chomsky argues that linguistics should be chiefly concerned with the study of competence rather than restrict itself to performance. That is, linguistic research should not be conducted on the basis of samples or collected data of language users' performance. Such samples are inadequate because they might contain many non-fluencies, changes of speech plan, slips of the tongue and other defects.

Chomsky argues that linguistics not only aims to provide an adequate account of competence in one language, but also attempts to establish principles of grammar shared by all languages, that is, the **universal grammar**, which can in the long term, shed light on the nature of human mind. The ambition that Chomsky cherishes stimulates a wide range of interest from scholars from many disciplines and has substantially influenced academic domains like psychology, pedagogy, computer science, artificial intelligence and even economics.

Another important pair of concept proposed by Chomsky is **deep structure** and **surface structure**. The major aim of generative grammar, according to him, is to provide a means of analyzing the process of deriving surface structures from deep structures. In his own practice in analyzing the English language, Chomsky put forward sets of generative rules and transformational rules, and it is precisely for this reason that Chomsky's theory is also termed **Transformational-**

generative (TG) grammar.

1.6.4 Functional Linguistics

Unlike generative linguistics, **functional linguistics** does not have one unanimously recognized leading figure, nor even generally acknowledged theoretical tenets. What we can be sure of is that early functional linguistics flourished chiefly in Europe, with scholars taking up Saussure's ideas and developing schools of thought that emphasized the study of functions of language in general, or the study of linguistic features in particular texts or contexts.

The first noteworthy school of functional linguistics is perhaps the **Prague School**, represented by linguists in Czechoslovakia, who founded the linguistic circle of Prague. Notably, the Prague School linguists emphasized the function of units and applied the idea to the study of phonology. The important concept of phoneme in distinguishing or demarcating words, for instance, is one of the contributions of the Prague School linguists. Leading figures in this school include Nikolais Trubetzkoy, Roman Jacobson and V. Mathesius, etc.

The **Copenhagen School** is a group of linguists who constituted the Copenhagen Linguistic Circle in the mid-1930s. Led by Louis Hjelmslev, the school developed a philosophical and logical basis for linguistic theory. They developed an approach to linguistics known as Glossematics or neo-Saussurean linguistics.

The **London School** is represented by the British linguist J. R. Firth and his followers. Distinguished from other theorists of his generation, Firth insisted that language should be studied as part of a social process. A linguist's data were for him events embedded in specific contexts and therefore he emphasized the importance of context in linguistic studies at all levels. In addition, he argued for the polysystemic principle of study, that is, the principle of analyzing language patterns with different systems within different contextual frameworks. Firth's influence is widespread and the **systemic linguistic school** established by his student M. A. K. Halliday has much in common with his notions and thus is sometimes termed the **neo-Firthian school.**

In America, functional linguistics flourished since the 1970s, when formalism still held sway, and became mature in the 1980s and 1990s. However, interest in functional approaches to language in America can be traced back to Franz Boas (1858—1942), Edward Sapir (1884—1939) and Benjamin Lee Whorf (1897—1941). In the 1960s—1970s, the contributions made by Dwight Bolinger, Wallace Chafe, Charles Fillmore and Charles Li paved the way for the development of functionalism in America. The major functional approaches include: Tagmemics, Case Grammar, Stratificational

Grammar, Discourse Grammar, Role and Reference Grammar, Cognitive Grammar, and so on.

Further Readings

Hudson, R. 1984. *Invitation to Linguistics*. Oxford: Blackwell.
Lyons, J. 1982. *Language and Linguistics*. Cambridge: Cambridge University Press.
Robins, R. H. 2002. *A Short History of Linguistics*. 北京:外语教学与研究出版社.
Traugott, E. C. & Pratt, M. L. 1980. *Linguistics for Students of Literature*. New York: Harcourt Brace Jovanovich, INC.
Yule, G. 2000. *The Study of Language*. 北京:外语教学与研究出版社.

Questions and Exercises

1. Define the following terms.
   - arbitrariness
   - duality
   - productivity
   - displacement
   - syntagmatic relation
   - paradigmatic relation
   - synchronic linguistics
   - diachronic linguistics
   - macrolinguistics
2. What is language?
3. How to tell the difference between human language and communication systems of animals?
4. Illustrate the design features of human language with examples.
5. In what sense is language arbitrary? Can you cite some examples to show that language is not arbitrary?
6. Why is displacement an important feature of human language?
7. Why is language seen as a distinctive property of human species? To what extent do you agree that language is a distinctive property of human species?
8. Among the different theories of the origin of language, which one do you think is most convincing?
9. In what sense is linguistics a science?
10. Say something about the difference between traditional grammar and linguistics.
11. Why is Saussure seen as the father of modern linguistics?
12. What is the significance of the distinction between diachronic and synchronic approaches to language study?
13. What are the differences between competence and performance? Is this dichotomy related in any way to Saussure's distinction between langue and parole?
14. What are the basic tenets of Structuralism?
15. Name some of the functional linguistic schools.

Chapter 2

Phonetics and Phonology: The Sounds and Sound Patterns of Language

2.1 Introduction

Human beings communicate with each other mainly in two modes of language—speaking and writing. In oral communication with someone from a different linguistic community, what first strikes us as different may not be that person's possibly different idea about something, but the exoticness of the speech sounds uttered.

Speech sounds are the sounds utilized by all human languages to represent meaning. They are the sounds produced or heard in using language to speak or understand, and are related by the language system to certain meanings. Anyone who knows a language knows what sounds are in the language and how they are "strung" together and what these different sound sequences mean (Fromkin & Rodman, 1983: 35). The study of human speech sounds can be done by examining the features of the sounds *per se* (Matthews, 2001: 33), which is adopted by the students of phonetics. The speech sounds can also be studied from the point of view of how they are actually used in different languages (Katamba, 1989: 66), including how some of the sounds interrelate and interact with each other within a given language system, which is adopted by the student of phonology.

2.2 Phonetics

The term "phonetics" is composed of *phone-*, which is from the Greek *phonê* meaning "sound" or "voice", and *-ics*, which means "a study of". So **phonetics** is the general study of the characteristics of speech sounds (Yule, 2006: 30). It is concerned with the physical properties of speech sounds (phones), and the processes of their physiological production, auditory reception, and neurophysiological perception. Thus, there are three branches of phonetics. The study of how speech sounds are made or "articulated" is called **articulatory phonetics**. The study of how speech sounds are perceived is called **auditory phonetics** (or **perceptual phonetics**). The study of the physical properties of speech sounds is called **acoustic phonetics**. The primary concern of

Chapter 2

Phonetics and Phonology: The Sounds and Sound Patterns of Language

phonetics is usually articulatory phonetics.

2.2.1 Speech Organs

The study of phonetics helps increase our awareness of the properties of speech sounds, which in turn can improve our ability to articulate them with accuracy by manipulating our **speech organs** more appropriately. The speech organs of the human beings consist of three major areas: the pharyngeal cavity (the throat), the oral cavity (the mouth) and the nasal cavity (the nose). The power source of our speech sounds is the flow of air from our lungs, and the air stream coming from the lungs may be modified in the cavities in various ways, resulting in different kinds of speech sounds.

In producing speech sounds, we start with the air pushed out of the lungs by the diaphragm, up through the trachea (or "windpipe") to the larynx. Inside the larynx are our vocal folds (also commonly known as vocal cords). When the vocal folds are spread apart, the air from the lungs passes without any restriction. Sounds thus produced are described as **voiceless**. Contrarily, if the vocal folds are drawn together, and the air from the lungs has to break through them repeatedly, creating a vibration effect, the sounds will be described as **voiced**. You can tell the distinction very easily between voiceless and voiced sounds by placing your fingertip gently on the tip of your "Adam's apple"—the part of the larynx in your neck below your chin. You will feel some vibration when you produce sounds like [z], but feel no vibration when you produce [s].

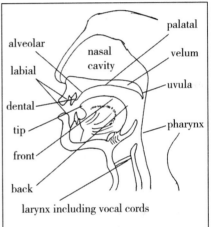

larynx including vocal cords

The oral cavity is made up of the tongue, the uvular, the soft palate (the velum), the hard palate (the palatal), the teeth ridge (the alveolar), the teeth (the dental) and the lips (the labial). Of these speech organs, the very flexible tongue is of particular importance, because the principal source of sound modification is the tongue, so much so that the word for it is often used as a synonym for language (Poole, 2000: 42).

The nasal cavity is a passage which is definitely open or closed, producing sounds either nasalized or non-nasalized.

All speech sounds are produced by manipulating the vocal tract while air is flowing through it. If this manipulation produces significant obstruction of the air stream, the result is a **consonant**. If it does not produce any obstruction, the result is a **vowel**. Thus, speech sounds can be classified into consonants and vowels according to whether the air stream coming from the lungs meets any obstruction in producing the sounds.

2.2.2 Consonants

Consonants can be described according to their **place of articulation** and **manner of articulation**, that is, where the air stream is modified and how it is modified.

2.2.2.1 Place of Articulation

After the air stream coming from the lungs passes through the larynx, it comes up and out through the mouth and/or the nose. Most of the 24 consonants in English are produced by using the tongue and other parts of the mouth to constrict the shape of the oral cavity through which the air is passing (Yule, 2006: 30). In other words, they are mostly articulated via closure or obstruction in the vocal tract. Consonants can be voiced or voiceless according to whether the vocal cords vibrate or not. The following terms are used to describe consonants in terms of where they are articulated.

A) Bilabials: These are sounds that are produced with the two (bi = two) lips (labia = lips). In English, bilabial consonants are [p], [m], [b], and [w]. Only [p] is voiceless, and the other three are all voiced.

B) Labiodentals: These are sounds that are produced with the lower lip and upper teeth. In English, there are only two labiodentals: [f] (voiceless) and [v] (voiced).

C) Interdentals: These are sounds that are produced with the tongue between (inter = between) the teeth, or just behind the upper teeth (also called "**dental**"), such as [θ] (voiceless) in words like *thin* and *bath*, and [ð] (voiced) in words like *there* and *then*.

D) Alveolars: These are sounds that are produced with the tongue tip at the alveolar ridge, behind the teeth. In English, there are 7 alveolars. They are [t], [d], [s], [z], [n], [l] and [r], of which [t] and [s] are voiceless and the others are all voiced.

E) Palatals: These are sounds that are produced with the front or body of the tongue raised to the palatal region. In English, palatals are [ʃ] (voiceless) in words like *ship* and *shout*, [tʃ] (voiceless) in words like *child* and *china*, [ʒ] (voiced) in words like *treasure* and *pleasure*, [dʒ] (voiced) in words like *bridge* and *joke*, and [j] (voiced) in words like *you* and *yet*.

F) Velars: These are sounds that are produced with the back of the tongue raised to the soft palate (also called "**velum**"). In English, there are three velars. They are [k] (voiceless) in words like *cold* and *kick*, [g] (voiced) in

Chapter 2

Phonetics and Phonology: The Sounds and Sound Patterns of Language

words like *go* and *bag*, and [ŋ] (voiced) in words like *sing* and *tongue*.

G) **Glottal**: In English, there is only one glottal, which is produced without an active use of the tongue and other parts of the mouth. It is [h] (voiceless). It is termed as such because the sound is produced with the glottis (the space between the vocal cords) open. In other words, there is no manipulation of the air passing out of the mouth.

2.2.2.2 Manner of Articulation

The 24 consonants can also be described in terms of how they are articulated, that is, how the air stream is modified. In producing consonants, the air stream from the lungs is either completely blocked (e.g. stops), partially blocked (e.g. laterals) or the opening is so narrow that the air escapes with audible friction (e.g. fricatives). With some consonants (e.g. nasals) the air stream is blocked in the mouth but allowed to escape through the nose.

A) **Stops**: Also called **plosives**, these are sounds produced by some form of "stopping" of the airstream very briefly then letting it go abruptly. Such sounds as [p], [b], [t], [d], [k], and [g] fall into this category.

B) **Affricates**: These are sounds produced by combining a brief stopping of the airstream with an obstructed release which causes some friction. The two consonants, [tʃ] and [dʒ], are affricates.

C) **Fricatives**: These are sounds produced by almost blocking the airstream and letting the air force through the narrow opening. They are termed as fricatives because when the air is pushed through, a kind of friction is produced. The fricative consonants are [f], [v], [s], [z], [ʃ], [ʒ], [θ] and [ð].

D) **Nasals**: These are sounds produced by allowing air to pass through the nose while blocked in the mouth. Nasal consonants are [m], [n] and [ŋ].

E) **Liquids**: These are sounds produced with a minimal constriction allowing air to pass freely. [l] and [r] are liquid consonants. In producing [l], the airstream flows around the sides of the tongue (it is called a lateral liquid); and in producing [r], the airstream flows through the center of the mouth.

F) **Glides**: These are sounds produced with a minimal constriction corresponding to a vowel (sometimes called "**semi-vowels**"). [w] and [j] are described as glides. The sound [h], as in *hello*, can also be classified as a glide because of the way it combines with other sounds.

Having described the consonants in terms of both the place and the manner of articulation, we can summarize the basic information in the chart below (−v = voiceless, +v = voiced):

	bilabial		labiodental		interdental		alveolar		palatal		velar		glottal	
	−v	+v	−v	+v	−v	+v	−v	+v	−v	+v	−v	+v	−v	+v
stops	p	b					t	d			k	g		
fricatives			f	v	θ	ð	s	z	ʃ	ʒ				
affricates									tʃ	dʒ				
nasals		m						n				ŋ		
liquids							l, r							
glides		w								j				h

(Yule, 2006: 34)

Thus, a consonant in English can be described according to whether it is voiced or voiceless, its place of articulation and manner of articulation, as shown in the following examples:

[b]: voiced bilabial stop
[f]: voiceless labiodental fricative
[n]: voiced alveolar nasal
[h]: voiceless glottal glide

2.2.3 Vowels

Different from consonants, **vowels** are sounds produced with no obstruction of the air stream, and they are all typically **voiced**. "To describe vowel sounds, we must consider the ways in which the tongue influences the 'shape' through which the airflow must pass" (Yule, 2006: 38). That is to say, what makes one vowel sound different from another is the size and shape of the space within your mouth: whether your tongue is higher or lower, whether you raise the front or the back of your tongue and whether you round or spread your lips. These variations affect how the air in your mouth resonates and they are responsible for the different qualities of the vowels.

2.2.3.1 Monophthongs

Most vowel sounds have only one "pure" vowel and are thus called **monophthongs** (mono = one), the articulation of which involves just one tongue position. Below is a chart of such simple vowels categorized in terms of the tongue position within the mouth.

Phonetics and Phonology: The Sounds and Sound Patterns of Language

```
              Front        Central      Back
High            i:                        u:
                  I                      ʊ
                              ɜ:
Mid               ɛ            ə
                               ʌ
                                           ɔ:
Low                æ
                                       ɑ:  ɒ
```

In this chart, high-mid-low refers to height of the tongue in the mouth; front-central-back refers to the part of the tongue. The symbol [:] suggests that the [i:], [u:], [ɜ:] and [ɔ:] are long vowels. Here are their English exemplifications.

[i:] eat, bee, key
[I] big, myth, village
[ɛ] dead, bet, said
[ɒ] cot, bomb, hot
[æ] dam, fast, pat
[ʌ] flood, but, rough

[u:] move, too, food
[ʊ] could, book, put
[ɜ:] dirt, hurt, verse
[ɔ:] saw, caught, ball
[ə] above, coma, suppose
[ɑ:] dark, heart, mark

When we look at the chart above, we should keep what Yule (2006: 39) says in mind: "Vowel sounds are notorious for varying between one variety of English and the next, often being a key element in what we recognize as different accent". For example, many Americans do not distinguish the vowels [ɒ] and [ɔ:], pronouncing *cot* and *caught* the same way.

2.2.3.2 Diphthongs

Vowel sounds may not be just one pure vowel. They can be complex speech sounds that begin with one vowel and gradually change to another vowel within the same syllable. In such cases, we have **diphthongs** (di = two). Altogether, English can be said to have 8 diphthongs. They are [eɪ], [əʊ] [aɪ], [aʊ], [ɔɪ], [ɪə], [ɛə], and [ʊə], which can be exemplified as follows:

[eɪ] date, slay, grey
[aɪ] buy, fly, eye
[ɔɪ] toy, spoil, noise
[ɛə] dare, hare, air

[əʊ] toe, slow, whole
[aʊ] how, proud, south
[ɪə] dear, fear, leukemia
[ʊə] tour, gourmet, moor

In passing, English also has a few **triphthongs**, where three vowel sounds [aɪə], [aʊə] come in succession in words such as *fire* and *power*. Anyway, it should be repeated here that when we pronounce most of the single vowel sounds, our vocal organs take only one position very briefly, but in pronouncing monosyllabic vowel combinations, our vocal organs will experience a quick but smooth movement, or glide, from one vowel to another.

2.2.4 Transcription of Speech Sounds

Typologically, English is a language whose written form (orthography) does not usually give us a secure clue to the actual pronunciation of its words (in contrast with Spanish and Italian, in which there is a consistent relationship between orthography and pronunciation). For this reason, **phonetic transcription** (or **phonetic notation**), the visual system of symbols for the sounds occurring in spoken communication, was invented to provide a function that orthography cannot. It displays a one-to-one relationship between symbols and sounds. The most common type of phonetic transcription uses phonetic symbols (such as the **International Phonetic Alphabet**, **IPA** for short). Incidentally, we enclose phonetic symbols within square brackets [ ], as distinguished from **phonemes** that are put between slash marks / / (e.g. /s/. See Section 2.3.1).

With phonetic transcription, we can step outside of orthography and examine differences in pronunciation between the numerous dialects within the language. In addition, we can identify changes in pronunciation that have taken place over time. Phonetic transcription can be broad or narrow. **Broad transcription** indicates only the more noticeable phonetic features of an utterance, whereas **narrow transcription** encodes more information about the phonetic variations of the specific **allophones** (see Section 2.3.2) in the utterance. For example, one particular pronunciation of the English word *little* may be transcribed using the IPA as [ˈlɪtl] or [ˈlɪtɫ]; the broad transcription indicates merely that the word ends with the phoneme /l/, but the narrow transcription (with a diacritic) indicates that this final /l/ ([ɫ]) is a dark sound. Thus, in narrow transcription, we make a distinction between the variations of the same phoneme. For example, the clear [l] and the dark [ɫ] belong to the same phoneme /l/, but the clear [l] occurs before a vowel, as in *lead* and *life*, and the dark [ɫ] occurs at the end of a word after a vowel or before a consonant, as in *tool* and *milk*.

The merit of the narrow transcription is that it can help learners to get exactly the right sound, and allow linguists to make detailed analyses of language variation. But the demerit is that it is rarely representative of all speakers of a language. The advantage of the broad transcription is that it allows statements to be made which apply right across a relatively diverse language community. It is thus most commonly adopted as the pronunciation data in foreign language dictionaries.

2.3 Phonology

Phonetics is interested in the speech sounds of all human languages: how they are pronounced; how they differ from each other; what phonetic features they possess; how they are classified, etc. However, in studying the speech sounds of a specific language, linguists may ask: What are the relationships between these speech sounds in the language? What is their linguistic function in the meaning structure of the language? What changes do they take in actual speaking? What sound patterns do these sounds form in the language? These questions are the major concerns of phonology.

Phonology is essentially the description of the system and patterns of speech sounds in a language. More specifically, it deals with the set of sounds that occur in a given language, the permissible arrangements of these sounds in words, and the rules or processes that affect sounds.

2.3.1 Phoneme

Before defining phonemes, we may as well know what phonemes usually look like. Phonemic representations are conventionally put between slash marks (e.g. /t/) as opposed to the square brackets for phonetic symbols (e.g. [t]). The symbol chosen for each phoneme is usually a phonetic symbol intended to suggest how the phoneme is most typically articulated. For example, the phoneme that occurs at the beginning of the word *pit* is commonly realized as a voiceless bilabial stop [p], and so the phoneme is represented as /p/. The entire word *pit* is represented as /pɪt/, with the three phonetic symbols for the three phonemes present in it.

Then, what is a phoneme? According to Aitchison (1992: 39), a **phoneme** is the smallest segment of sound which can distinguish two words. This seemingly simple definition actually tells us two marked features about phonemes: one is that they are basic and the other is that they are meaning-distinguishing. That is to say, the essential property of a phoneme is that it functions contrastively (Yule, 2006: 44). For example, we know that there are two phonemes /b/ and /p/ in English because they can be used to make contrasts in meaning between the words *big* and *pig*, or *bond* and *pond*. This contrastive property is the basic operational test that is used in determining the phonemes in a language. If the substitution of one sound for another results in a change in meaning, then these two sounds represent two different phonemes. That is to say, phonemes have distinctive features: phonemes are capable of distinguishing meaning, and the distinctive features differentiate one phoneme from another.

As can be seen, the two words *big* and *pig* we cite for illustration are identical in form except for a contrast in one phoneme, occurring in the same position. Two words which are different in meaning and identical in form except for one sound segment are referred to as a **minimal pair**. More examples of minimal pair are: *tick—dick*, *pat—pad*, *tap—top*, *site—side*. If we have a group of, not just two, words that can be differentiated by changing one phoneme (always in the same position in the word), then we have **a minimal set**, such as *bate—mate—date—late—rate—wait—gate—hate—fate*.

2.3.2 Phone and Allophone

It should be kept in mind that **phoneme** is an abstract unit or sound type ("in the mind"), and a phoneme is not or need not always be realized in the same manner phonetically. In other words, one abstract sound type can have different versions in actual speech ("in the mouth"). These different versions are described as **phones** (Yule, 2006: 45). Take the English phoneme /p/ as an example. It is phonetically an aspirated plosive [p^h] in the word *pit* ("aspirated" means you will feel a puff of air if you put your hand before your mouth when pronouncing it), but an unaspirated plosive [p] in the word *spit*. So we have two phones [p^h] and [p], both of which are versions of one phoneme /p/.

This example indicates that there are often differences in the way a phoneme is pronounced in a specific context. The variant pronunciations of a phoneme are called **allophones** (*allo-*means "other" or "variation") of that phoneme. So we can say that [p^h] and [p] are allophones of /p/. They are the variants of the same phoneme and occur in **complementary distribution.** "When two sounds are in complementary distribution, they are barred from occurring in identical environments: there is a rigid division of labor, as it were, so that one sound appears in certain contexts and the other in some different, clearly defined contexts" (Katamba, 1989: 19). In our example, the aspirated plosive [p^h] always occurs at the beginning of a syllable and is followed by a stressed vowel (as in the word *pit*) while the unaspirated plosive [p] occurs in other situations (as in the word *spit*).

"The crucial distinction between phonemes and allophones is that substituting one phoneme for another will result in a word with a different meaning (as well as a different pronunciation), but substituting allophones only results in a different (and perhaps unusual) pronunciation of the same word" (Yule, 2006: 45).

2.3.3 Phonotactics

In learning a language, it is not enough just to learn its vocabulary. We

Chapter 2
Phonetics and Phonology: The Sounds and Sound Patterns of Language

have to learn the grammatical rules so that we can arrange the words in proper sequences for meaningful communication. By the same token, it is not enough to learn how to articulate the speech sounds of a language, for we also need to learn the rules that govern the sequences of sounds in the language. On this account, phonology can be regarded as the grammar of phonetic patterns. The particular branch of phonology which studies the permissible sound combinations is called **phonotactics** (in Greek *phone* = voice and *tactic* = course). To put it differently, phonotactics is a branch of phonology that deals with restrictions in a language on the permissible combinations of phonemes.

In the English language, *fig*, *wig*, *rig*, *dig* and *pig* are both phonotactically acceptable and semantically meaningful words. Another two forms that can be added to the minimal set are *lig* and *vig*. Though they are not English words, they are phonotactically permissible. One day, as Yule (2006: 47) says, they might come into use. "They might, for example, begin as invented abbreviations (I think Bubba is one very ignorant guy. —Yeah, he is a big *vig*)". On the other hand, the forms like *bned* and *sthring* do not exist and are unlikely ever to come into existence because they violate the phonotactical restrictions.

The examples indicate that phonotactic restrictions always operate on a unit that is larger than the single phoneme. The phonemic features that occur above the level of one sound segment are called **suprasegmentals**. Suprasegmental features include **syllable** and **prosodic features** known as **stress**, **tone** and **intonation**. Phonotactic constraints typically operate on the suprasegmental unit of syllable.

A syllable is a unit in speech which is often longer than one sound and smaller than a whole word. All words can be divided into one or more syllables. Words with one syllable (*dog*, *bright*) are **monosyllabic**, while words with more than one syllable (*little*, *today*) are **polysyllabic**. The syllable is defined by the way in which vowels and consonants combine to form various sequences. In English, a syllable must contain a vowel or vowel-like sound. The most common type of syllable in language also has a consonant (C) before the vowel (V), and is typically represented as CV. Technically, the basic elements of the syllable are the **onset** and the **rhyme**. The onset can be one consonant, like [p] in *put*, or a combination of more than one consonant called a **consonant cluster**, like [sk] in *sky* and [spr] in *spring*. The rhyme consists of a vowel, which is treated as **nucleus**, plus any following consonant(s), described as **coda** (Yule, 2006: 47). The structure of a typical syllable can be represented as follows:

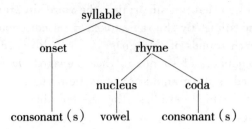

Now we are in an easy position to list some of the phonological rules in English (Note: the list is by no means exhaustive), which are extremely helpful in describing the possible words in English.

1) All the sounds in English can be at the beginning of the syllable except the nasal consonant /ŋ/. So /ŋʌt/ is "ungrammatical".
2) Long vowels (such as /iː/) and diphthongs cannot be followed by /ŋ/.
3) The vowel of *house* does not occur before a final /b/, /p/, /m/, /f/, or /v/.
4) The vowel /ə/ does not occur in stressed syllables.
5) One vowel sound alone can constitute a syllable, like /ə/. But a consonant cannot, though sometimes a consonant can serve as the nucleus, as in the second syllable of *kitten*.
6) In English, there are many possible CC onset combinations, as in *blanket*, *brag*, *dwarf*, *track*, *twinkle*, *fly*, *freight*, and *through*. /l/, /r/ and /w/ are used in the second position, and cannot serve as the first consonant in the CC onset combinations.
7) In a CC onset combination, if the first consonant is /s/, the second consonant can only be /f/, /k/, /l/, /m/, /n/, /p/, /t/, or /w/ (e. g. *sphere*, *school*, *scope*, *slender*, *small*, *snow*, *spin* and *sway*). Though /sr/ is possible, it exists only in some exotic words like *Sri Lanka* and *Srinager*.
8) In a CC onset combination, if the first consonant is /θ/, the second consonant can only be /r/ or /w/ (e. g. *thrive* and *thwart*).
9) If the onset is a consonant cluster with three consonants (CCC), the first consonant must always be /s/, the second can be /t/, /p/, /m/ or /k/ and the third one should be /j/, /l/, /r/ or /w/ (e. g. *skewer*, *smew*, *spew*, *student*, *street*, *splash*, *squad*, *scratch* and *spring*).
10) If /j/ is at the end of an onset (/pj/, /bj/, /tj/, /dj/, /kj/, /fj/, /vj/, /θj/, /sj/, /hj/, /mj/, /nj/, /lj/, /spj/, /stj/, /skj/), it must be followed by /uː/ or /ʊə/ (e. g. *pure*, *bureau*, *tutor*, *duke*, *cute*, *fusion*, *view*, *thew*, *suit*, *hew*, *muse*, *new*, *lure*, *spurious*, *studious*, and *skew*).

11) English normally permits up to two consonants in the coda (e. g. *belt*, *dump*) and sometimes even more consonants can pile up at the end of words (e. g. *sixths*, *melts*, *texts*, *strengths*).

2.3.4 Prosodic Features: Stress, Tone and Intonation

Prosodic features refer to phonological variations mainly in stress, tone and intonation, that is, relative loudness of syllables, changes in the pitch of a speaker's voice and the choice of pitch level, and so on. They are features that are sometimes loosely synonymous with suprasegmental features.

Almost every English word has at least one syllable which is noticeably more prominent than the other syllables. The relative prominence that a particular syllable has in pronunciation is called the **stress** of the word. The syllable that receives a stress is the stressed syllable. The word *dictionary*, for example, has four syllables and the stress falls on its first syllable in pronunciation. English-speaking people see eye to eye with each other on the stress of most words in the language, but they may have different opinions on the stress of words like *exquisite*, *vagaries* and *controversy*—some people stress the first syllable while others give prominence to the second syllable. Stress is sometimes indeed an issue of controversy!

If a word has several syllables, it often has both its **primary stress** (or **main stress**) and a **secondary stress**. For example, *explanation* has the main stress on the third syllable but a secondary stress on the first one.

Stress is a helpful means for us to distinguish words that have the same forms but belong to different grammatical categories. For instance, 'ex*port* and 'sub*ject* are nouns but ex'*port* and sub'*ject* are verbs. Stress is sometimes even essential in distinguishing words that are completely different, such as '*billow* from be'*low*.

Apart from the ordinary word-stress, there is also sentence-stress in actual English communication: people may place a strong stress on a particular word within an utterance for the sake of emphasizing that word. For instance, *John met Mary at the school gate yesterday* can be uttered with different sentence-stresses, and the implications will be certainly different:

JOHN met Mary at the school gate yesterday. (John rather than anybody else)

John MET Mary at the school gate yesterday. (John didn't do anything else)

John met MARY at the school gate yesterday. (Mary rather than anybody else)

John met Mary at the SCHOOL gate yesterday. (Not any other gate)

John met Mary at the school GATE yesterday. (Not anywhere else)

John met Mary at the school gate YESTERDAY. (Not any other day)

Tones are pitch variations, which are caused by the differing rates of vibration of the vocal cords. When we listen to people speaking, we can hear some sounds or groups of sounds in their speech to be relatively higher or lower than others. This relative height of speech sounds as perceived by a listener is called pitch. Pitch variations can distinguish meaning. For example, Chinese is a tone language which makes use of four tones to distinguish words or meanings: high level (yī, meaning "one"), rising (yí, meaning "move"), falling-rising (yǐ, meaning "already") and falling (yì, meaning "idea").

Intonations are pitch differences that extend over phonological units larger than the syllable. By means of intonation, syllables are grouped into phrases, and phrases into sentences. Intonation distinguishes meaning through **intonation patterns**, which are usually expressed by variations in pitch, loudness, syllable length, and sometimes speech rhythm. Intonation is used to perform grammatical functions, that is, to indicate whether an utterance is a question, or a statement. It can also be used to show the speaker's attitude to the subject matter discussed or to the listener.

2.3.5 Co-articulation Effects

So far we have discussed the speech sounds in syllables and words as if they are articulated very carefully and slowly. But normally, we do not speak like that unless we are talking to someone from a different linguistic community with little knowledge of our language or to a person of much lower cognitive ability such as a baby. In spontaneous connected speech, we usually speak fast, moving from one sound to the next without stopping. In other words, when we are preparing to articulate a phoneme, we are already thinking of the one which follows it. Take the English word *map* for example. As the nasal consonant [m] precedes the vowel [æ], some of its nasality will be carried forward so that the vowel will begin with a smidgen of nasal quality. When such simultaneous or overlapping articulations are involved, we can feel the **co-articulation effects**. Thus, co-articulation effects involve the phonological processes of spreading phonetic features to neighboring segments. There are two major types of co-articulation effects: assimilation and elision.

2.3.5.1 Assimilation

Assimilation, just as its name implies, is a phonological process by which a sound becomes more similar to its nearby sound in terms of some phonetic features. It is the process of one sound exercising influence on another and as a result, the two sound segments occurring in sequence sound more alike. This process happens because our speech organs usually do the job with higher

Phonetics and Phonology: The Sounds and Sound Patterns of Language

speed, greater ease and better efficiency in connected speech.

Assimilation in which a following sound brings about a change in a preceding one is called **regressive assimilation** or **anticipatory co-articulation**. Take *black people* as an example. If we pronounce the two words individually, *black* will be [blæk]. But if we articulate the phrase at a normal speed, the last phoneme of the word, [k], will take the feature "labial" of the following consonant sound /p/ in *people*, and the two words will be perceived by the ear as [blæp pʰiːpl]. What happens is labial assimilation. In the same way, the normal articulation of *this year* [ðɪʃjɪə] involves palatal assimilation.

Assimilation in which a preceding sound brings about a change in a following one is called **progressive** or **perseverative assimilation**. For example, whether a preceding consonant is voiced or voiceless will influence a following sound, as exemplified by the difference between the [s] in words like *pets* and *books* and the [z] in *toads* and *frogs* and the difference between the final [t] in *jumped* and the final [d] in *sobbed*.

2.3.5.2 Elision

The word "elision" is derived from the verb "elide", meaning "to leave out" (e− = out, −lide = strike). **Elision**, then, is a phonological process that involves the omission of a phoneme (frequently unstressed vowels or medial consonants) in connected speech or verse. It is the process of not pronouncing a sound segment that might be present in the deliberately careful pronunciation of a word in isolation (Yule, 2006: 49). You can try the phrase *you and me*. If you speak fairly quickly, you will find yourself uttering [juː æn miː]. The stop sound [d] in the word *and* is omitted. The elision of the sound has much to do with its phonological environment: it is both preceded by the nasal [n] and followed by another nasal [m]. Efficiency will lead you not to devote speech energy to including the stop sound [d]. Try *East China* and you will hear yourself speaking [iːstʃaɪnə].

2.4 Summary

From the introduction above, we can see clearly that phonetics is a discipline that studies how possible speech sounds are articulated and perceived. It provides us with methods for their classification and description. By studying it we can get a picture of the physical properties of speech sounds. Phonology, on the other hand, deals with systems of linguistically significant sounds (Kaye, 1989: 10). In other words, phonology investigates the ways in which speech sounds are used systematically to form words and utterances (Katamba, 1989: 60), and its primary aim is to discover the principles that govern the way sounds are organized in language, and to explain the variations that occur.

Even though sounds in themselves have no meaning, and even though the associations between sounds and meaning in language are arbitrary and conventional, there are ways of using sounds to complement meaning (Traugott & Pratt, 1980: 69). To quote Alexander Pope in his *An Essay on Criticism*, "The sound must seem an echo to the sense". This phenomenon is called **sound symbolism** (See Chapter 1). Take the sound [ʃ] as an example. This palatal fricative, if combined with short vowels, is often suggestive of an unpleasant event or a speedy motion like *shout*, *smash*, *crush*, *dash* and *rush*. In pronouncing words that contain several consonants and only one or two short vowels, we have to be swift and the swiftness in sound is often a clue to its meaning, such as *abrupt*, *fast*, *crash*, *slap* and *jump*.

Here we wish to point out that phonetics and phonology are not esoteric academic disciplines with no relevance to the real world. They have actually found their use in such fields as language teaching, drama performance, speech therapy, communications engineering, forensic pathology, etc. (Katamba, 1989: 75—77).

Further Readings

Clark, J. & Yallop, C. 2000. *An Introduction to Phonetics and Phonology*. 北京:外语教学与研究出版社.
Gimson, A. C. & Arnold, E. 2000. *An Introduction to Phonetics and Phonology*. 北京:外语教学与研究出版社.
Katamba, F. 1989. *An Introduction to Phonology*. London and New York: Longman.
Roach, P. 2000. *English Phonetics and Phonology: A practical course*. 北京:外语教学与研究出版社.
Roach, P. 2001/2003. *Phonetics*. 上海:上海外语教育出版社.
Yule, G. 2006. *The Study of Language* (Third Edition). Cambridge: Cambridge University Press.

Questions and Exercises

1. Define the following terms:
   speech sound   prosodic features   complementary distribution
   phoneme   allophone   phone
   minimal pair   interdentals   consonant
   vowel   manner of articulation   phonetic transcription
   phonotactics   suprasegmentals   syllable
2. Describe the following sound segments in English.
   1) [ɛ] _____   2) [uː] _____
   3) [m] _____   4) [p] _____
   5) [dʒ] _____   6) [ð] _____
3. How is phonetics related to phonology and how do they differ from each other?

Phonetics and Phonology: The Sounds and Sound Patterns of Language

4. How are vowels classified in the English language?
5. How are consonants classified in the English language?
6. What are co-articulation effects? Illustrate them with your own examples.
7. Why are the following sound combinations not possible in English?
   1) [ŋaʊt]
   2) [tʃiːŋ]
   3) ['mɛtɪ]
   4) [θnaɪv]
   5) [tjʊl]
   6) [maʊp]

Chapter 3

Morphology: The Word Structure of Language

3.1 Introduction

Morphology, which literally means "the study of forms", is about the structure of words. More specifically, it refers to the study of the internal structure of words, and the rules by which words are formed. Morphology is the area of grammar that attempts to answer the following questions: How is a word structured? What is the basic component part of a word? How are the component parts put together to form words? What are the word-formation processes in a language? How is the form of a word affected when it is used with other words or in a sentence?

3.2 The Words of Language

It is difficult to define the term "**word**". For some people, words are physically definable units, whose boundaries are usually recognized by spaces in writing or slight pauses in speech. For others, a word is a unit of meaning and a unit of sound. There are still others who regard words as grammatical units that can function in a sentence. Stockwell and Minkova (2001: 56) characterize a word as the smallest unit that one thinks of as being basic to saying anything. It is the smallest unit of sentence composition and the smallest unit that we are aware of when we consciously try to create sentences. To put things together, we can define a word as the smallest of the linguistic units which can occur on its own in speech and writing (Richards et al., 1985: 311). For example, *care*, *careless* and *careful* are smallest linguistic units in speech and writing, so they are all words. Some people may argue that *careless* and *careful* are not smallest, because *careless* is made up of *care* and *-less*, and *careful* is made up of *care* and *-ful*. However, in speech and writing we do not use *care* and *-less*, or *care* and *-ful* separately, as *-less* or *-ful* cannot stand on its own. Some people may also argue that many words like *the*, *so*, *of* can hardly occur on their own, because they are almost always used with other words in speech and writing. This is true, but in this definition, "occur on its own" means that distinct from units like *-less* and *-ful*, a word is an individual

Chapter 3

Morphology: The Word Structure of Language

unit of meaning that is not bound to any other units. This definition may not be perfect, but it captures the basic characteristics of a word. That is, a word is a sound-meaning unit and a fundamental unit of speech and writing.

In discussing words, the following terms are also frequently used, and sometimes distinctions are made as follows:

- **Lexis**: the vocabulary of a language, in contrast to its grammar or syntax.
- **Lexicon**: the set of all the words and idioms of any language, often used interchangeably with vocabulary.
- **Lexeme**: the smallest unit in the meaning system of a language, an abstract unit that remains constant. For example, *give* is the lexeme of its variants *gave*, *given*, *giving*.
- **Vocabulary**: A complete inventory of the words in a language.

Words can be classified into **content words** and **function words**. Content words are words which refer to a thing, quality, state, or action and which have stable lexical meaning or semantic content. They mainly include nouns, verbs, adjectives, and adverbs. Content words are also called lexical words or full words. Content words are also **"open-class" words**, because new words can be added to these classes.

Function words are words whose role is primarily to express grammatical relationships and such words have little meaning on their own except their grammatical meaning. They mainly include conjunctions, prepositions, auxiliaries and articles. Function words are also called **form words, empty words, grammatical words, structural words** or **structure words**. Function words are **"closed-class" words** because new words are not usually added to these classes.

3.3 The Structure of Words

Although words are the smallest of the linguistic units in speech and writing, they have an internal structure. That is, they are said to be made up of meaningful units of their own, as exemplified in the following:

careful → care + ful
sadness → sad + ness
realize → real + ize
disobey → dis + obey
unthinkable → un + think + able

These examples show that a word can be analyzed into minimal units of meaning. In *disobey*, there are two minimal units of meaning, one being *dis-* (meaning "not"), the other being *obey*.

When words are used in sentences, the word-forms such as *works*, *worked*, *working* can also be analyzed into minimal units of meaning. In this case, the word-forms consist of one element *work*, and a number of other elements such as *-s*, *-ed*, *-ing*, which indicate various grammatical meanings.

Thus, a word can be analyzed into the most elemental units of meaning. Some words are composed of one unit of meaning, like *help*, *the*, *happy*, *apple*. Some words consist of two or more than two units of meaning. For example, *happily* contains two minimal units of meaning, and *ungentlemanliness* contains five minimal units of meaning. The minimal unit of meaning is traditionally called **morpheme**. Thus, it can be said that a word is composed of at least one morpheme and it may be composed of more than one. Words that are formed by one morpheme only and cannot be analyzed into parts are called **opaque words**. Words that consist of more than one morpheme and can be segmented into parts are called **transparent words**.

3.4　Morpheme, Morph and Allomorph

A **morpheme** is the smallest meaningful linguistic unit that cannot be further segmented. For example, the word *morpheme* itself contains two morphemes, *morph-*, meaning "form", and *-eme*, meaning "unit". We sometimes can predict the meanings of a word by identifying its morphemes.

A morpheme is an abstract concept. The concrete form of a morpheme is called **morph**. That is to say, morphs are the actual forms used to realize morphemes. A morpheme may take different shapes or forms, which are called **allomorphs**. Thus, an allomorph is any of the variant forms of a morpheme.

Why is there an abstract-concrete distinction here? One possible answer is that such a distinction is necessitated by morphological description. For example, the following group of words have one grammatical meaning in common: *dogs*, *buses*, *sheep*, *men*, *geese*, *children*, *phenomena*. They are all plural forms expressing the grammatical meaning of "more than one..." The plural meaning is expressed by *-s* in *dogs*, but by *-es* in *buses*. Things become more complicated when we look at the other words: what makes *sheep* the plural of *sheep*, or *geese* the plural of *goose*? Can we say that the plural meaning in all these words is expressed by different morphemes? Certainly not. There is only one morpheme involved here, and we may call it the morpheme "plural". It can be attached to a number of lexical morphemes to produce structures like "dog + plural", "sheep + plural", "goose + plural", and so on. The morpheme "plural" takes different forms in actual realization, called morphs, and they are all allomorphs of the one morpheme. We can say that "dog + plural", "sheep + plural", "goose + plural" are abstract analyses at the morpheme-level, and are realized as *dogs*, *sheep*, *geese* at the morph-level (Yule, 2000: 79). This two-level analysis makes morphological description much easier, but very often the term "morpheme" is used for convenience when we actually refer to a morph. So many people refer to forms like *-s* and *-ed*, which are morphs, as morphemes.

3.5 Classification of Morphemes

3.5.1 Free Morphemes and Bound Morphemes

A **free morpheme** is a morpheme which can stand by itself as an independent word, e.g. *water*, *child*, *attack*, and *berry*. A **bound morpheme** is a morpheme which cannot stand on its own as a word, but which is typically attached to another form, e.g. *-dom* in *freedom*, *-hood* in *childhood*, *-ship* in *friendship* and *un-* in *undo*. On the morphemic level, words can be classified into simple words, compound words and complex words according to the number and type of morphemes words contain:

- A **simple word** consists of a single morpheme (which is certainly a free morpheme), e.g. *hill*, *walk*, *great*, *element*.
- A **compound word** is composed of two or more free morphemes, e.g. *blackboard*, *sunset*, *headstrong*, *forget-me-not*.
- A **complex word** consists either of a free morpheme together with one or more than one bound morpheme, or of two bound morphemes, e.g. *cats*, *careful*, *unfriendly*, *contain*, *conceive*, *prelude*.

3.5.2 Roots and Affixes

A **root** is the basic unchangeable part of a word, and it conveys the main lexical meaning of the word. It is the part of a word remaining when all affixes have been removed. A root can be a free morpheme, e.g. *work* in *worker*, *think* in *unthinkable*, or a bound morpheme, e.g. *ceive* in *perceive*, *tain* in *retain*, *vit* in *vital*.

An **affix** is a bound morpheme that is used only when added to another word or morpheme. It is used to mark the grammatical function of a word or create a new word. Affixes can be further classified into inflectional morphemes and derivational morphemes.

3.5.3 Inflectional Morphemes and Derivational Morphemes

When a word appears in a variety of forms depending on its grammatical role in the sentence, we say that it inflects or undergoes inflection (Radford et al., 2000: 154). Thus, an **inflectional morpheme** is an affix that indicates aspects of the grammatical function of a word, such as *-s* for plurality of countable nouns, *-ed* for past tense of verbs, *-er* and *-est* for the comparative and superlative degrees of adjectives or adverbs. An inflectional morpheme does not form a new word when it is added to another word, nor does it change the part of speech of the word to which it is affixed (with a few exceptions like *-ing* and *-ed*, as in *the learning of a language*, and *the golden-haired woman*). The part of a word to which an inflectional affix is added is called a **stem**, e.g. *talk* in *talked*, *farmer* in *farmers*, *classmate* in *classmates*.

A **derivational morpheme** is one that is used to form a new word. For example, *-ment* is added to *move* and the new word *movement* is derived. English is a language rich in derivational morphemes. Some derivational morphemes appear before another form, while others after another form. Thus, derivational morphemes can be classified into **prefixes** and **suffixes** according to their positions in the derived words. In addition, some derivational morphemes produce words of a different class from the word to which they are affixed, while others do not. All these properties of the derivational morpheme will be illustrated in the discussion of word formation.

On the basis of what has been discussed above, we can make a classification of morphemes as shown in the following diagram:

$$
\text{morpheme}\begin{cases} \text{free} \begin{array}{l} \text{free root} \\ \text{bound root} \end{array} \Big\} \text{root} \\ \text{bound} \begin{cases} \text{affix} \begin{cases} \text{inflectional} \\ \text{derivational} \begin{cases} \text{prefix} \\ \text{suffix} \end{cases} \end{cases} \end{cases} \end{cases}
$$

3.6 Word Formation Processes

With the development of society, science and technology, new words constantly emerge and many new words gain popularity and find their way into the English language. A new word or expression is often referred to as a **neologism**, which can be a coinage, i.e. a word or phrase that has been recently invented, or a word used with a new meaning. For example, *glass ceiling* and *laptop* are recent coinages, while *mouse* and *memory* used in computer science are words with new meanings.

Word formation is an area of derivational morphology which studies the processes of word building and the rules governing the formation of new words. New words are formed according to morphological rules which determine how morphemes combine to form new words. In English, there are

Chapter 3
Morphology: The Word Structure of Language

major word formation processes which are productive, such as derivation, compounding and conversion, and minor word formation processes which are less productive, such as blending, clipping, back-formation and acronymy.

3.6.1 Derivation

Derivation, also called affixation, is a process of word formation by which a new word is created by adding an affix to a **base**. A base is that part of a word to which a derivational affix is added. Some people regard the term base as an alternative to root or stem, although they are not always the same. For example, in *modernize*, the base form is *modern*, and in *modernization*, the base form is *modernize*.

Derivational morphemes can be classified into prefixes and suffixes according to their positions in the derived words. A morpheme added to the left of a base is a **prefix**, e.g. *re-* in *reopen*, *en-* in *enable*. Thus, the formation of a new word by adding a prefix to the base is called **prefixation**. A morpheme added to the right of a base is a **suffix**, e.g. *-ize* in *civilize*, *-ness* in *illness*. Thus, the formation of a new word by adding a suffix to the base is called **suffixation**.

Prefixation usually produces words of the same class as the base, while suffixation very often produce words of a different class from the base, as can be seen in the examples below.

Base	Affix	Derived word	Word class
gold	-en	golden	N→ Adj
deep	-en	deepen	Adj→ V
fool	-ish	foolish	N→ Adj
snow	-y	snowy	N→ Adj
ill	-ness	illness	Adj→ N
biology	-ist	biologist	N→ N
excite	-ment	excitement	V→ N
weather	-wise	weatherwise	N→ Adv
civil	-ize	civilize	Adj→ V
valid	-ate	validate	Adj→ V
opinion		opinionate	N→ V
path	by-	bypath	N→ N

续表

Base	Affix	Derived word	Word class
touchable	un-	untouchable	Adj→ Adj
dress		undress	V→ V
able	en-	enable	Adj→ V
danger		endanger	N→ V
wear	out-	outwear	V→ V
marine	sub-	submarine	N→ N
loyal	dis-	disloyal	Adj→ Adj
obey		disobey	V→ V
compose	de-	de-compose	V→ V
hero	anti-	antihero	N→ N
character	non-	non-character	N→ N
practical	im-	impractical	Adj→ Adj
angle	tri-	triangle	N→ N
head	fore-	forehead	N→ N

From these examples, we can see that derivation has several properties. First, most words derived through suffixation have a different part of speech from the base, while most words derived through prefixation have the same part of speech as the base. Second, phonological factors sometimes work simultaneously with the derivational process. One example is that the suffix *-en* often goes with the monosyllabic adjectives which only have an obstruent at the end to derive words like *darken*, *widen*, *deepen*, and *broaden*. Another example is that the word stress is changed with some English suffixes like *-itarian* "ˈhuman → ˌhumaniˈtarian", *-ation* "conˈdense → ˌcondenˈsation", *-cal* "psyˈchology → ˌpsychoˈlogical". Third, some derivational processes may involve a change in the lexical meaning. For example, negative affixes like *dis-*, *un-*, *in-*, *non-* and *-less* can be used to form words with a negative meaning.

3.6.2 Compounding

Compounding is a word formation process by means of joining two or more words to form a new word. Words formed in this way are called **compounds** or **compound words**, e. g. *greenhouse*, *daybreak*, *moonlight*, *round-the-clock*. Words can be combined in various ways to form compounds, as shown in the following examples:

Chapter 3

Morphology: The Word Structure of Language

	-Noun	-Verb	-Adjective
Noun-	eyeball horseman lighthouse spotlight	daybreak spoon-feed lip-read chain-smoke	ice-rich war-weary headstrong thread-bare
Verb-	pick-pocket crybaby tell-tale	snapshot crashland sleepwalk	carryall
Adjective-	greenhouse black-hole blueprint	whitewash dry-clean fine-tune	bitter-sweet all-new deaf-mute

There are primarily three types of compound words: noun compounds, verb compounds, and adjective compounds. The word class of a compound can be (but not always) predicted according to the following principles: (a) When the two words belong to the same class, the compound will belong to this class: noun + noun — *masterpiece, paper-clip, end-product*; adjective + adjective — *icy-cold, gray-brown, red-hot*. (b) When the two words fall into different classes, the class of the compound is generally determined by the class of the second or final word: verb + noun — *driveway, pick-pocket*; noun + adjectives — *snow-white, life-long*.

Compounds differ from phrases in terms of stress patterns. The primary stress usually falls on the first part of a compound. Thus, a ʹhot-line with a stress on *hot* refers to a frequent communication by phones, while a hot ʹline with a stress on *line* can refer to a line, metal, plastic, or cotton that is hot, rather than cold. Pinker (1994: 133) provides us with a simple way to tell whether something is a compound word or a phrase: compounds generally have stress on the first word, phrases on the second. A *dark* ʹroom (phrase) is any room that is dark, but a ʹ*dark room* (compound word) is where photographers work.

A compound is structurally stable and is used as a single unit. For example, *greenhouse* cannot be modified by adverbs. Although *a very green house* can be regarded as a phrase, * *a very greenhouse* is unacceptable as *greenhouse* is a compound noun. Nor can we use the comparative and superlative forms of *green* in the compound. Thus, * *a greenerhouse* does not exist as a compound, and *a greener/greenest house* becomes a phrase. This is also the case with other compounds like *fine art* and *loud speaker*.

As a chunk expressing a single idea, the meaning of a compound cannot be inferred from the individual component of the compound. A *no-nonsense* teacher does not refer to a teacher who does not talk nonsense, but one who is reliable, dependable, and strict with students. And a *songbird* may refer to a woman singer, not a bird that sings. Again, a *sandpiper* is a small wading bird having a slender bill and piping call, with a sense that has little to do with sand beach and a musical instrument. Similar analysis can be made of compounds like *dog days* and *blue blood*.

3.6.3 Conversion

Conversion is word formation by means of converting words of one class into another. As conversion involves the shift of word class without the addition of an affix, it is also variously called zero derivation, root formation, functional shift, or derivation by zero suffix. This process often occurs between a number of word classes.

a. **noun to verb conversion**
   can: to can apples
   shelter: to shelter an orphan
   butter: to butter bread
   weed: to weed the garden
   elbow: to elbow the door open
   mother: to mother a child

b. **verb to noun conversion**
   doubt: to have no doubt
   walk: to take a walk
   bet: to lay a bet
   cover: to find a cover
   divide: a divide between two rivers

c. **adjective to noun conversion**
   poor: the poor
   wounded: the wounded
   native: a returned native

d. **adjective to verb conversion**
   idle: to idle away
   dim: to dim out
   free: to free the slaves
   warm: to warm the house

There are also other types of conversion as shown in the following examples: *to up a hill*, *to face the ups and downs of life*, *the then president*. One thing worthy of note is that conversion may bring about shift of word stress, as shown in the following examples: per'mit (verb)-'permit (noun), re'cord (verb)-'record (noun), ex'port (verb)-'export (noun).

3.6.4 Blending

Blending is the formation of new words by combining parts of two words or a word plus a part of another word. Words formed in this way are called **blends**. Blending involves parts of two words called "head" and "tail". Head is the first part of a word, and tail is the final part of a word. Thus, blending can have the following types according to different kinds of combination.

a. **head + tail**: motor + hotel = motel
　　　　　　　smoke + fog = smog
　　　　　　　breakfast + lunch = brunch
b. **head + head**: situation + comedy = sitcom
　　　　　　　communications + satellite = comsat
　　　　　　　formula + translator = Fortran
c. **head + word**: medical + care = medicare
　　　　　　　Europe + Asia = Euroasia
　　　　　　　automobile + camp = autocamp
d. **word + head**: sky + laboratory = skylab
　　　　　　　mass + culture = masscult
　　　　　　　laser + computer = lasercomp
e. **word + tail**: lunar + astronaut = lunarnaut
　　　　　　　work + welfare = workfare
　　　　　　　tour + automobile = tourmobile

3.6.5 Backformation

Backformation is a process of word formation by the deletion of a supposed affix. It reverses the process of derivation in the sense that it forms new words by removing rather than adding an affix. For example, *edit* is from *editor*, *burgle* from *burglar*, *peddle* from *peddler*, *emote* from *emotion*, *free-associate* from *free-association*, *reminisce* from *reminiscence*, *grue* from *gruesome*, *gangle* from *gangling*, and *attrit* from *attrition*.

3.6.6 Abbreviation or Shortening

Abbreviation or **shortening** is a word formation process by making a word shorter. It reflects the tendency of simplification in language use, as can be exemplified by clipping and acronymy

Clipping is a process of maintaining a single syllable, while removing the rest in a polysyllabic word. For example, *fax* is shortened from *facsimile*, *ad* or *advert* from *advertisement*, *vet* from *veterinarian*.

Acronymy is the process of forming new words by joining the initial letters of words. Words formed in this way are called **initialisms** or **acronyms**, depending on the pronunciation of the newly formed words. Initialisms are words formed from the initial letters of words and pronounced as letters. For example, *BBC* is from *British Broadcasting Corporation*, *POW* from *prisoner of war*, *CEO* from *chief executive officer*, *WTO* from *World Trade Organization*. Acronyms are words formed from the initial letters of words and pronounced as words. For example, *NATO* is from *North Atlantic Treaty Organization*, *OPEC* from *Organization of Petroleum Export Countries*, *laser* from *light amplification by stimulated emission of radiation*.

3.7 Summary

Morphology studies the structure of words in language and it can be broadly classified into **derivational morphology** and **inflectional morphology**. Derivational morphology is concerned with how a word is formed and the word-formation processes. Inflectional morphology is concerned with how the form of a word may be affected when it is used with other words or in a sentence. That is to say, words vary with their grammatical roles in sentence formation. As Crystal (1997: 90) puts it, inflectional morphology studies the way in which words vary (or "inflect") in order to express grammatical contrasts in sentences. A word inflects or undergoes inflection when it appears in a variety of forms depending on its grammatical role in the sentence. Carstairs-McCarthy (2002: 30) takes inflection as a process of dealing with the inflected forms of words, that is, the kind of variation that words exhibit on the basis of their grammatical context. In some languages like Greek, Latin and French, inflection plays a major role in sentence formation, because such languages rely on overt inflectional forms as markers of syntactic relations. Modern English is not an inflected language, but there are still inflectional morphemes indicating the grammatical function of a word. According to Yule (2000: 77), English has eight inflectional morphemes, illustrated in the following:

Let me tell you about Jim**'s** two sister**s**.
One like**s** to have fun and is always laugh**ing**.
The other lik**ed** to study and has always tak**en** things seriously.
One is the loud**est** person in the house and the other is quiet**er** than a mouse.

It can be noticed that inflection in English takes place in nouns, verbs and adjectives. Nouns inflect for possessive (-*'s*) and plural (-*s*). Verbs inflect for third person present singular (-*s*), present participle (-*ing*), past tense (-*ed*) and past participle (-*en*). Adjectives inflect for comparative (-*er*) and superlative (-*est*) degrees. Thus, word forms like *Jim's*, *sisters*, *likes*, *laughing*, *liked*, *taken*, *loudest* and *quieter* are grammatically conditioned

Chapter 3
Morphology: The Word Structure of Language

variants of the basic word forms, that is, the stems.

Further Readings
Adams, V. 1973. *An Introduction to Modern English Word-Formation*. London: Longman.
Carstairs-McCarthy, A. 1992. *Current Morphology*. London: Routledge.
Carstairs-McCarthy, A. 2002. *An Introduction to English Morphology: Words and Their Structure. Edinburgh*: Edinburgh University Press.
Matthews, P. H. 2000. *Morphology* (Second Edition). 北京:外语教学与研究出版社.
Radford, A. et al. 2000. *Linguistics: An introduction*. 北京:外语教学与研究出版社.

Questions and Exercises
1. Define the following terms.

content words	function words	opaque words
transparent words	morpheme	allomorph
morph	neologism	word formation
derivation	compounding	conversion
backformation	clipping	blending
eponym	affix	acronymy

2. How is morpheme classified?
3. Here is a list of words:
   (a) aftershock   (e) survivor   (i) deoxyribonucleoprotein
   (b) tower   (f) bedridden (j) uncopyrightable
   (c) original   (g) antirehabilitationism (k) antidisestablishmentarianism
   (d) government   (h) ninths (l) floccinaucinihilipilificationalizationalize
   (1) How many morphemes are there in each word?
   (2) Which of these morphemes are free morphemes?
4. Illustrate the properties of derivation with examples?
5. In English, the prefix *un-* can be added to some adjectives. Consider the possibility of attaching it to each of the following adjectives and then answer the questions.
   (a) bad   (b) interesting   (c) inhabitable   (d) glad   (e) important
   (f) good   (g) sympathetic   (h) strong   (i) reliable
   (1) Which words can take the prefix *un-*?
   (2) What does the prefix *un-* mean in the derived words?
   (3) How does this *un-* differ in meaning from the *un-* in *unbutton*, *undo*, and *unfasten*?
6. Explain how stress placement can change the meanings of the following words or expressions in Column A and Column B.

Column A	Column B
a black ˈboard	a ˈblackboard
a white ˈhouse	The ˈWhite House
a silk ˈworm	a ˈsilkworm
a toy ˈfactory	a ˈtoy factory
a dark ˈroom	a ˈdark room

7. Illustrate different types of conversion with examples.
8. Illustrate different types of blending with examples.
9. How is the form of a word affected when it is used with other words or in a sentence?

Chapter 4

Syntax: The Sentence Structure of Language

4.1 Introduction

The word "syntax" is from the Ancient Greek *sýntaxis*, which literally means "arrangement" or "setting out together". In linguistics, **syntax** is the study of how words combine to form sentences and the rules which govern the formation of sentences. Most languages have a finite number of basic words, but these words can be put together to make an infinite number of sentences. This is because there are rules and patterns that can be used in a recursive way to create new sentences. Syntax studies the rules governing the way words are combined to form sentences in a language. Generally, there are four major approaches to syntax, namely, the traditional approach, the structural approach, the transformational-generative approach, and the functional approach.

What is the relationship between syntax and **grammar**? According to Lyons (1968), the term "grammar" goes back (through French and Latin) to a Greek word which may be translated as "the art of writing". Quite early in the history of Greek scholarship this word acquired a much wider sense and came to embrace the whole study of language. More recently, the term "grammar" has developed a narrower interpretation: it tends to be restricted to that part of the analysis of language which was handled in classical grammar under the headings of inflection and syntax. According to the traditional distinction, inflection deals with the internal structure of words, and syntax accounts for the way in which words combine to form sentences. Thus, in a restricted sense, grammar refers to a level of structural organization which can be studied independently of phonology and semantics, and generally divided into the branches of syntax and morphology. In this sense, grammar is the study of the way words, and their component parts, combine to form sentences. This is the usual popular interpretation of the term "grammar", which is contrasted with a general conception of the subject, where grammar is seen as the entire system of structural relationships in a language, and thus subsumes phonology and semantics as well as syntax.

Chapter 4
Syntax: The Sentence Structure of Language

4.2 Sentence Structure

4.2.1 Definition of Sentence

Most syntactic studies have focused on sentence structure, for this is where the most important grammatical relations are expressed.

In the traditional and popular view, a **sentence** is "a series of words in connected speech or writing, forming the grammatically complete expression of a single thought" (Matthews, 1981). Modern syntax avoids this semantic definition based on thoughts or ideas, because of the difficulties involved in saying what "thoughts" are. For example, *an apple* can express a thought, but it would not be considered as a complete sentence; *He came late, because he overslept* is one sentence, but it could easily be analyzed as two thoughts.

Most linguistic definitions of sentence show the influence of American structuralism: a sentence is the largest structural unit to which syntactic rules apply. That is, a sentence is the maximal unit of syntax, "an independent linguistic form, not included by virtue of any grammatical construction in any larger linguistic form" (Bloomfield, 1933). This definition also has its problems. In particular, it does not allow for elliptical sentences such as *To town* as the answer to *Where are you going?* and minor sentences such as *Help!*, *All aboard!*, *Happy Birthday!* In reaction to the problem concerning the notion of completeness, some linguists classify sentences into two types: complete and incomplete. Other linguists propose to make a systematic distinction between sentence and **utterance**: sentence is a theoretical unit, defined by a grammar, while utterance is a physical unit, a matter of speech production, or performance. In this view, utterances can be analyzed in terms of sentence, but utterances do not "consist of" sentences.

Most analysts agree on the need to recognize a functional classification of sentences into statement, question, command and exclamatory types. Although sentences may be incomplete, normally a sentence consists of at least one subject and its predicate. Most analyses also recognize the classification of "sentence patterns" into **simple** versus **complex** or **compound** types, i.e. consisting of one subject-predicate unit, as opposed to more than one.

4.2.2 The Linear Structure of Sentence

The linear structure of sentence is concerned with the word order of sentences: the sequence in which grammatical elements such as subject, verb, and object occur in sentences. Sentences are not just strings of words which occur in a random order. As Fromkin and Rodman (1983) put it, sentences are more than merely words placed one after another like beads on a string. There are syntactic rules determining the correct order of words in a sentence. These syntactic rules account for how different parts of a sentence are related, that is, "who" does "what" to "whom". These are grammatical relations of a sentence and they reveal how each part of the sentence functions grammatically, or syntactically. Grammatical relations are usually referred to as "subject of" and "object of", etc. In *It tastes nice* the relationship of *it* to *tastes* is that of a subject to a predicator. The pronoun is the subject of the verb. The relationship of *tastes* to *nice* is that of a predicator to its complement. The adjective is the complement of the verb. This sentence can then be said to have a "subject-predicator-complement" construction, whose elements (subject, predicator, complement) are successive functions established by the individual grammatical relations.

Different models of analysis use different terms in characterizing the linear structure of sentence. For example, generative grammar uses "NP + VP", and systemic-functional grammar uses terms like "actor-process-goal".

4.2.3 The Hierarchical Structure of Sentence

Sentences demonstrate a linear structure because words of a sentence are arranged one after another in a sequence by means of grammatical relations. However, grammatical relations can also be considered as parts of a larger unit. For example, in *It tastes nice* the pronoun is the "subject of" the verb, but it can also be described as "the subject" within the clause or sentence as a whole. In the same unit, the adjective is at once the "complement of" the verb (relation of part to part) and also "the complement" within the clause (relation of part to whole). The linear structure "NP + VP" can also be regarded as a larger unit made up of the smaller units NP and VP. In other words, a sentence can be analyzed into constituents. Conversely, constituents at different levels can combine to form increasingly larger units.

4.3 The Traditional Approach

Traditionally, syntax refers to the branch of grammar dealing with the ways in which words, with or without appropriate inflections, are arranged to show connections of meaning within the sentence (Matthews, 1981). Often known as **traditional grammar**, the **traditional approach** refers to the range of attitudes and methods found in the prelinguistic era of language study. Traditional grammar goes back to Greece of the fifth century before Christ, and includes the work of classical Greek and Roman grammarians, Renaissance grammarians, and eighteenth-century prescriptive grammarians. This approach

Chapter 4
Syntax: The Sentence Structure of Language

emphasizes such matters as correctness, linguistic purism, literary excellence, the use of Latin models and the priority of written language.

The traditional grammar is essentially a grammar of prescription. The term **"prescriptive"** is used by linguists to characterize any approach which attempts to lay down rules of correctness as to how language should be used. Using such criteria as purity, logic, history or literary excellence, **prescriptivism** aims to preserve imagined standards by insisting on norms of usage and criticizing violations of these norms. Prescriptive rules for English sentences, for example, mainly come from the following sources:

- Greek and Latin, which are regarded as models of linguistic excellence. According to the Latin standards, for example, you should use *It is I* or *He runs faster than I* and not *It is me* or *He runs faster than me*; You are not allowed to split an infinitive as in *He wants to quickly finish the work*, nor are you allowed to end a sentence with a preposition as in *What did you do this for?*
- The written language, which is more careful, prestigious and permanent than speech. You should say *Whom did you meet?* instead of *Who did you meet?*
- Logic, which means that language should follow the principles of logic. You should say *I didn't eat anything* or *I ate nothing* and not *I didn't eat nothing* because double negatives make a positive.

Modern linguistics owes a large debt to traditional grammar, because many basic concepts used by modern linguists can be traced back to traditional grammar. Modern linguistics is especially indebted to traditional grammar for the following:

- The modern notion of sentence, which is typically defined in traditional grammar as an independent group of words expressing a complete thought. It is customary in traditional grammar to begin with notional definitions of the sentence and its components.
- **Grammatical category**, which is a class or group of items which fulfill the same or similar functions or share a common set of grammatical properties in a language. Traditional grammar provided modern linguistics with a number of grammatical categories including the parts of speech, number, person, tense, voice, gender, subject and predicate.
- The notion of **concord** or **agreement**, which is associated with the requirement that the forms of two or more words in a syntactic relationship should agree, or be in concord, with each other in terms of some grammatical categories. For example, in the sentence *The boy speaks good English*, the verb *speaks* agrees with the noun *boy*. The

agreement is based on the grammatical categories of number and person. That is, the noun *boy* is third person singular, and the verb *likes* agrees with the noun. Agreement can also be found in noun phrases, so we say *a book* and *this book*, but *three books*, *these books* and *some books*.

- **Paradigm analysis**, which is the analysis of the different forms that a word can have in a grammatical system. A **paradigm** is a set or list of linguistic elements showing the forms which a word can have. Paradigms typically show a word's inflections. For example, in Latin:

<u>singular</u>   <u>plural</u>
amō "I love"   amāmus "we love"
amās "You love"   amātis "you love"
amat "he, she, it loves"   amant "they love"

To some extent, the terminology and analytical procedures of traditional grammar provide a useful framework for describing the outward structure of sentences and continues to serve as the point of departure for all schools of grammatical analysis. However, traditional grammar differs from modern linguistics in some essential aspects (See Chapter 1).

4.4 The Structural Approach

The **structural approach** to the analysis of language was started by the Swiss linguist Ferdinand de Saussure, "the father of modern linguistics", in the beginning of the twentieth century. The structural approach regards linguistic units as interrelated with each other in a structure.

While traditional grammar is a grammar of prescription, the structural approach analyses the structure of different languages through description. The **descriptive approach** focuses on the actual samples of language and attempts to describe the regular structure as it is used, not according to some view of how it should be used.

4.4.1 Immediate Constituent Analysis

The structural approach is most closely associated with American structuralism from the 1920s to the late 1950s (See Chapter 1). The technique frequently used in the analysis of the structure of sentences was **immediate constituent analysis** (IC analysis), which is a method of analyzing sentences into their component parts. This approach works through the different levels of structure within a sentence in a series of steps. At each level, a construction is divided into its major constituents, and the process continues until no further division can be made. In general, the division is binary. The two parts that are

Chapter 4
Syntax: The Sentence Structure of Language

yielded after each cut are the immediate constituents, and the smallest grammatical units obtained through segmentation are ultimate constituents. To sum up, immediate constituent analysis is the segmentation of a sentence into immediate constituents by using binary cuttings until obtaining its ultimate constituents. For example, to make an IC analysis of the sentence *The horse kicked the dog*, we carry out the following steps:

(a) Identify the two major constituents, *the horse* and *kicked the dog*.
(b) Divide the next-biggest constituent into two, viz. *kicked the dog* into *kicked* and *the dog*.
(c) Continue dividing constituents into two until we can go no further, viz. *the horse* into *the* and *horse*, *the dog* into *the* and *dog*.

The order of segmentation can be summarized using lines or brackets. If the first cut is symbolized by a single vertical line, the second cut by two lines, and so on, the sentence would look like this:

The||| horse | kicked || the ||| dog.

However, a much clearer way of representing constituent structure is through the use of tree diagrams:

Through IC analysis, the internal structure of a construction can be demonstrated clearly. Furthermore, IC analysis can help account for ambiguities. For example, the construction *more modern music* is ambiguous because it can be analyzed differently in terms of its constituent structure, as demonstrated below:

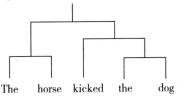

4.4.2 Endocentric and Exocentric Constructions

A **construction** is any syntactic structure such as a sentence or phrase. There are generally two types of constructions according to their structure: endocentric and exocentric.

An **endocentric construction** is a group of syntactically related words where one of the words is functionally equivalent to the group as a whole. As there is a definable "center" or head inside the group, which has the same distribution as the whole, an endocentric construction is also called a **headed construction**.

For example, *the fat lady in the park* is an endocentric construction, because, there is one central element (the head *lady*) which is distributionally (functionally) equivalent to the phrase as a whole.

Endocentric constructions can be divided into **subordinate constructions** and **coordinate constructions**. Subordinate constructions are endocentric constructions in which there is only one head, with the head being dominant and the other constructions dependent. For example, *the trees in the park*, *the book we are discussing*, *run away quickly*, *afraid of the dark*. Coordinate constructions are endocentric constructions in which there are more than one head, and they are of equal syntactic status, with no one dependent on the other. In other words, both are capable of serving as the head. For example, *man and woman*, *hit and run*.

An **exocentric construction** is a group of syntactically related words where none of the words is functionally equivalent to the group as a whole. That is to say, there is no definable "center" or head inside the group. The following are some typical examples of exocentric constructions:
- Basic sentence structures: *The man fell*
- Subordinate clauses: *If he is going*
- Prepositional phrases: *on the table*
- Verb + Object: *kick the ball*
- Verb + adjective: *seemed angry*.

4.5 The Transformational-generative Approach

4.5.1 The TG Model of Grammar

As introduced in Chapter 1, **transformational-generative grammar** is a theory of grammar proposed by the American linguist Noam Chomsky in his book *Syntactic Structures* (1957). The primary goal of TG grammar is to explain, with a system of rules, the knowledge which a native speaker of a language uses in forming grammatical sentences, and the ultimate goal is to provide a universal grammar for the description of all languages. **Universal grammar** (UG) is a theory of linguistics aiming to establish principles of grammar shared by all languages and thought to be innate to humans. The ultimate goal of universal grammar is to specify precisely the possible form of a human grammar, so as to provide a theory of the human language faculty and shed light on the nature of human mind. Chomsky views language as a system capable of producing an infinite number of sentences. The syntactic component is one of the three major organizational units within a grammar (the others being phonological and semantic), containing the phrase structure rules and

Syntax: The Sentence Structure of Language

transformational rules for the generation of syntactic structures.

TG grammar has undergone five stages of development since 1957. The Classical Theory (1950s) established the notion of generative grammar and the concepts of phrase structure rules and transformations. The Standard Theory (1960s) recognized the deep structure and surface structure in sentences, related by transformations, and introduced the semantic component at the level of deep structure in order to constrain the generation of ill-formed sentences. The Extended Standard Theory (1970s) recognized the role of surface structure in semantic interpretation and introduced the trace theory. The Government and Binding Theory (1980s), also called the principles and parameters theory, introduced the concepts of principles and parameters, including X-Bar Theory, θ-Theory, Case Theory, Binding Theory, Movement Theory. The Minimalist Program (1990s and after) is a theory of grammar whose core assumption is that grammars should be described in terms of the minimal set of theoretical and descriptive apparatus necessary.

Although many of the ideas and concepts in the early periods of TG grammar are no longer used in the recent framework, they serve as a good starting point for the understanding of the analytical procedures in TG grammar.

In the original TG model, grammar works in this way: **phrase structure rules** generate the basic sentence structures and sentences are formed through transformations. This means that each sentence is considered to have two levels of structure: **deep structure** and **surface structure**. Deep structure is the abstract syntactic representation of a sentence, that is, an underlying level of structural organization displaying all the factors that govern how a sentence should be interpreted. Surface structure is the syntactic structure of a sentence we actually articulate or hear. It is the final stage in the syntactic derivation of a sentence. The original TG model of grammar can be summarized as follows: the phrase structure rules generate deep structures which are transformed into surface structures by applying a set of **transformational rules.**

Phrase structure rules are also called PS rules, rewrite rules or categorical rules. They are rules for the generation of the deep structure of a sentence. Phrase structure rules not only present information about the constituent structure of a sentence, but also information about the constituents such as words and phrases. For example:

S → NP + VP
NP → Det + N
VP → V + NP
Det → the, a, this, that ...
N → man, tree ...

V → hit, walk ...

These rules mean that a sentence (S) can be analysed (or rewritten) as consisting of a noun phrase (NP) and a verb phrase (VP); a noun phrase can be further rewritten as a determiner (Det) and a noun (N); a verb phrase can be further rewritten as a verb (V) and a noun phrase; a determiner can be rewritten as *the* or *a*, and so on. Thus, to form the deep structure for *The man escaped*, the following phrase structure rules are needed:

S → NP + VP
NP → Det + N
VP → T (ense) + V
Det → the
N → man
T → PAST
V → escape

The following **tree diagram** can be used to show the deep structure for the sentence *The man escaped* and how the rules are applied:

(1)
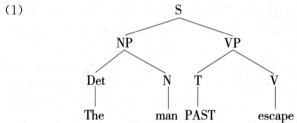

The deep structure is not an actual English sentence yet, and transformational rules will be applied to change the deep structure in to the surface structure *The man escaped*.

Apart from the phrase structure rules and transformational rules, there is also a phonological component which is responsible for the articulation of sentences at the level of surface structure.

4.5.2　Syntactic Structure

4.5.2.1　Phrase Structure

Words can be combined according to phrase structure rules to form phrases. For example, we can form the verb phrase (VP) *speak English* by merging the verb *speak* with the noun *English*. The head of the phrase is the verb *speak*, because it determines the grammatical category of the phrase. The phrase *speak English* is a projection (i.e. a phrasal expansion) of the verb *speak*. The **merging operation** can be illustrated in the following labeled tree diagram:

Chapter 4
Syntax: The Sentence Structure of Language

(2)
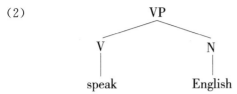

In the example of (2), the phrase *speak English* is formed by merging two words. Larger phrases can also be formed in the same way by merging two categories together. For example, we can form the infinitive phrase (IP) *to speak English* by merging the infinitive particle (I) *to* with the verb phrase *speak English*, with the infinitive particle *to* as the head.

(3)
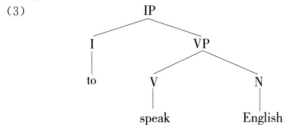

The infinitive phrase in (3) can be combined with the verb *learn* to form a larger verb phrase: *learn to speak English*:

(4)
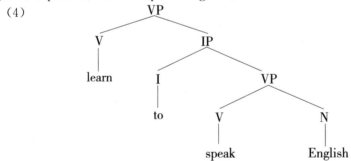

From the discussion above it can be assumed that phrases can be formed by merging pairs of categories together, no matter how complex the phrases are. With the help of category labels (V, N, I, VP, IP), tree diagrams (also called **phrase-markers**) can show how categories are combined together to form larger categories. Each point in the tree diagram that carries a category label is called a **node**. Nodes at the bottom of the tree are called terminal nodes (e. g. V, N, I), and nodes that branch into two (i. e. dominate other nodes) are nonterminal nodes (e. g. VP, IP).

The tree diagrams also show that categories are combined in a pairwise fashion to form larger categories. That is, syntactic structure is binary, which is captured by the **Binary Principle**: all nonterminal nodes are binary-branching (Radford, 2002: 98).

4.5.2.2 X-bar

According to the Binary Principle, phrases are formed by combining pairs of constituents. Many phrases are formed by merging a **head** (e. g. a noun, or verb, or preposition, or an infinitive) with a constituent following the head. The constituent which follows the head is called a **complement**. These various phrases named NP, VP, PP and IP, etc. can be given one name: XP, where X is a word category serving as the head of a phrase. Thus, the basic structure for an XP can be illustrated in Figure 4.1:

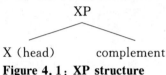

X (head)　　　complement

Figure 4.1: XP structure

Thus, in the NP *loss of face*, *of face* is the complement of the head *loss*; in the PP *at a meeting*, *a meeting* is the complement of the head *at*.

Apart from the head and complement, there may also be a constituent positioned to the left of the head. This constituent is called a **specifier**, because it specifies relevant information of the head. It is easy to find such phrases in the English language as the following:

XP	Specifier	Head	Complement
NP	government	decision	to ban guns
AP	very	curious	of the matter
VP	both	speak	English
PP	right	in	the middle
DP	such	a	pity

It is obvious that all the phrases above are made up of three elements: specifier + head + complement. However, this seems to contradict with the Binary Principle of phrase structure. So how is a complex phrase like *government decision to ban guns* formed? We might suppose that the head *decision* combines with its complement *to ban guns* to form an intermediate level called **N-bar** (also labeled as N'). The full NP would be formed by merging the specifier *government* with the N-bar:

Chapter 4
Syntax: The Sentence Structure of Language

(5)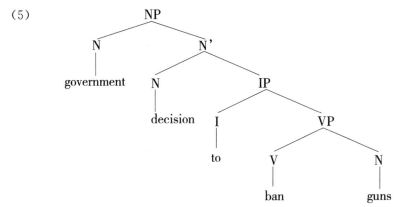

As shown in (5), the N-bar *decision to ban guns* is an immediate level larger than the noun *decision* but smaller than the full noun phrase *government decision to ban guns*. This way of analysis applies to all phrases of the form specifier + head + complement. Thus, **X-bar** is a level of structure formed by merging the head (X) with its complement. It is an immediate level or category larger than the head but smaller than the full XP. This can be formulated as follows and illustrated in Figure 4.2:

XP → specifier + X'
X' → X (head) + complement

```
            XP
           /  \
    specifier  X'
              /  \
        X (head)  complement
```

Figure 4.2: X-bar

The X-bar theory assumes that every phrase is headed, and hence endocentric. This view of phrase structure is quite different from the structural approach which makes a distinction between endocentric and exocentric structures.

4.5.2.3 Sentence Structure

It can be assumed that sentences are formed in the same way as phrases are formed, that is, by the binary operation of merging pairs of categories together. The head of a sentence is the inflectional category (shortened as INFL or I) in the sentence. By definition, INFL is a category comprising auxiliaries (inflected for tense and agreement) and the infinitive particle *to* (Note that the infinitive particle *to* functions in the same way as auxiliaries do). In a sentence, the head INFL takes an NP (the subject) as its specifier and a VP category as its complement, as illustrated in (6).

(6)
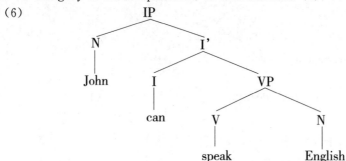

As a sentence is formed in the same way as does a phrase, a sentence can be regarded as an **inflection phrase** (shortened as IP) with INFL as its head. Thus, the sentence in (6) is formed by merging the head (the auxiliary *can*) with its complement (the VP *speak English*) to form the inflection phrase *can speak English*. According to the X-bar theory, *can speak English* is an intermediate inflection phrase in the sense that it is larger than the head and smaller than a full IP, so it is an I-bar (I'). Besides, it is an incomplete inflection phrase in the sense that it cannot be used as a sentence, because auxiliaries require a subject (or specifier). The IP is finally formed by merging the noun *John* (both subject and specifier) with the I-bar.

4.5.2.4 Complementizer Phrase

It has been shown that a sentence can be regarded as an inflection phrase (IP) of the form subject + INFL + complement. In the English language, some sentences are introduced by **complementizers** such as *that* (e.g. *John thought* **that** it was raining), for (It is important **for** you to go) *or* if/whether (I asked **if** you could help me). Thus, the framework of merging should be extended to explain this kind of structure.

A complementizer is a functional element which is typically used to introduce a complement clause. In terms of merging operations, a complementizer merges with a sentence (IP) to form a **complementizer phrase** (CP), with the complementizer (C) as its head, as shown in (7).

Chapter 4
Syntax: The Sentence Structure of Language

(7)
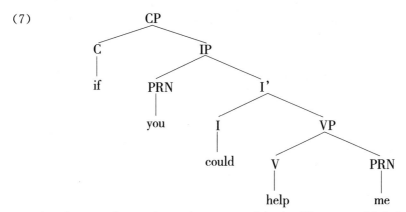

In (7), the complementizer *if* merges with the IP *you could help me* to form the complementizer phrase *if you could help me*.

4.5.2.5 C-command

The structure of a sentence can tell us how constituents are related. One apparent structural relation is **dominance**, which is the hierarchical or top-to-bottom ordering of constituents as demonstrated in a tree diagram. For example, dominance relation in the sentence *John's father doesn't like him* can be illustrated in (8):

(8)
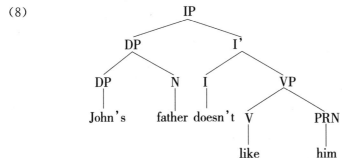

To simplify the matter, we may use (9) to show the structural relation of dominance in (8):

(9)
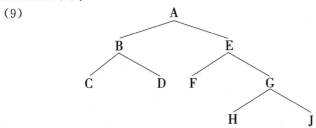

(Radford, 2002: 99)

The dominance relation between nodes in a tree diagram is manifested by whether one node occurs higher up in the structure than another. Thus, in (9), node A dominates all other nodes; node B only dominates nodes C and D; node E dominates nodes F, G, H and J; node G dominates nodes H and J. Nodes C, D, F, H and J are terminal nodes, so they dominate no other nodes.

A more complex structural relationship which can be used to account for the grammaticality of sentences is **c-command** (or **constituent command**). C-command can be defined as follows:

α c-commands β iff (= if and only if) α does not dominate β and every γ that dominates α dominates β. (Chomsky, 1986: 8)

This can be illustrated in the following tree diagram in Figure 4.3.

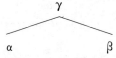

Figure 4.3: C-command

C-command can be easily understood with the help of the train network analogy drawn by Radford (2002). If you think of α and β as different stations in a train network, we can say that α c-commands β if you can get from α to β by taking a northbound train from α, getting off at the first stop, and then taking a southbound train to β (on a different line). We may use the tree diagram in (9) to further illustrate this structural relationship. We can say that C c-commands D; B c-commands E, F, G, H and J; F c-commands G, H and J; H c-commands J.

We now return to (8) to see how c-command works. The pronoun (PRN) *him* is ambiguous in that it can either refer to *John* or someone else. Certainly it cannot refer to the determiner phrase (DP) *John's father*. If we look at the structural relation here, *him* is c-commanded by the DP *John's father*. It can be assumed that a pronoun like *him*, called a **pronominal**, cannot be c-commanded by an **antecedent** within the same sentence. As *John* does not c-command *him*, it can be the possible antecedent for the pronominal. However, if we change the pronominal *him* into the reflexive *himself*, it becomes unambiguous, and the reflexive only refers to *John's father*. In *John's father doesn't like himself*, the DP *John's father* c-commands the reflexive *himself*. Thus, different from pronominals, reflexives are c-commanded by an antecedent. Reflexives like *himself*, *themselves*, *myself* and reciprocals like *each other* and *one another* are called **anaphors**. They cannot be used to refer directly to an entity in the outside world, but rather must be bound by or refer to an antecedent elsewhere in the same phrase or sentence. Otherwise, the resulting sentence is ungrammatical. The binding of anaphors by their antecedents can be explained in terms of the **c-command condition on binding**:

A bound constituent (= anaphor) must be c-commanded by an

appropriate antecedent.

The c-command condition on binding can tell us why (10a) is grammatical while (10b) is ungrammatical.

(10) a. The president can congratulate himself.
  b. * Supporters of the president can congratulate himself.
(Radford, 2002: 75)

In (10a), the DP *the president* c-commands the PRN *himself*, so the c-command condition on binding is satisfied, as shown in (11) below:

(11)
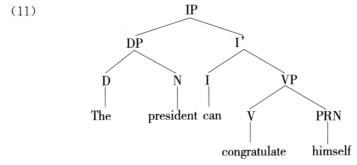

(12)
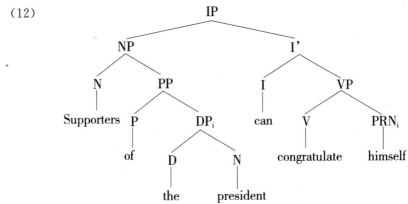

In (10b), however, *the president* cannot be the antecedent of *himself*, because *the president* does not c-command *himself*, as shown in (12). Although *supporters of the president* c-commands *himself*, it is not a suitable antecedent because it is a plural expression, and *himself* requires a singular antecedent. Thus, the c-command condition on binding is not satisfied, hence the ungrammaticality of (10b).

4.5.3 Movement

Merge and move are said to be the two central syntactic operations in forming sentences. So far, we have shown how sentences are formed by means of merging operations. However, not all sentences are formed by merging constituents together. Some sentences such as yes-no questions and wh-questions are formed through the syntactic operation of movement. By definition, **movement** is an operation by which a word or phrase is moved from one position in a structure to another. In deriving a sentence, certain elements may be moved, and they may only be moved to certain positions.

4.5.3.1 Head Movement

In English, yes-no questions involve auxiliary inversion. That is, the auxiliary is traditionally said to move into the position in front of the subject. Thus, in *Could you help me*? the auxiliary *could* is said to have been inverted and have moved from the post-subject position into the pre-subject position.

In TG grammar, a yes-no question is formed by moving an inverted auxiliary from the head I position in IP into the head C position in CP. When movement occurs, the moved constituent leaves behind an empty trace (labeled as *t*) of itself in the position out of which it moves. Thus, the sentence *Could you help me*? has the structure in (13).

(13)

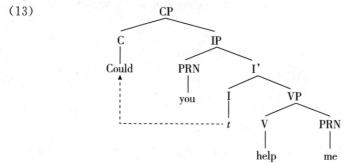

This type of movement in (13) involves movement of a word from the head position in one phrase into the head position in another phrase, and so is known as **head movement** (or **head-to-head movement**).

When yes-no questions are formed from statements containing no overt auxiliary, the dummy auxiliary *do* is used. For example:

(14) a. Birds fly.
     b. *Do* birds fly?

Since the head I is left empty in (14a), as shown in (15), the yes-no question in (14b) is formed by generating the auxiliary *do* in I and then raising it from I to C, as shown in (16).

(15)

(16)

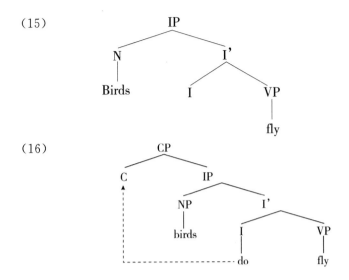

4.5.3.2 Operator Movement

A yes-no question can be regarded as a CP consisting of a head C (filled by an inverted auxiliary) and an IP complement. However, another constituent can occur before the head C constituent, and form a question like (17):

(17) **Which book** can you read?

Example (17) is an interrogative often called a wh-question. Words like *what* and *which* are called interrogative operators or wh-operators, and expressions like *which book* are called operator phrases. What kind of movement operation has taken place in wh-questions?

In (17), the operator phrase *which book* functions as the complement of the verb *read*. That is, the operator phrase originally occupies the complement position after the verb, as shown in (18):

(18) You can read *which book*?

In forming the wh-question, two kinds of movement are involved: one is the head movement of the auxiliary *can* from the head I position in IP to the head C position in CP; the other is the movement of the operator phrase to a position before the inverted auxiliary *can*. As the inverted auxiliary occupies the head C position in CP and the position before the head is typically occupied by specifiers, it can be reasonably assumed that the operator phrase is moved into the specifier position in CP. Thus, sentence (17) will be derived as in (19).

Please note that according to the X-bar theory, the head merges with its complement to form an X-bar, and an XP is formed by merging the specifier with the X-bar. In (19), the head C merges with its IP complement to form a C-bar (C'), which merges with the specifier DP (determiner phrase) to form the CP.

(19)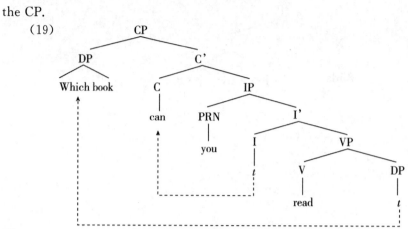

Thus, in deriving wh-questions, the operator phrase moves into the specifier position in CP. This movement operation is called **wh-movement** or **operator movement**.

In a wh-question like (17), the operator phrase functions as the complement of the verb. However, the operator phrase can also function as the subject of the verb. For example:

(20) a. Who saw it?
b. What languages are easy?

Wh-questions in (20) are called wh-subject questions. It seems plausible to suggest that in deriving the wh-subject questions in (20), only the operator phrases (*who* and *what languages*) move into the specifier position in CP, and no auxiliary movement is involved. This is shown in (21):

(21)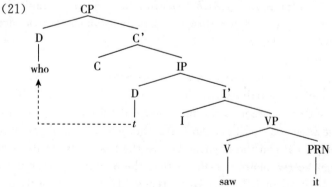

More recently, wh-subject questions are said to have the status of IPs, and thus have the structure in (22) below:

(22)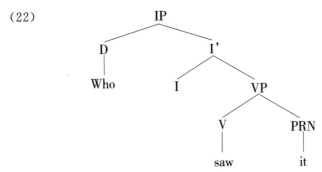

In (22), the wh-operator *who* occupies the specifier position of IP. Since the IP has the wh-operator *who* as its specifier, the IP is interpreted as a question without moving the wh-operator into the specifier position in CP. This is different from the other type of wh-question (e. g. *What can you read?*), in which the wh-operator moves into the specifier position in CP in order to generate a structure containing a wh-operator as its specifier.

4.5.3.3 Conditions on Movement

It can be said that all movement operations have in common the property of moving a category from one position to another. Thus, all movement operations can be reduced to a single general process called **Move α**, where α stands for any category. Move α can be simply defined as "move any category anywhere". However, this does not mean that movement is not constrained. Appropriate conditions are needed in order to prevent Move α from generating ungrammatical sentences. These conditions make sure that only certain categories move from certain positions to certain other positions over a certain distance.

The conditions on movement can be illustrated by the **economy principle** in the minimalist program, which is summarized as follows:

> Minimise grammatical structure and movement operations (i. e. posit as little structure as possible, and move as few constituents as possible the shortest distance possible) (Radford et al., 1999: 333).

As far as movement is concerned, the economy principle is also variously called the principle of shortest movement, minimal link condition, or the minimality condition.

In head movement, for example, an auxiliary can only move from the head I position into the nearest head C position of CP. This can explain why (23a) derived from the movement operation of (23b) is grammatical, while (24a) derived from the movement operation of (24b) is not:

(23) a. Does John know that Mary will come?
　　 b. [CP Does [IP John t know [CP that [IP Mary will come]]]]

(24) a. * Will John knows that Mary come?
　　 b. [CP Will [IP John knows [CP that [IP Mary t come]]]]

In operator movement, the economy principle makes sure that in questions containing more than one wh-operator, only one operator can be moved and it is the nearest wh-operator that moves into the specifier position of CP. This explains why (25a) is grammatical, but (25b) and (25c) are ungrammatical:

(25) a. Who do you think will say what?
　　 b. * What who do you think will say?
　　 c. * What do you think who will say?

In (25b), two wh-operators are involved in the movement. In (25c), it is the further wh-operator (*what*) that moves to the specifier position of CP. The difference between (25a) and (25c) is clear in (26):

(26) a. Who do you think t will say what?
　　 b. * What do you think who will say t ?

4.6 The Functional Approach

The **functional approach** looks at how language enables us to do things—to share information, to enquire, to express attitudes, and so on. It is concerned with how people use language for certain purposes, that is, how language is used to fulfill our social needs or to perform various functions. At the heart of a functional model of language is an emphasis on meaning and on how language is involved in the construction of meaning. It sees language as a resource for making meaning. The functional approach to language is not concerned with a set of rules which prescribe correct and incorrect usage. More specifically, a functional model of language describes how language operates at the text level, not at the level of individual words and sentences in isolation (Derewianka, 1990: 3—4).

4.6.1　Functions of Language

As far as the function of language is concerned, traditional accounts of language typically tend to view language as a means of communication. On this view, the essential feature of language is that it is used in communication. As regards verbal communication, Jakobson (1960) suggests that there are six essential factors in any act of verbal communication. The ADDRESSER sends a

Chapter 4
Syntax: The Sentence Structure of Language

MESSAGE to the ADDRESSEE. To be operative, the message requires a CONTEXT referred to; a CODE fully, or at least partially, common to the addresser and addressee (or in other words, to the encoder and decoder of the message); and finally, a CONTACT, a physical channel and psychological connection between the addresser and the addressee, enabling both of them to enter and stay in communication. This is the code model of communication, as is illustrated in Figure 4.4 below:

CONTEXT
MESSAGE
ADDRESSER ·················· ADDRESSEE
CONTACT
CODE

Figure 4.4: The code model of communication

According to Jakobson, each of these six factors determines a different function of language. The **REFERENTIAL**, or "**denotative**" function, oriented towards the CONTEXT, is the use of language to convey information, and thus forms the basis for verbal communication. The **EMOTIVE** or "**expressive**" function, focused on the ADDRESSER, is the direct expression of the addresser's attitude towards what he or she is speaking about. The **CONATIVE** function, oriented towards the ADDRESSEE, is the use of language in order to achieve a result in the addressee, in accord with the addresser's wishes. Corresponding to CONTACT is the **PHATIC** function of language to establish an atmosphere or maintain social contact rather than to exchange information or ideas (e.g. greetings, comments on the weather, or enquiries about health). Whenever the addresser or addressee needs to check up whether they use the same code, speech is focused on the CODE: it performs a **METALINGUAL** function (e.g. *I don't follow you—what do you mean?* or *Do you know what I mean?*). The last function of language, the **POETIC** function, which focuses on the MESSAGE, is any aesthetic or creative linguistic use of the spoken or written medium.

Owing to the diversity of things we can do with language, it is difficult to make a clear-cut classification of all the functions of language. In systemic functional linguistics, Halliday (1994) proposes a classification of three **metafunctions**, so called because these are the fundamental functions of every natural language, and they are used as the basis for exploring how meanings are created and understood. Thus, all the more specific functions of language can be assigned to one or other of the three metafunctions:

- **The experiential function**: we use language to talk about our experience of the world, including the worlds in our own minds, to describe events and states and the entities involved in them.

- **The interpersonal function**: we use language to interact with other people, to establish and maintain relations with them, to influence their behavior, to express our own viewpoint on things in the world, and to elicit or change theirs.
- **The textual function**: in using language, we organize our messages in ways which indicate how they fit in with the other messages around them and with the wider context in which we are talking or writing.

(Thompson, 2008: 30)

This also means that people use language to make three kinds of meanings simultaneously. Experiential meanings are meanings about how we represent experience in language. Interpersonal meanings are meanings about role relationships with other people and our attitudes to each other. Textual meanings are meanings about how our message is organized and how it relates to the linguistic or non-linguistic context.

4.6.2 Functional Analysis of Syntactic Structure

Functional linguistics aims to describe the specific matches of function and wording. That is, the fundamental question functional linguistics attempts to answer is: how is language structured to make meaning? According to Halliday (1994), language is structured to make three kinds of meanings simultaneously: experiential, interpersonal, and textual. Each of these three types of meanings or functions corresponds to one particular type of wording in grammar. To sum up, people use language to make meanings: to make sense of the world and of each other. Language is structured in such a way that enables people to make meanings with each other.

We now use Thompson's (2008: 31) example to illustrate how language is structured for use. Suppose a child in class complains that someone has taken her calculator while she was not looking. In such a context, the teacher is expected to identify the child responsible and make him or her return the calculator. There are obviously many options open to the teacher as to how he goes about this, but let us assume that the teacher guesses that one of the students, say, Jim, is guilty, and questions the other students about this:

- **In experiential terms**, the teacher wants to refer to the action that has happened (taking) and the thing that the action was done to (the calculator); and he also wants to refer to the possible doer of the action. He will thus opt for an experiential structure which expresses the event, the doer and the done-to: we can symbolize this as *Jim/take/her calculator*.
- **In interpersonal terms**, the teacher wants his addressees, the children, to tell him whether Jim was the doer or not; and he will opt for a yes/

no question structure with the ordering of Finite^Subject: *Did Jim (take her calculator)?*
- **In textual terms**, the teacher's starting point is the part of the clause which shows that this is a question, since the questioning is presumably uppermost in his mind; so there is no reason to move the Finite^Subject combination from its most natural position at the beginning of the utterance.

As a result of these simultaneous choices, the teacher produces the wording: *Did Jim take her calculator?* Following this line of analysis, we can have three kinds of structure for the clause, each corresponding to one of the meanings being made, as shown in Figure 4.5.

Type of structure	Did	Jim	take	her calculator?
experiential→		Actor	Process	Goal
interpersonal→	Finite	Subject	Predicator	Complement
textual→	Theme		Rheme	

Figure 4.5: Three kinds of structure in the clause(Thompson, 2008: 34)

It can be seen that this kind of analysis in Figure 4.5 not only brings out the constituent structure of the clause, but also neatly labels the functions of the constituents. In experiential terms, *Jim* is labeled as Actor, *her calculator* as Goal, and *take* as Process. That is, we are looking at the clause from the experiential perspective of something or someone doing something. In interpersonal terms, the Finite^Subject ordering indicates the interrogative mood of the clause, which suggests that the teacher demands information from the children and wants the children to confirm or deny the guess *Jim took her calculator*. In other words, we are looking at the clause from the interpersonal perspective of how the speaker interacts with the listener. In textual terms, *Did Jim* is labeled as "Theme", showing that the starting point for the message is the part of the clause which signals that this is a question. The remaining part of the clause is labeled as "Rheme", indicating what is said about the Theme (See Chapter 7 for a detailed discussion of Theme and Rheme). In other words, we are looking at the clause from the textual perspective of how the speaker organizes the message by ordering the various constituents of the clause.

4.7 Summary

Syntax studies the structure of a sentence. Although there have been various approaches to syntax, currently two approaches seem to be dominant:

the formal approach and the functional approach. The formal approach is represented by Chomsky's TG grammar, which aims to explain the knowledge of native speakers in forming grammatical sentences. The formal approach regards language as an autonomous system containing rules for the generation of syntactic structures. Thus, the formal approach studies sentence structures without taking account of language-external factors. The functional approach, however, maintains that syntactic structure is related to language-external factors, especially the use of language in context. Thus, the functional approach studies syntactic structure in relation to the functions of language.

Further Readings

Bloor, T. & Bloor, M. 2001. *The Functional Analysis of English: A Hallidayan Approach*. 北京:外语教学与研究出版社.

Halliday, M. A. K. 1994. *An Introduction to Functional Grammar*. London: Edward Arnold.

Radford, A. 2002. *Syntactic Theory and the Structure of English: A Minimalist Approach*. 北京:北京大学出版社.

Radford, A. et al. 2000. *Linguistics: An Introduction*. 北京:外语教学与研究出版社.

Thompson, G. 2008. *Introducing Functional Grammar* (Second Edition). 北京:外语教学与研究出版社.

胡壮麟、朱永生、张德禄、李战子,2005,《系统功能语言学概论》。北京:北京大学出版社。

石定栩,2002,《乔姆斯基的形式句法》。北京:北京语言大学出版社。

Questions and Exercises

1. Define the following terms.

traditional grammar	IC analysis	endocentric construction
exocentric construction	universal grammar	phrase structure rules
transformational rules	deep structure	surface structure
X-bar	c-command	head movement
operator movement	Move α	experiential function
interpersonal function	textual function	

2. What is the relationship between syntax and grammar?
3. How is sentence defined?
4. Illustrate the linear structure and hierarchical structure of sentence with examples.
5. In what sense is traditional grammar prescriptive? Where did the prescriptive rules for English sentences come from?
6. What contributions did traditional grammar make to modern linguistics?
7. Analyze the following ambiguous sentences using immediate constituent analysis.
   (a) He arrived late last night.
   (b) Tom or Dick and Harry will go.
   (c) He saw the man with a telescope.
8. Illustrate how the following phrases are formed through merging operation with tree diagrams:
   (a) plan to build a house
   (b) decide to go home

(c) try to find the book
(d) vote against the plan
9. Draw tree diagrams to represent the structures of the sentences below.
   (a) The president has resigned.
   (b) He is reading a book.
   (c) You may see her.
   (d) John has tried to catch the bus.
10. Draw tree diagrams to represent the structures of the following sentences and explain how the c-command condition on binding constrains the meaning or grammaticality of these sentences.
    (a) John's father doesn't like him.
    (b) John's father doesn't like himself.
    (c) * He doesn't like herself.
    (d) The president may blame himself.
    (e) * Supporters of the president may blame himself.
11. Draw tree diagrams to represent the structures of the following sentences and use arrows to show what has moved from where to where.
    (a) Can you hear me?
    (b) Does it hurt?
    (c) What can you do?
    (d) Which way do you think John went?
    (e) * Which way do you wonder why John went?
12. What are the functions of language according to the code model of communication?
13. What are the three metafunctions of language?
14. How is language structured to make meaning?

Chapter 5

Semantics: The Meaning of Language

5.1 Introduction

Generally, **semantics** is a branch of linguistics, which is concerned with the study of meaning in language. As meaning plays a central part in human communication, semantics is at the center of the study of communication. In human communication, utterances are produced because they convey meaning. Semantics studies the nature of meaning and why particular linguistic expressions have the meanings they do.

Semantics is said to be a discipline that has fascinated philosophers since the beginning of Western civilization. Philosophers are mainly interested in the relation between linguistic expressions, such as the words of a language, and persons, things, and events in the world to which these words refer. Within the domain of linguistics, semantics is mainly concerned with the analysis of meaning of words, phrases, or sentences and sometimes with the meaning of utterances in discourse or the meaning of a whole text.

5.2 Approaches to Meaning

Everyone who knows a language can understand what is said to him or her and can produce strings of words that convey meaning. However, the definition of meaning has long plagued linguists and philosophers, because "meaning" covers a variety of aspects of language and there is no general agreement about the nature of meaning. Various different interpretations have thus far arisen.

According to **the naming view**, language might be thought of as a communication system with on the one hand the signifier, and on the other the signified. The signifier is a word in the language and the signified is the object in the world that it "stands for", "refers to" or "denotes". Words, that is to say, are "names" or "labels" for things. The naming view is obviously limited because it seems to apply only to nouns (or nominal expressions in general). It is difficult, if not impossible, to extend the theory of naming to include these other parts of speech. Even if we restrict this approach to nouns alone, some

Chapter 5
Semantics: The Meaning of Language

nouns, e. g. *unicorn, goblin, fairy, courage, nonsense, imagination, love,* do not refer to objects in the world at all.

Different from the naming view which relates words and things directly, **conceptualism** holds that words and objects are related through the mediation of concepts of the mind. Ogden and Richards (1923) were the first to develop what can be called a **"referential"** theory of meaning illustrated by the classic **"semiotic triangle"**, which looks upon the relation between words and objects as a triangle:

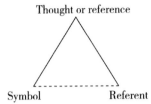

The SYMBOL refers to the linguistic element (word, sentence, etc.), the REFERENT refers to the object in the world of experience, and THOUGHT or REFERENCE refers to the concept. The relation between the symbol and the referent is not direct. Rather, the symbol signifies the referent by way of the thought or reference, the concept in the mind of the speaker of a language.

This theory has taken a step further than the naming view, but it also poses a difficult question: what precisely is the link between symbol and concept? Some people say that it is a psychological one, that when we think of a name we think of the concept and vice versa. But what exactly is meant by "thinking of" a concept? To answer this question, some scholars have proposed the image theory of meaning. That is, language users have some kind of image of a chair when they talk about chairs. But this is certainly false. A word may evoke a certain image in our mind, but it is not true that whenever we utter or hear a word we would visualize a certain image in our mind. If this were a necessary part of talking, it would be impossible to communicate ideas between people or to give a lecture on linguistics. Moreover, to people from different social-cultural backgrounds, the same word may call up different images. If so, the same word would be said to have different meanings and communication between these different people would be impossible. Worst of all, there are many words with which it is impossible to associate any image at all —*and*, *or*, *because*, *therefore*, etc. Yet they are by no means meaningless.

There are still other approaches to meaning which take into account the use of language or the context in which language is used. **The behaviouristic** or **mechanistic approach** of the American structural linguists represented by Bloomfield defines meaning by using the behaviourist notions of "stimulus" and "response", and thus the meaning of a linguistic sign is "the situation in which the speaker utters it and the response which it calls forth in the hearer". **The**

contextual theory of meaning associated with Wittgenstein and Firth defines meaning of a word as its use in the language and argues that one can derive meaning from or reduce meaning to observable contexts, and therefore it is useless to study the meaning of words in isolation of their context of use.

5.3 Sense and Reference

To explicate the complicated nature of meaning, two different aspects of meaning can be proposed: **sense** and **reference**. Reference is the relationship between language and the world. It deals with the relationship between the linguistic elements, words, sentences, etc., and the non-linguistic world of experience. Sense is the relationship inside the language. By the sense of a word we mean its place in the system of relationships with other words in the vocabulary. In other words, sense relates to the complex system of relationships that hold between the linguistic elements themselves (mostly the words); it is concerned only with intra-linguistic relations.

In the vocabularies of all languages, there are certain items that can be used to refer to the physical world. When a sentence like *John is a teacher* is uttered, the speaker refers to a certain individual existent in the situation or known by both the speaker and hearer. Although not all words can be used in this way, it is fair to say that words are related in one way or another. Whether a word has reference or not, we can ask whether the word has meaning in a certain context. A word can enter into paradigmatic relations with other words which can also occur in the same context. A word can also enter into syntagmatic relations with other units of the same level in a linear or sequential structure. For example, in such contexts as *a ... of milk*, the word *pint* forms paradigmatic relations with such other words as *bottle*, *cup*, *gallon*, and syntagmatic relations with *a*, *of* and *milk*.

Thus, in discussing meaning, we may relate our language to our experience or talk about sense relations. To illustrate, let's consider the words *ram* and *ewe*. These on the one hand refer to particular kinds of animals and derive their meaning in this way. But they also belong to a pattern in English that includes *cow/bull*, *sow/boar*, *mare/stallion*, etc. But there are other kinds, e.g. *duck/duckling*, *pig/piglet* (involving adult and young), or *father/son*, *uncle/nephew* (involving family relationships), and these are not usually thought to be grammatical. They are rather a part of the "semantic structure" of English.

It is very difficult to make a clear-cut distinction between sense and reference. The categories in language correspond, to some degree at least, to real-world distinctions. The fact that we have *ram/ewe*, *bull/cow* is part of the semantic structure of English, but it also relates to the fact that there are male and female sheep and cattle in the real world. The understanding of the semantic anomaly of a sentence like *John's printer has bad intentions* not only depends on the language user's ability to interpret the sense relations within the sentence, but also the ability to relate the sentence to the world of experience. However, we have to remember (1) that not all languages will make the same distinctions, (2) that there is considerable indeterminacy in the categorisation of the real world: some things (e.g. the mammals) fall into fairly natural classes, while others do not. It is because of this that we can distinguish sense and reference, yet must allow that there is no absolute line between them, between what is in the world and what is in language.

5.4 Word Meaning

In talking about **word meaning**, we are actually dealing with **lexical semantics**, which is concerned with the meanings of words and the relations between the meanings of words. Word meaning is made up of various components which are interrelated and interdependent. These components are commonly described as types of meaning.

5.4.1 Grammatical Meaning and Lexical Meaning

Generally speaking, word meaning can be classified into two broad types: grammatical and lexical. **Grammatical meaning** refers to that part of the word meaning which indicates grammatical concepts or relationships such as word-class, gender, number, case, tense and all other grammatical forms known as inflectional paradigm. A grammatical or inflectional **paradigm** is the set of grammatical forms of a word that indicates singular and plural meaning of nouns, or tense meanings of verbs, and so on.

Lexical meaning is that part of the meaning of a word that remains constant in all forms of one and the same word. That is to say, for the same word, the lexical meaning is the same throughout the paradigm; that is, all the word-forms of one and the same word have the same lexical meaning. This is different from the grammatical meaning of the word, which varies from one word-form to another. For example, the word *walk* has the same lexical meaning no matter what grammatical forms it may take.

5.4.2 Classification of Lexical Meaning

According to Leech (1981), lexical meaning falls into two broad categories: **conceptual meaning** and **associative meaning**. Conceptual meaning is the meaning given in the dictionary and forms the core of word meaning.

Associative meaning is the secondary meaning beyond the conceptual meaning. It is open-ended and indeterminate as it is liable to the influences of such factors as culture, experience, belief, background, education, etc. Associative meaning is a cover term for connotative meaning, social meaning, affective meaning, reflected meaning and collocative meaning. Leech also mentions another type of meaning called thematic meaning, which is related to the organization of the message in a sentence. Altogether, there are seven types of lexical meaning.

Conceptual meaning has been given various names such as denotation, cognitive meaning, denotative or denotational meaning. It refers to that part of meaning of a word or phrase that relates it to phenomena in the world. Conceptual meaning is used when the emphasis is on the relationship between language, on the one hand, and the things, events, or processes, which are external to the speaker and his language, on the other. For example, the conceptual meaning of the English word *sun* is "a heavenly body which gives off light, heat, and energy", a meaning which is understood by anyone who speaks English. Conceptual meaning is constant and relatively stable, and as such, it forms the basis for linguistic communication simply because the same word has the same conceptual meaning to all speakers of the same language.

Connotative meaning, traditionally known as connotation, is the emotional association which a word or phrase suggests in one's mind. It is the supplementary value which is added to the purely denotative meaning of a word. For instance, the denotative meaning of the word *mother* is "female parent", but it generally connotes love, care, and tenderness. Connotations associated with a certain word can be different from culture to culture, or from person to person. For example, the word *dog* is associated with different overtones in Chinese and English. Even in the same culture or community, the word *mother* will have different connotations for different people because of their individual experiences. For most people, this word has the connotations of love, care and tenderness, but for those other people whose mothers are strict or cruel, this word may have totally different connotations.

Social or **stylistic meaning** is that which a piece of language conveys about the social circumstances of its use. Many words have social or stylistic features that make them appropriate for certain contexts. We recognize some words or pronunciation as being dialectal, i. e. as telling us something of the geographical or social origin of the speaker; other features of language tell us something of the social relationship between the speaker and the hearer. Because of socio-stylistic variation, it is not surprising that we rarely find words which have both the same conceptual meaning and the same stylistic meaning. For example, *horse*, *nag*, *gee-gee* and *steed* are synonyms, and they have the same conceptual meaning, but the social meanings associated with them differ: *horse* is a word for general use, while *nag* is a slang word, *gee-gee* is baby language, and *steed* is used in poetry. Thus, in language use, we should choose words properly to fit different contexts or situations.

Affective meaning indicates the speaker's feelings or attitudes towards the person or thing in question. There are a small number of words in English (chiefly interjections, like *Aha*! *Alas*! and *Hurrah*!) whose main function is to express emotion. Some words explicitly convey emotive meanings: *love*, *hate*, *boast*, *gang*, *niggardly*, *pleasure*, *good*, *bad*, *modest*, *honest*, *angel*. These words, often called **purr words** or **snarlwords**, are used not as a mere statement of fact, but to express the speaker's approval or disapproval of the person or thing being talked about. Affective meaning falls into two categories: the **appreciatory meaning** is expressed by the purr words, i. e. words of positive or favourable overtones, showing appreciation or attitude of approval; the **derogatory** or **pejorative meaning** is expressed by the snarlwords, i. e. words of negative or unfavourable associations, implying disapproval, contempt or criticism. This contrast of affective meaning can be illustrated by the following pairs of words: *famous/notorious*, *black/nigger*, *slender/skinny*, *determined/pigheaded*, *statesman/politician*, *confidence/complacency*. It is obvious that the first word in each pair is appreciatory while the second is derogatory.

Reflected meaning is that which is communicated through association with another sense of the same expression. Reflected meaning arises in cases of multiple conceptual meaning, when one sense of a word forms part of our response to another sense. People generally choose to use **euphemistic expressions** or avoid using **taboo words** to keep away from the reflected meanings associated with certain words. Thus taboo words concerned with sex or some parts of the body or religion are seldom used simply because they usually conjure up uncomfortable associations. On certain occasions, people tend to use mild, vague or indirect words or phrases in place of what is required by truth or accuracy. Thus *belly* is replaced by *abdomen*, *water-closet* by *wash-room*, and so on.

Collocative meaning consists of the associations a word acquires on account of the meanings of words which tend to occur in its environment. Words have collocative meanings because they tend to co-occur with other words in the expression of meaning. This co-occurrence or mutual expectancy of words, which is called collocation, is part of the meaning of a word. For example, *pretty* and *handsome* share common ground in the meaning "good-looking", but they have different collocative meanings, as they are distinguished by the range of nouns with which they are likely to collocate: *pretty* is usually used with *girl*, while *handsome* is usually used with *boy*. Further examples are quasi-synonymous verbs such as *wander* and *stroll* (*cows* may *wander*, but may not *stroll*) or *tremble* and *quiver* (one *trembles* with *fear*, but *quivers* with *excitement*).

Thematic meaning refers to what is communicated by the way in which a speaker or writer organizes the message, in terms of ordering, focus, and emphasis. For example, an active sentence such as *The rain destroyed the crops* has a different meaning from its passive equivalent *The crops were destroyed by the rain*, although in conceptual content they seem to be the same. The difference lies in the communicative values because the two sentences suggest different contexts: the active sentence seems to answer an implicit question *What did the rain do?* while the passive sentence seems to answer an implicit question *What happened to the crops?* Thematic meaning is mainly a matter of choice between alternative grammatical constructions such as passive and active voices, inversion, cleft sentences, and so on.

5.4.3 Sense Relations

Sense relation is concerned with paradigmatic relations of words in language. Words can be categorized on the paradigmatic axis into synonyms, antonyms, hyponyms and meronyms according to the relationships between their senses, in terms of the semantic relations of similarity, contrast, inclusion and part-whole relation. Sense relations also include such phenomena as polesemy and homonymy. Polesemy has to do with how different meanings of the same word are related, while homonymy has to do with how different meanings are related to words of the same phonological and/or spelling form.

5.4.3.1 Synonymy

Synonymy is used to mean "sameness of meaning". A **synonym** is a word which has the same, or nearly the same, meaning as another word. In the process of the development of the English language, its vocabulary has mainly come from two different sources: Anglo-Saxon on the one hand and French, Latin and Greek on the other. As a result, English is rich in synonyms, with pairs of, or even triples of words from different origins expressing the same meaning. For instance, *brotherly* and *fraternal*, *buy* and *purchase*, *world* and *universe*, *driver* and *chaufeur*, *kingly*, *royal* and *regal*, and many others.

There are few, if any, **absolute** or **complete synonyms**, and the so-called absolute synonyms are restricted to highly specialized vocabulary, such as *scarlet-fever* and *scarlatina* in medicine. Strictly speaking, no two words have exactly the same meaning and most synonyms in the English language are actually relative synonyms or near-synonyms. There are a number of ways in which synonyms can be seen to differ.

First, synonyms may embrace different shades of meaning, and thus vary in the range and intensity of meaning. For example, *want*, *wish*, *desire* are synonymous, but differ in terms of range and intensity. Of the three words, *want* is the most general and has the widest range of meaning while *wish* and *desire* are narrower in sense but are stronger in intensity, and *desire* is the strongest of all.

Secondly, synonyms may belong to different dialects of the language. People, depending on where they live, will select different regional varieties in talking about the same thing. The most obvious example is the difference between American English and British English. American people use *fall* while British people use *autumn*.

Thirdly, some synonyms have the same cognitive meaning but express different degrees of formality. That is, they have different stylistic meanings. For instance, *gentleman*, *man*, *chap* have the same cognitive meaning, but *gentleman* is formal, *man* is general, while *chap* is colloquial.

Fourthly, synonyms may have the same cognitive meaning but different emotive or evaluative meanings. A ready example is *bravery* and *foolhardiness*, of which *bravery* implies approval, while *foolhardiness* implies disapproval.

Fifthly, synonymous words may collocate with different other words in their actual usage. That is, some synonyms occur in different environments or have different distributions. For example, *rancid* collocates with *bacon* or *butter*, *addled* with *eggs* or *brains*, *sour* with *milk*. For "groups" of animals, we have synonyms occurring with different types of animals, such as *a flock of sheep*, *a herd of cows*, *a shoal of fish*, and *a swarm of bees*.

5.4.3.2 Antonymy

Antonymy is used for "oppositeness of meaning". Words having opposite meanings are **antonyms**. Antonyms can be classified into three types on the basis of semantic opposition.

A. Contraries

Contraries (or **contrary terms**) show a type of oppositeness of meaning, illustrated by such pairs as *wide/narrow*, *old/young*, *big/small*, etc. They can be seen in terms of degrees of the quality involved. Thus a road may be wide or very wide and may be wider than another. This shows that the semantic polarity in contraries is relative and the opposition is gradual. Contraries are also known as graded antonyms. This means that contraries can be placed at both extremes of a scale, between which there may be gradable lexical items. For example, between the antonymic pair *beautiful—ugly*, there may be such gradable adjectives as *pretty—good-looking—plain*. One may also grade the intensity of feeling as in *love—attachment—liking—indifference—antipathy—hate*. It can be seen from above that contraries always imply comparison with some norm. There is one thing that is particularly interesting about contraries: one member of a pair, usually the member for the positive degree, is more basic and frequent, and is thus unmarked. Generally, we ask the age of a person, however young or old the person is, by saying *How old are you?* instead of *How young are you?* The latter question will not be used unless we deliberately emphasize the point that the addressee is surprisingly or unexpectedly young.

B. Complementaries

Also called **contradictory terms**, **complementaries** (or **complementary terms**) represent a type of binary semantic contrast which admits of no gradability between the items, e. g. *male—female, boy—girl, single—married*, etc. *Male* is said to be "the complementary of" *female*, and vice versa. In such a relationship, the assertion of one of the items implies the denial of the other.

C. Conversives

Also called **relative terms** or **converse terms**, **conversives** display a type of oppositeness of meaning, illustrated by such pairs as *buy — sell, give — receive, parent—child, debtor—creditor, above—below*, etc. *Buy* is said to be "the converse of" *sell* and vice versa: If A sells a watch to B, B buys a watch from A. The same applies to the pair *above—below*: If A is above B, B is below A. In such a relationship, found especially in the definition of reciprocal social roles, spatial relationship and so on, there is an interdependence of meaning, such that one member of the pair presupposes the other member. In this respect, "converseness" contrasts with complementarity, where there is no such symmetry of dependence.

5.4.3.3 Hyponymy

Hyponymy is a relationship between two words, in which the meaning of one of the words includes the meaning of the other word. For example, in English the words *animal* and *dog* are related in such a way that *dog* refers to a kind of *animal*, and *animal* is a general term. That is to say, if any object is a *dog*, then it is necessarily an *animal*, so the meaning of *animal* is included in the meaning of *dog*. The specific term, *dog*, is called a **hyponym**, and the general term, *animal*, is called a **superordinate**. One point worthy of note is that meaning inclusion is opposite to class membership: the class of animals includes the class of dogs.

A superordinate term can have many hyponyms. Hyponyms having the same sperordinate are called **co-hyponyms**. For example:

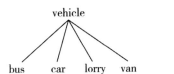 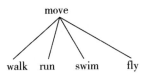

All hyponymy is transitive in the sense that there is a hierarchical relation between different terms. If a relation holds between the superordinate X and the hyponym Y, and Y in turn is the superordinate of Z, then X is also the superordinate of Z. For example:

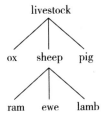

From this example we can see that one term may be a hyponym in one hierarchical relation but a superordinate in another.

5.4.3.4 Meronymy

Meronymy is a term from the Greek words *meros* (part) and *onoma* (name). It is a relation in semantics that expresses the part-whole relation that lexical items may have. In this relation, the part is called the **meronym**, and the whole is called the **holonym**. For example, *limb* is a meronym of *tree* because a limb is part of a tree.

The same entity may be made up of different components, which means that a holonym can have many meronyms. Words denoting parts of the same entity are **co-meronyms**, as in the case of *tree*, *limb*, *root*, where *limb* and *root* are co-meronyms. Similarly *palm* and *finger* are co-meronyms of *hand*.

Meronymy is different from hyponymy in that the relation of meronymy captures the idea of "is part of", while the relation of hyponymy captures the idea of "is a kind of". For instance, a *ram* is a kind of *sheep*, but a *finger* is part of the *hand*.

5.4.3.5 Polysemy

Polysemy refers to the phenomenon that the same word may have a set of different meanings. For instance, *mouth* is a **polysemic word**, as it has several different meanings: "organ of body", "entrance of cave", etc.

The meanings of a polysemic word are usually related in one way or another. There is usually a primary meaning, and all other meanings are derived from it. For example, the word *face* originally means "the front of the head", and a number of derived meanings spring from this basic meaning, such as "the expression of the countenance", "a surface of a thing", "the appearance", "dignity", etc., a whole bunch of meanings you can find in a dictionary. In some cases, a word originally having an abstract meaning may be used to express a concrete meaning, and vice versa. This can be illustrated by *credit* and *ear* in "The student is a *credit* to the university" and "She has an *ear* for music". In other cases, in the meanings of a polysemic word, one meaning may be more general or specific than other meanings. That is, a distinction is made between general meaning and specific meaning. The word *case*, for example, is used in a general sense to mean "instance" or "example", but it is also used in a specific way to mean "an instance of disease" or "a legal suit". Furthermore, the meanings of a polysemic word may be related in such a way that a figurative meaning is derived from its literal meaning through transference of meaning. For example, the word *blanket* literally means "a kind of bed covering", but we can use it figuratively in *a blanket of snow*. Similar examples include *a cool reception*, *the bed of a river*, *the cock of a gun*, *a saddle in the mountains*, so on and so forth.

5.4.3.6 Homonymy

Lexical items which have the same phonological and/or spelling form, but differ in meaning are called **homonyms**. Such a linguistic phenomenon, i.e. identity of form and diversity of meaning is referred to as **homonymy**. There are three types of homonyms in English:

A. Homographs

Words that have the same spelling, but differ in sound and meaning are called **homographs**, e.g. *bow* /baʊ/ *v.* (bend the head or body in respect) — *bow* /bəʊ/ *n.* (a device for shooting arrows); *lead* /liːd/ *v.* (guide or direct) — *lead* /led/ *n.* (a heavy, soft, malleable, bluish-gray chemical element); *wind* /waɪnd/ *v.* (turn or make revolve) — *wind* /wɪnd/ *n.* (air in motion).

B. Homophones

Words that have the same phonological form, but differ in spelling and meaning are called **homophones**, e.g. *air*—*heir*, *sea*—*see*, *ore*—*oar*, *cent*—*scent*.

C. Full Homonyms

Words that are identical in sound and spelling but different in meaning are called **full** (or **perfect**) **homonyms**, e.g. *ball* (a round object used in games) — *ball* (a gathering of people for dancing); *match* (a short thin stick, usually of wood, with a head covered by chemicals) — *match* (a game or sports event).

Chapter 5
Semantics: The Meaning of Language

5.4.4 Semantic Field

Semantic field is concerned with paradigmatic relations. In any language, words sharing the same concept can be classified into meaning areas or semantically related sets. The semantic field is the organization of words as a system of interrelated lexical networks, and words of a semantic field are joined together by a common concept. For example, kinship terms such as *father*, *mother*, *brother*, *sister*, *uncle*, *aunt* belong to a semantic field whose relevant features include generation, sex, membership of the father's or mother's side of the family. Another often quoted example is the color terms which belong to the same semantic field of colors in English: *green*, *blue*, *black*, *gray*, *orange*, *rose*, *olive*, *purple*, *lemon*, *emerald*, *sandy*, *coral*, and so on. In all these examples we have a list of words referring to items of a particular class dividing up a semantic field.

In a semantic field, words are incompatible. We cannot say "This is a *red* hat" and of the same object "This is a *yellow* hat". Nor shall we allow a creature to be described both as a *lion* and as an *elephant*. The incompatibility of terms within a semantic field is often clearly indicated in language. Thus "It was on *Saturday* that she went there" implies that she did not go there on Monday or any other day of the week (but not that she did not go there in August), while "Bill **punched** Mary" (with a contrastive stress) implies that he did not kick her or slap her: *punch*, *kick* and *slap* all belong to the same semantic field.

It is also important to note that there are sometimes differences in the ways in which two languages divide up a particular field. For example, in English, the items dividing up the kinship field include: *father*, *mother*, *grandfather*, *grandmother*, *brother*, *sister*, *uncle*, *aunt*, *cousin*, *nephew*, *niece*, etc., while the Chinese kinship field is made up of 父亲,母亲,祖父,祖母,兄,弟,姐姐,妹妹,叔父,伯父,舅父,姨父,姑父,伯母,婶娘,姨母,舅母,堂(表)兄弟,堂(表)姐妹,侄子,外甥,侄女,甥女,etc. Thus, in English, *uncle* is an inclusive term which is correspondent to the terms 叔,伯,舅父,姨父,姑父 in the Chinese language.

5.5 Sentence Meaning

5.5.1 Definition of Sentence Meaning

Every day, we produce a great number of sentences, some of which have never been said or heard before. Normally, these sentences could be understood without much difficulty. How does a sentence express its desired meaning? How is the meaning interpreted by the addressee? Perhaps the most naïve answer is that the meaning of a sentence is the sum total of the meanings of the individual words, and that if we know the meaning of each word we will naturally understand the meaning of the sentence. However, sentences made up of the same words may express quite different meanings owing to variations in word order. For example, it is obvious that *John kissed Mary* and *Mary kissed John* differ in meaning, although they consist of the same set of words. The two sentences demonstrate different word orders, which brings about two major consequences. First, in grammatical terms, *John* is subject in the first sentence but object in the second sentence, and *Mary* is object in the first sentence but subject in the second sentence. Secondly, the grammatical elements play different semantic roles in the two sentences. In the first sentence, *John* is the actor performing an action on the goal *Mary*, but in the second sentence, the roles are reversed, with *Mary* as the actor performing an action on the goal *John*.

It can be said that grammatical meaning plays a vital role in sentence meaning. As Saeed (2009) puts it, the meaning of a sentence is determined by the meaning of its component parts and the way in which they are combined. Thus, any grammatical form imposed in the generation of a sentence makes a contribution to the meaning of the sentence.

5.5.2 Semantic Relations at the Sentential Level

As there are sense relations between words, so sense relations also exist between sentences. There are five major types of sense relations between sentences: entailment, presupposition, synonymy, inconsistency and implicature.

5.5.2.1 Entailment

Entailment means that the meaning of one sentence is contained in that of another, as is illustrated by the following two sentences with sentence (a) entailing sentence (b).

(a) Helen has three nice children.
(b) Helen has children.

In the semantic relation of entailment, one sentence follows logically from another: when (a) is true, (b) is necessarily true; when (a) is false, (b) may be true or false; when (b) is true, (a) may be true or false; when (b) is false, (a) is false.

5.5.2.2 Presupposition

Presupposition refers to the conditions that must be met in order for the intended meaning of a sentence to be regarded as acceptable. For example, in the following pair of sentences, sentence (a) presupposes sentence (b).

(a) Martha regrets drinking John's home brew.

(b) Martha drank John's home brew.

If sentence (b) is not true, that is, Martha didn't drink John's home brew, sentence (a) would not be acceptable in the real world. Presupposition is similar to entailment in that when (a) is true, (b) is true in both cases. However, there is an important difference between them, that is, in presupposition, when (a) is false, (b) is still true. In other words, both (a) and its negation presuppose (b). Furthermore, when (b) is true, (a) can either be true or false; when (b) is false, no truth value can be said about (a), i. e. (a) is neither true nor false.

5.5.2.3 Synonymy or Paraphrase

Sentences may be synonymous or form paraphrases. A **paraphrase** is an alternative version of a sentence that does not change its meaning. Synonymous sentences or paraphrases have the same truth value. For example:

(a) I am an orphan.

(b) I am a child and have no father or mother.

Sentences (a) and (b) mean approximately the same thing, differing only in emphasis. The semantic relation of synonymy or paraphrase may be expressed as the following: if (a) is true, (b) is true; also if (a) is false, (b) is false; and vice versa.

5.5.2.4 Inconsistency or Contradiction

Inconsistency or **contradiction** means that if one sentence is true, the other must be false. That is, if (a) is true, (b) is false; also if (b) is true, (a) is false. The two sentences below are inconsistent or contradictory in terms of their sense relation.

(a) Wilkins does not wish to sell his farm.

(b) Wilkins hopes to sell his farm.

It can be said that if two sentences are inconsistent or contradictory, one sentence does not follow logically from the other.

5.5.2.5 Implicature

Implicature is largely a relation of pragmatic implication, worked out through the inference of the addressee in a certain context. For example, in the following pair of sentences, sentence (a) implicates (b).

(a) Few men marry blonde heiresses.

(b) Some men marry blonde heiresses.

As a semantic relation, implicature can be defined as the implied meaning inferred from a sentence in terms of the speaker's and the hearer's assumptions and beliefs.

5.6 Ambiguity

Ambiguity involves expressions with more than one normal interpretation. In other words, a word, phrase, or sentence which has more than one meaning is said to be ambiguous. Lexical ambiguity is usually caused by polysemy or homonymy. Sentences may be lexically ambiguous because they contain one or more ambiguous words. For example, *The girl found a book on Main Street* can be interpreted in three ways:

(a) The girl found a book which was lying on Main Street.

(b) The girl found a book while she was on Main Street.

(c) The girl found a book whose subject matter concerned Main Street.

A phrase or sentence may also be grammatically ambiguous if more than one structural analysis can be assigned to it. For example, *old men and women* could be analysed either as *old [men and women]* (i.e. both are old) or *[old men] and women* (i.e. only men are old). This can also be illustrated by the following sentences:

(d) He arrived late last night.

(e) Tom or Dick and Harry will go.

Sentence (d) can be interpreted as: "It was last night that he arrived late" vs. "It was late last night that he arrived". Sentence (e) can be interpreted as: "Either Tom will go or Dick and Harry will go" vs. "Either Tom or Dick will go and Harry will go".

There are some ambiguous sentences whose grammatical ambiguities are revealed only by their underlying structures. This can also be illustrated by Chomsky's famous example *Flying planes can be dangerous*, which can be paraphrased as "Planes which are flying can be dangerous" or "To fly planes can be dangerous". More examples of this kind are as follows:

(f) It is too hot to eat.

(g) They hated the shooting of the hunters.

Sentence (f) can be related to two different underlying structures: "It is too hot for it to eat its food" vs. "It is too hot for someone to eat it". Sentence (g) can also be disambiguated in a similar way: "The hated the fact that the hunters shot" vs. "The hated the fact that the hunters were shot".

It is a universally recognized and demonstrable fact that many of the acceptable utterances of English and other languages are ambiguous. Frequently, though not always, their ambiguity passes unnoticed in everyday language behaviour, because the context can exclude those irrelevant or improbable interpretations.

5.7 Semantic Analysis

5.7.1 Componential Analysis

Componential analysis is an approach to the study of meaning which analyses a word into a set of meaning components or semantic features. The word *man*, for example, has the following semantic features: [Human], [Adult], [Male].

Semantic features constitute the linguistic meaning of a word. They are a set of abstracted characteristics that distinguish the category that the word names from all other categories. Semantic features are established on the basis of binary opposition. For example, we can factor out Male/Female as the binary opposition that holds between the noun pairs:

man	woman
boy	girl
rooster	hen
bull	cow

To capture this generalization, a binary feature [±Male] can be established. With the same list we can factor out an opposition between Human and Non-human:

man	rooster
woman	hen
boy	bull
girl	cow

and the opposition Adult/Non-adult as in:

man	boy
woman	girl

We can thus set up three binary semantic features: [±Male], [±Adult], [±Human]. The "meaning" of a word can then be specified by indicating a "plus" or "minus" for the presence or absence of all the semantic properties that define the word. Using these features we can characterize *man*, *woman*, *boy*, *girl*, *bullock* and *cow* semantically as, among other things:

man [+Male, +Adult, +Human]
woman [−Male, +Adult, +Human]
boy [+Male, −Adult, +Human]
girl [−Male, −Adult, +Human]
bullock [+Male, −Adult, −Human]
cow [−Male, +Adult, −Human]

Componential analysis can be used to explain such sense relations as hyponymy, synonymy, entailment, inconsistency, tautology, presupposition, and semantic anomaly. For example, from the point of view of componential analysis, hyponymy refers to the relationship which exists between two meanings if one componential formula contains all the features present in the other formula. *Woman* is hyponymous to *grown-up*, because the two features making up the definition *grown-up* [+Human, +Adult] are both present in the definition *woman*: [+Human, +Adult, −Male].

In practice componential analysis has not been used simply in order to restate the sense relations in a language. Rather it has been used to bring out the logical relations that are associated with them. Thus by marking *man* as [+Male] and *pregnant* as [−Male], we can rule out contradictions such as *pregnant man*. Similarly by marking *boy* as [+Male, −Adult, +Human] and *child* as [−Adult, +Human], we can establish that *There were two boys* entails *There were two children*.

5.7.2 Predication Analysis

5.7.2.1 Proposition and Predication

According to Crystal (1997), perhaps the most important trend in modern semantics is the investigation of sentence meaning using ideas derived from philosophy and logic. In this kind of approach, a distinction is usually drawn between sentences and **propositions**. A sentence is a grammatical unit, while a proposition is a semantic unit. Lyons (1977) defines proposition as what is expressed by a declarative sentence when that sentence is uttered to make a statement. More specifically, a proposition is the unit of meaning that identifies the subject matter of a statement; it describes some state of affairs, and takes the form of a declarative sentence. A very important property of the proposition is that it has a truth value. It is either true or false. Sentences having the same underlying proposition have the same truth value, because they share a description of the same state of affairs. For example:

(a) Caesar invaded Gaul.
(b) Gaul was invaded by Caesar.
(c) It was Gaul that Caesar invaded.
(d) It was Caesar that invaded Gaul.
(e) What Caesar invaded was Gaul.
(f) The one who invaded Gaul was Caesar.

All these sentences have the same proposition that can be expressed as
    invade (Caesar, Gaul)

Propositions can be a useful way of capturing part of the meaning of sentences. They are more abstract than sentences because the same proposition can be represented by several different statements.

However, if we restrict sentence meaning to propositions, non-statements such as questions and commands will be excluded in the study of sentence meaning. In actual language, questions and commands are just as important as statements, because language is not simply concerned with providing information.

In order to describe the meaning of sentences, Leech (1981) regards **predication** as the major unit in the semantic analysis of sentence meaning. Predication is the common category shared by propositions, questions, commands, etc. In the three sentences *The children ate their dinner*, *Did the children eat their dinner?* and *Eat your dinner, children*! there is a common content which can be expressed in the open sentence "Children eat dinner". Similarly, the predication "Girl ride horse" can be exemplified as the following:

(a) The girl rode a horse
(b) The girl didn't ride a horse
(c) Did the girl ride a horse?
(d) The girl's riding of a horse
(e) For the girl to ride a horse

5.7.2.2 Predicate and Argument

Predication analysis is an important approach to the analysis of sentential meaning. This kind of analysis consists in breaking down predications into their constituents: **argument** (a logical participant) and **predicate** (a relational element linking the arguments). Between them, the predicate is the major or pivotal element and governs the arguments. According to the number of arguments governed by the predicate, we may distinguish three general types of predicates: a **two-place predicate** which governs two arguments, a **one-place predicate** which governs one argument, and a **no-place predicate** which has no argument at all. What appear to be three-or four-place predications usually turn out to be combinations of two-place and one-place predications. For instance, *make* and *hit* can be regarded as two-place predicates, *walk* and *tremble*, one-place predicates, and *rain* in *It is raining* a no-place predicate, because *it* here has no meaning independent of the predicate and only fulfils the syntactic requirement.

5.7.2.3 Advantages of Predication Analysis

According to Leech (1981), the theory of predication analysis is believed to be able to explain a number of sense relations existing between sentences, especially those commonly viewed as semantic deviations.

From the perspective of predication analysis, entailment, for example, can be defined as follows: A relation of entailment exists between two propositions which differ only in that an argument of one is hyponymous to an argument of the other. Thus, *She saw a boy* entails *She saw a child*, because the argument *boy* is hyponymous to the argument *child*. Similarly, the hyponymy relation can also be between predicates, as is shown by the relation between *steal* and *take* ("stealing" is a kind of "taking"). As a result, *John stole a horse* entails *John took a horse*, because the first predication includes all the features of the second predication. To sum up, the entailment holds by virtue of the semantic inclusion of one predication in the other.

Inconsistency can also be defined in a similar way as the relation between two propositions whenever the predicate of one is incompatible with that of the other. For example, *Mary dislikes work* is inconsistent with *Mary likes work*, because the predicate *dislike* is incompatible with the predicate *like*.

Contradiction arises when the information contained in an argument of a predication is incompatible with the information contained in the predicate. In a one-place predication, it means the argument is incompatible with the predicate, as in *The woman you love is male*. In a two-place predication, a contradiction means the qualifying predication semantically excludes the rest of the main predication, as in *Tennis-lovers hate tennis*.

Tautology refers to the unnecessary repetition of a word or idea. A statement is said to be tautological if the speaker unnecessarily says the same thing twice using the same or different words. For example, sentences like *Boys are boys* and *He sat alone by himself* are tautological because they all involve unnecessary repetition of meaning. Tautologies are uninformative, and should be avoided in linguistic communication. However, some tautologies can be used for specific purposes. For example, *Boys are boys* may convey the implicature like "Boys are naughty and mischievous by nature". From the perspective of predication analysis, tautology arises when information contained in an argument of a predication includes the information contained in the rest of the predication. In a one-place predication, it means the argument is hyponymous to the predicate, as in *The woman you love is female*. In a two-place predication, a tautology arises whenever a qualifying predication within one of its arguments semantically includes the rest of the main predication. For example, *A butcher sells meat* is a tautology, because its argument *a butcher* contains the qualifying predication "a man who sells meat".

Finally, sentences that violate possible semantic relations are said to be anomalous. One frequently cited example is Chomsky's famous sentence *Colorless green ideas sleep furiously*. In this sentence, each successive pair of

Chapter 5
Semantics: The Meaning of Language

words involves a semantic contradiction. Anomalous sentences are considered to be meaningless and are not used except in literary writings. In terms of predication analysis, **semantic anomaly** arises when one of the arguments or the predicate of the main predication is self-contradictory, i. e. containing two contrasting features such as [+Human] and [−Human], or contains two downgraded predications which semantically exclude one another, as exemplified by *Human horses feed on oat* and *This programme is for the music-lover who dislikes music*.

Further Readings
Palmer, F. R. 1981. *Semantics*. (Second Edition). Cambridge: Cambridge University Press.
Lyons, J. 1995/2000. *Linguistic Semantics: An Introduction*. 北京:外语教学与研究出版社.
Saeed, J. I. 2009. *Semantics*. (Third Edition) 北京:外语教学与研究出版社.
Simpson, J. M. Y. 1984. *A First Course in Linguistics*. Edinburgh: Edinburgh University Press.

Questions and Exercises
1. Define the following terms

the semiotic triangle	grammatical meaning	lexical meaning
conceptual meaning	associative meaning	connotative meaning
social meaning	affective meaning	reflected meaning
collocative meaning	thematic meaning	sense relation
synonymy	antonymy	hyponymy
meronymy	polysemy	homonymy
homographs	homophones	full homonyms
semantic field	entailment	presupposition
tautology	ambiguity	componential analysis
semantic features	predication analysis	proposition
predication		

2. How does the naming view approach the meaning of language? Why is it limited?
3. How does conceptualism approach the meaning of language? What problems does it have?
4. What is sense? What is reference? How are they related?
5. What are the differences between lexical meaning and grammatical meaning?
6. Illustrate the difference between denotation and connotation with examples.
7. How are synonyms differentiated?
8. How are antonyms classified?
9. Explain how the following pairs of words are related in meaning.

brave-bold	hand-finger	husband-wife
son-sun	sleeve-shirt	man-woman
bird-robin	deep-shallow	wall-house

10. How are the meanings of a polysemic word related?
11. The meaning of a sentence is determined by the meaning of its component parts and the way in which they are combined. Comment on this statement with examples.

12. What are the sense relations between sentences?
13. Disambiguate the following sentences.
    a. He hit the man with a stick.
    b. He saw the man with a telescope.
    c. You can't get fresh fruit and vegetables these days.
    d. They are moving pictures.
    e. These are synthetic buffalo hides.
    f. Visiting relatives can be awful.
    g. I know Simon better than you.
    h. John loves Jane more than Tony.
14. Illustrate the uses of componential analysis with examples.
15. Comment on the advantages of predication analysis.

Chapter 6

Pragmatics: The Use of Language in Context

6.1 Introduction

As a linguistic term, "**pragmatics**" originated with Morris (1938). As the Latin root *pragma*- means "act" or "action", pragmatics can be broadly defined as the study of language use or act of communication. In its early days, pragmatics was profiled as a rag-bag or waste-basket: whenever you cannot explain a linguistic phenomenon using regular, accepted linguistic theories, you can have recourse to pragmatics. Now pragmatics has risen from the status of the Cinderella of linguistics to a vigorous area of linguistic research. As Leech (1983: 1) puts it, we cannot really understand the nature of language itself unless we understand pragmatics: how language is used in communication. In modern linguistics, pragmatics has come to be applied to the study of language from the viewpoint of the users, especially the choices they make, the constraints they encounter in using language in social interaction, and the effects their use of language has on other participants in an act of communication (Crystal, 1985: 240).

6.2 Pragmatics as a New Branch of Linguistics

6.2.1 Defining Pragmatics

As a relatively new branch of linguistics, pragmatics has been defined in many ways by various scholars. The diversity of definitions reflects the different dimensions of language use and the different focal concerns of scholars, and thus contributes to the understanding of pragmatics from varied perspectives.

a. Pragmatics is the study of contextual meaning (Yule, 1996: 1) **or meaning in context** (Thomas, 1995: 1—2). Put differently, it addresses how context determines the way meaning is conveyed and interpreted. Compare the following exchanges:

(1) A: Your mother is a doctor. What about your father?

B: He's a lawyer.
(2) A: I've got some trouble with my contract with the bank. Can your father help me?
B: He's a lawyer.
(3) A: My computer has gone wrong. Can you ask your father to help me?
B: He's a lawyer.

While the same utterance *He's a lawyer* is employed, it is interpreted differently in each context: a direct answer about the father's profession, an indirect affirmative answer, and an indirect negative answer respectively. Now, consider Jack's utterance in (4):

(4) Jack: The hamburger didn't order onion, Kate.

Without the knowledge of the proper context, say, a McDonald's, Kate would fail to understand what Jack intends to communicate (i.e. he intends to remind Kate that the customer who ordered the hamburger did not order onion). Possibly, she would assume that this utterance might have occurred in a children's story. The reason why Jack produces the utterance this way is that he may not know the name of the customer concerned, and in the very type of context, it is relatively easy or customary to identify a customer by the food he or she orders. Thus, it is clear that pragmatics devoted to the study of the role of context can help understand "the relations between language and context that are basic to an account of language understanding" (Levinson, 1983: 21).

In the domain of pragmatics, **"context"** is profuse in meaning. Essentially, it can be seen as encompassing the following layers: situational or physical, social, mental, and linguistic. In (4), the situational context is where the conversation takes place. Some language forms, notably deictic or indexical expressions depend crucially on the context for interpretation. The term **"deixis"** is often used for a deictic or indexical expression, whose referent is identifiable only in the context concerned. That is, the function of deixis is to relate an utterance to a referential context of person, time and place. For example:

(5) This and this, are yours. That's mine.
(6) Come here now.

In (5), one cannot make sense of *this*, *yours*, *that* or *mine* unless we know who speaks to whom and what the speaker keeps pointing at. In (6), *Come here* may mean come to this desk or come to this classroom or come to this city according to the context, and *now* may mean the time of speaking or today or the time following the time of speaking according to the context.

The social aspect of context concerns social distance, social roles, social relations, etc. As Mey (1991: 6) puts it, "pragmatics studies the use of

language in human communication as determined by the conditions of society."
In (4), the social distance between Jack and Kate is close because they are colleagues, which enables him to use a familiar form of address (i.e. "Kate").

The mental aspect of context has to do with background knowledge, beliefs, interests, wants, etc. In (4) again, Kate can interpret what Jack means on the basis of some background knowledge (e.g. hamburger and onion are foods served in the McDonald's; one may refer to a customer by the food ordered.)

Finally, the linguistic context, or co-text, is the preceding utterance(s) and/or the following one(s). In (1)—(3), *he* is used as a substitute of *your father*. Also, B's utterance gets different interpretations largely because it is found in different linguistic contexts.

It is important to note that pragmaticians generally take context to be dynamic and ever-changing rather than static or stable. For one thing, the production and comprehension of a new utterance entails the selection and participation of new background knowledge. For another, as communication proceeds, each new utterance will be situated in a new co-text. Also, it is worthy of mention that interlocutors may diverge on the construction of context. Specifically, a hearer may activate different background knowledge from the speaker when understanding an utterance. This well explains why misunderstanding occurs from time to time.

b. Pragmatics is the study of speaker meaning (Yule, 1996: 1). That is, it deals with what people mean by what they say. A similar approach to the definitional job is to portray pragmatics as the study of how more gets communicated or interpreted than is said (Yule, 1996: 1). That is, it examines how listeners can make inferences about what is said in order to arrive at an interpretation of the speaker's intended meaning. Consider (7) and (8):

(7) George: Let's go out drinking tonight.
   Pat: My grandmother is here.
(8) A: How did Mary and Bill do in the math exam?
   B: Mary did fine.

Clearly, what Pat means in (7) is not exactly the information that his grandmother is with him. Rather, by providing this information, he actually intends to mean that he cannot go out drinking with George. In other words, what he means is different from, if not unrelated to, what he says. In (8), B not only conveys the message that Mary did fine in the math exam, but also implicitly communicates that Bill did not do fine. That is to say, what B communicates here is more than what he says.

To sum up, as a new discipline of linguistic study, pragmatics is characterized by the consideration of the role both context and language users play in verbal communication. Also, it is characteristic of pragmatics to view communication as not only involving encoding and decoding, but often crucially depending on principle-governed inference as well. This largely explains why the speaker meaning is sometimes only partially or even wrongly interpreted, as evidenced by frequent occurrence of misunderstanding in daily communication.

6.2.2　Syntax, Semantics and Pragmatics

Pragmatics as a branch of study has its origin in semiotics. Morris (1938) categorized pragmatics as one of the three components of semiotics, the other two being syntax and semantics:

- Syntax: the study of the relationships between linguistic forms, how they are arranged in sequence and which sequences are well-formed.
- Semantics: the study of the relationships between linguistic forms and entities in the world, how words literally connect to things.
- Pragmatics: the study of the relation of linguistic units to their users

(Davis, 1991: 3)

Thus, the three branches, interconnected in fundamental ways, are responsible for different aspects of language and its usage. Primarily, syntax accounts for the grammaticality of sentence making; semantics explains the meaningfulness of sentence building; and pragmatics studies the felicity conditions or appropriateness conditions governing language use. For instance, while sentences (9) and (10) are linguistically ill-formed, the utterance in (11) is pragmatically problematic because *come* and *there* are inherently contradictory in the direction of movement so that the execution of the act is impossible.

(9) * John sing well.
(10) * John is an orphan whose father is a teacher.
(11) ?? Come there please! (Levinson, 1983: 7)

It is interesting to note that linguistically ill-formed sentences may be found in actual use. If someone uses (9), though almost unlikely (10), we can understand it (though we may think the user is probably not a good speaker of English). On the other hand, people sometimes intentionally "misuse" language for some special effect. The following sentences are telling examples:

(12) Boys will be boys.
(13) Golf plays John.
(14) I'm loving it. (McDonald's slogan)

Not only are uses of ungrammatical sentences explicable in pragmatic terms, but syntactic choices are also essentially a matter of pragmatic

consideration. For example:
(15) a. I'm familiar with Jack.
b. Jack is familiar to me.

The two ways of communicating basically the same message are different in communicative effects. They correspond to different perspectives from which we report the message. Thus, we are led to highlight that pragmatics is "the study of those relations between language and context that are grammaticalized, or encoded in the structure of a language" (Levinson, 1983: 9).

As regards the relation between semantics and pragmatics, we tend to assign abstract, literal, linguistic meaning, truth conditions, etc. to the former, and contextual, non-literal, speaker-intended meaning to the latter. For some scholars, pragmatics is "the study of all those aspects of meaning not captured in a semantic theory" (Levinson, 1983: 12). The following are outward criteria proposed by Leech (1981: 320—321) for judging whether a particular discussion of meaning takes us into the realm of pragmatics:

(a) Is reference made to addressers or addressees, or SPEAKERS or HEARERS?
(b) Is reference made to the INTENTION of the speaker or the INTERPRETATION of the hearer?
(c) Is reference made to CONTEXT?
(d) Is reference made to the kind of ACT or ACTION performed by means of or by virtue of using language?

If the answer to one or more of these questions is *yes*, there is reason to suppose that we are dealing with pragmatics.

6.3 Speech Act Theory

The first major theory of pragmatics is the one that goes by the name of **Speech Act Theory** (SAT for short), initiated by the prestigious British philosopher John Austin in the late 1950s, and further developed chiefly by his American pupil John Searle in the 1960s and 1970s. A **speech act** can be regarded as a unit of utterance in communication that performs a certain function, that is, an act of doing things with words. Thus, a primary tenet of Speech Act Theory is the argument that we "do things with words" (Austin, 1962).

6.3.1 Constatives and Performatives

Many philosophers believe that we use language to represent the world, and it is essential that we make true statements about the state of affairs in it.

One of the central arguments of formal semantics is thus that we will know the meaning of a sentence if we know under what conditions the statement expressed by the sentence is true.

However, a hard fact about language use is that we are not confined to making true or false statements about the world. According to Austin (1962), whereas some instances of language use are **constative**, that is, they are statements, assertions or the like that do not change the state of affairs, other uses of language are **performative**, in the sense that they bring about some immediate change to the state of affairs. For instance, compare the following:

(16) China is the biggest country in Asia.

(17) You're fired. (said by a boss to his employee who has just made a serious mistake)

Clearly, (16) makes a true statement about China. It is informative, and the statement as such does not make China the biggest country in Asia. By contrast, the boss's saying of (17) attains the immediate effect of dismissing the employee. In other words, the words said constitute an act in itself, given the right context. These are what we mean by speech acts, i.e. actions performed via utterances (Yule, 1996: 47). Other typical ones include thanking, apology, request, compliment, invitation, promise, congratulating, etc.

Austin's dichotomy between constative and performative uses of language won much approval. Yet, he was soon criticized on various grounds. Among others, it was pointed out that even constatives are performative in some ways. For example, (16) can be said to perform the speech act of stating or asserting, because the saying of it can at once change the knowledge state of the addressee. In other words, all utterances we use in context are analyzable as speech acts. Also, an utterance involving the use of a certain type of performative verb like *promise* does not necessarily appear performative in the way indicated by the verb, as in (18):

(18) I promise I will take two points off your final score if you are late again.

Here, a threat rather than a promise is being issued by the speaker, because a promise is generally, by definition, in the interests of the addressee. Thus, we can perform one type of speech act by performing another. This is what Searle (1979) later termed **"indirect speech act"**. Such examples abound in daily communication. Language users are indirect for various reasons, like avoiding bluntness, reducing imposition, creating humor, etc.

6.3.2 Locution, Illocution, and Perlocution

After the collapse of the dichotomy, John Austin proposed a new

framework for the analysis of speech acts. Given that virtually all utterances are explicitly or implicitly "performative", one might treat every single utterance as performing three related acts simultaneously: a locutionary act, an illocutionary act, and a perlocutionary act.
- **The locutionary act** is the linguistic aspect of an utterance, i.e. the act of verbally saying something.
- **The illocutionary act** is the behavioral aspect of an utterance involving the intentions of the speaker, i.e. the act of doing something or having someone do something.
- **The perlocutionary act** is the consequential aspect of an utterance in terms of the effects the speaker achieves on the listener, i.e. the act of bringing something to happen.

Consider the following example:
(19) Mary: I'm hungry.
   John: I can get you something to eat.
   Mary: Thank you.

We may just focus on Mary's first utterance. Its locution is the linguistic expression itself; its illocution is an indirect request for John to get her some food; and its perlocution is the outcome: John offers to get Mary some food.

6.3.3 Felicity Conditions

As we may find, the locution of an utterance may not literally correspond to its illocution. Also, it is to be remembered that the perlocutionary act may sometimes fail to achieve the effect the speaker intends to obtain because it has to depend on the cooperation of the addressee (Gu, 1993). Speech acts are not always properly or successfully performed in daily communication. They must satisfy the **felicity** or **appropriateness conditions**. These include:
- **Preparatory condition**: the condition that must exist beforehand (e.g. the speaker has the authority to perform the speech act).
- **Propositional content condition**: the requirement that what is said needs to be relevant to what is intended to be done (e.g. to make a promise, the speaker must predicate a future action of himself).
- **Sincerity condition**: the requirement that one means what one says, that is, the speech act should be performed sincerely (e.g. the speaker is not lying).
- **Essential condition**: the requirement that the speaker is committed to a certain kind of belief or behaviour, having performed a speech act (e.g. accepting an object one has just requested, or performing the action as one has promised).

All these conditions must be fulfilled in order for a speech act to be satisfactorily performed or realized. For instance, if Jack orders Joan to close a window, the preparatory conditions may include at least the following: Joan is able to do it at the moment; the window is open; Jack has the power to order Joan around. The propositional content condition is that Jack's order is about the closing of a window, rather than about anything else. The sincerity condition is that he really intends Joan to close the window. The essential condition is that Jack's utterance counts as an attempt to get Joan to close the window. Suppose Jack has no power over Joan. Then, the perlocutionary act as performed by his order will probably not obtain the intended (perlocutionary) effect.

6.3.4 Classification of Speech Acts

Speech acts that utterances are used to perform fall into five major categories, namely representatives, directives, commissives, expressives, and declarations (Searle, 1979).

Representatives or **assertives** are those kinds of speech acts that state what speakers believe to be the case or not, covering claims, reports, descriptions, assertions, conclusions, etc. (Yule, 1996: 53; Huang, 2007: 106).

Directives are those kinds of speech acts that speakers perform to get someone else to do something, covering such acts as commands, orders, requests, suggestions, etc. (Yule, 1996: 54).

Commissives are those kinds of speech acts that speakers perform to commit themselves to some future action, such as promises, threats, refusals, pledges, and offers (Yule, 1996: 54; Huang, 2007:107).

Expressives are those kinds of speech acts that speakers perform to state their psychological states, such as pleasure, pain, likes, dislikes, joy, or sorrow (Yule, 1996: 53). Typical expressives include apologizing, blaming, congratulating, praising, and thanking (Huang, 2007: 107).

Declarations or declaratives are those kinds of speech acts that speakers perform to change the world via their utterance (Yule, 1996: 53) or effect immediate changes in the current state of affairs (Huang, 2007: 108). Typical declarations include dismissing (an employee), declaring (a war), nominating (a candidate), naming (a ship), marrying (a couple), etc. These acts are generally governed by some social conventions or rules in the course of their execution. The language used is often formulaic or quite predictable.

The classification of speech acts, as presented above, has some defects. Among others, there might be overlapping between two types. For instance, the act of complaining in a specific context might be categorized as belonging to either the category of expressives or that of directives. Another problem is that the classification may not have exhausted all possible types of speech acts. For example, accepting an offer made by the speaker does not seem to belong to any of the five types. Indeed, the classification has largely ignored response acts. In addition, it is important to know that whereas classifying one type of speech act is one thing, recognizing it is another. In other words, we need to take into account the dynamic, sequential context of the ongoing interaction when identifying a particular type of act. This partly explains why recent research on speech acts often adopt a conversation analysis (CA) approach instead of just focusing on an isolated utterance or purely conducting discourse completion tests (DCTs) that involve no naturally occurring data.

Finally, it is worth mentioning that we can perform one category of speech act, e.g. a representative act like the description of one's hunger (e.g. *I'm hungry*), in order to perform another, e.g. a directive act like a request to get someone to bring the speaker some food, resulting in an **indirect speech act**.

6.4 Theory of Conversational Implicature

6.4.1 The Notion of Implicature

The second best-known theory in the field of pragmatics is that of **conversational implicature** developed by Herbert Paul Grice (1967) in his seminal paper "Logic and Conversation". Often defined as "an additional conveyed meaning" (Yule, 1996: 35) "beyond the semantic meaning of the words uttered" (Thomas, 1995: 57), it is more precisely what the speaker intends to communicate by and beyond saying these words. In other words, it is not just an "additional" layer of the meaning; rather, it is exactly what the speaker wants to mean by what he literally says (note that Grice initially used "implicature" to refer to the speaker's act of implying and "implicatum" to refer to what is implied or understood by the hearer as implied. However, as in his own writing, the distinction has not been strictly maintained later on, such that implicature is also used to refer to the product of the process of implying.). Take (20) for example:

(20) Jack: Can I get a ride with you?
   Mary: My car's not working. (Adapted from Green, 1989: 92)

In the normal case, we interpret Mary's utterance as conveying the conversational implicature that she is not able to give Jack a ride. This implicature is what Mary conveys to Jack via her utterance. She is not, however, doing these two things at the same time: informing Jack that her car is not working and refusing to give him a ride. Or, the latter is just an additional meaning she conveys. Rather, she does the latter indirectly through doing the former literally.

Conversational implicatures may be of two types: **generalized conversational implicatures** and **particularized implicatures**. The former require no special contextual information on the part of the hearer for their inference, whereas the latter require the hearer to have the relevant background knowledge of the particular context involved. Compare the exchange in (21) with that in (20):

(21) Pat: How did Mary and Bill do in the math exam?
Jack: Mary did fine.

The case of (21) is somewhat different from that of (20). Jack not only means what he literally says (i.e. Mary did fine in the math exam), but also typically conveys an additional meaning or implicature (i.e. Bill did not do fine in the math exam). To reach this implicature, which belongs to the generalized type, Pat can rely on her own question and Jack's answer. By contrast, in (20), Jack not only needs to have in mind what he and Mary each said, but also has to depend on the world knowledge that once a car does not work, it cannot be used.

Conversational implicatures are said to have some properties. First, they are cancelable or defeasible. For instance, in (21), Jack could cancel the implicature by adding *And Bill did fine, too* or *But I've no idea about Bill*. Secondly, conversational implicatures are calculable or deducible because we generally can work out what the speaker implies by considering his or her utterance in the context. Thirdly, conversational implicatures are non-conventional in the sense that they are not part of what is said and that they are different from the literal meaning of the utterance used. Last but not least, they are reinforceable; that is, we can follow up with an explicit expression of the implicatures without causing redundancy. In (21), Jack could have naturally said *Mary did fine but Bill didn't*.

In a way, conversational implicatures are similar to **presuppositions** because both are implicit information conveyed by utterances. By presupposition we mean, pragmatically, the premise or precondition on which we produce an appropriate utterance. Compare the following:

(22) a. Jack's cousin speaks good French.
b. The king of France speaks good French.

In (22a), the speaker presupposes that Jack has a cousin. If this is not the case, the utterance would be counted as infelicitous or invalid. Thus we can explain why (22b) does not make sense because it is known to all that France does not have a king today. Interestingly, presupposition can generally survive the so-called negation test. Take (22a) for example. Suppose the speaker says *Jack's cousin does not speak good English*. He or she still presupposes that Jack has a cousin. Clearly, the presupposed information is not explicitly communicated by the speaker. Rather, one needs to make some inference. Yet, this inference is predominantly based on the linguistic forms (often termed "presupposition triggers") the speaker employs. In (22a), a definite description ("Jack's cousin") suggesting the existence of some entity serves as the presupposition trigger. Unlike the inference of presuppositions, that of conversational implicatures depends crucially on some contextual information as well as what has been said. Moreover, implicatures are what we intend to convey whereas presuppositions are what we assume to exist in order to communicate some new information, implicatures included.

6.4.2 Cooperative Principle and Its Maxims

For competent language users, it is almost intuitive to arrive at Jack's intended meaning or conversational implicature in (21). However, a theory needs to be more explicit about the ways this implicit meaning is derived. Paul Grice's solution is the presumption of a **Cooperative Principle** (CP for short) at work. Simply put, in conversation, one is supposed to talk in a way in accordance with the mutually accepted purpose of the exchange or interaction (Grice, 1967). Observance of this general principle can be measured by whether one abides by its four **conversational maxims**:

A. **Maxim of Quality**: Be truthful.
   a. Do not say what you believe to be false.
   b. Do not say that for which you lack adequate evidence.
B. **Maxim of Quantity**: Be informative.
   a. Make your contribution as informative as required (for the current purposes of the exchange)
   b. Do not make your contribution more informative than is required.
C. **Maxim of Relation**: Be relevant.
   Make sure that whatever you say is relevant to the conversation at hand.
D. **Maxim of Manner**: Be perspicuous.
   a. Avoid obscurity of expression.
   b. Avoid ambiguity.
   c. Be brief (i.e. avoid unnecessary prolixity).
   d. Be orderly.

It is worth mentioning that the Cooperative Principle as well as its four maxims is not something that prescribes how people must talk in conversation. Rather, it reveals that people are more or less aware of the need to be cooperative in order for their conversation to run smoothly. Also, the "cooperative" in the Cooperative Principle should not be confused with "cooperative" in the folk sense of jointly engaging in an activity with a common purpose for each other (Culpeper & Haugh, 2014: 93).

Since its appearance, the Cooperative Principle has come under attack. One criticism is that it assumes a European-centered norm of communication, as shown by a clause of its maxim of quantity stipulating that one is not expected or supposed to say more than necessary. In many Asian cultures, people are often generous with the offer of extra information as a token of hospitality. Another problem with the theory is that there are overlaps between the maxims such as quantity and relation. More often than not, the additional amount of information is not directly or essentially relevant. Last but not least, the inclusion of four maxims instead of three, five, or more seems arbitrary. There might be other candidate maxims worth considering.

The problems with the Cooperative Principle have led scholars to develop new versions of the theory, of which the neo-Gricean pragmatics and the post-Gricean Relevance Theory are best-known and most influential. The former is represented by Lawrence Horn and Stephen Levinson, whereas the latter is led by Dan Sperber, Deidre Wilson, and Robyn Carston. For more information, refer to Chen (2009).

6.4.3 Flouting the Maxims

Indeed, the Cooperative Principle and its four maxims are by no means inviolable. Two major types of violation are possible. The first type is the total rejection or ignorance of the general principle, not to mention its maxims. This may take either an explicit form, as shown by the opt-out way of saying *I don't want to talk about it* or *No comment*, or an implicit form, as found in cases where the speakers tell lies in order to deceive or mislead the hearers.

The second type is that one deliberately fails to fulfill a certain maxim while still observing the general principle. There may be two reasons. The first reason is that one may face a conflict or clash of maxims. For instance, one would infringe the Maxim of Quality if one risks being as informative as is required in the absence of enough information. The solution is to strike a balance between the two, as shown by B's answer in (23):

(23) A: Where does Tome live?
     B: Somewhere in the suburbs of the city.

The second reason is that one wants to convey some conversational implicature. The solution is to blatantly or openly flout (i. e. ignore) some maxim, as manifested by B's answer in (24):

(24) A: Let's get the kids something.
     B: Okay, but I veto I-C-E-C-R-E-A-M.

Here, B is flouting the Maxim of Manner, because B not only uses a big word ("veto") probably unintelligible to the kids concerned, but also pronounces the familiar word *ice-cream* in a way that may again baffle the kids.

The following conversational exchanges also involve blatant flouting or exploitation of some maxims:

(25) Peter: What do you think of Jack?
Mark: He's a fox.

In (25), Mark is flouting the Maxim of Quality, because Jack is a human being rather than an animal, implying that Jack is a cunning person.

(26) John: Where were you last night?
Jane: I was out.

In (26), Jane is flouting the Maxim of Quantity, because she must know the specific place she went to last night, implying that she does not want to tell John where she went last night.

(27) Jack: Let's play tennis.
Pat: I have a stomachache.

In (27), Pat is flouting the Maxim of Relation, because his answer is apparently about a totally different topic, implying that he does not want to play tennis with Jack.

It is worthy of note that second/foreign language learners may sometimes fail to make proper inference when native speakers convey their message by means of implicature. One reason is that the learners tend to interpret non-native-language utterances literally. Another reason is that they may lack the same background knowledge as presupposed by the native speakers. Language teachers are therefore supposed to promote the learners' awareness of implicature derivation.

6.5 Politeness Principle

Why do people not say literally what they mean? Why do people opt to flout or exploit some maxims in order to convey what they mean? These are questions that we are interested to ask and yet that Paul Grice did not address in his theory. The answer was provided by Leech (1983): as social beings, people need to talk politely.

6.5.1 Politeness: The Principle and the Maxims

According to the **Politeness Principle** (PP for short), one needs to minimize (other things being equal) the expression of impolite beliefs and maximize (other things being equal) the expression of polite beliefs (Leech, 1983: 81). Specifically, the principle is composed of six maxims:

A. **Tact Maxim**: Minimize cost to other; Maximize benefit to other.
B. **Generosity Maxim**: Minimize benefit to self; Maximize cost to self.

C. **Approbation Maxim**: Minimize dispraise of other; Maximize praise of other.
D. **Modesty Maxim**: Minimize praise of self; Maximize dispraise of self.
E. **Agreement Maxim**: Minimize disagreement between self and other; Maximize agreement between self and other.
F. **Sympathy Maxim**: Minimize antipathy between self and other; Maximize sympathy between self and other.

While the Tact Maxim may involve a scale of material or physical benefit-cost (For instance, asking someone to take a rest is more polite than asking someone to clean the window, because the former maximizes benefit to other while the latter maximizes cost to other.), its linguistic realization as marked by a scale of indirectness is more relevant to pragmatic study. Compare the following set of utterances:

(28) a. Show me the way to the railway station, Tom.
 b. Can you show me the way to the railway station, Tom?
 c. Could you possibly show me the way to the railway station, sir?

As the degree of indirectness increases from (28a) to (28c), the utterances sound more and more polite. But it is to be noted that the use of polite forms needs to be appropriate. For a person to use (28c) as a request to someone intimate to him or her might not be interpreted as sincerely polite.

Also, the difference between (29a) and (29b) can be explained by the Generosity Maxim:

(29) a. Could I have some more soup?
 b. Is there some more soup?

Whereas the speaker of (29a) explicitly mentions himself as the beneficiary, that of (29b) does not. In accordance with the Generosity Maxim, the latter utterance is more polite.

Also worthy of special mention here is the Agreement Maxim. Since on many occasions we cannot agree with others, it is polite that we soften the tone of disagreement by using expressions like *Yes, but ...* or *What you said is partly right, but ...* and so on.

6.5.2 Clashes Between the Maxims

As in the case of the CP maxims, the PP maxims are sometimes at odds with each other, too. Take the following exchange as an example:

(30) Kate: What a nice skirt you're wearing!
 Lucy: Thank you.

After hearing Kate's compliment, Lucy faces a dilemma in that she would either infringe the Agreement Maxim or fall short of the Modesty Maxim. In actuality, she opts to observe the former at the cost of the latter. In the

Chinese culture, though, people might often prefer to give priority to the latter.

Thus, it is essential that we give full recognition to the role culture plays in the understanding and theorizing of politeness. Indeed, Leech has been criticized for downplaying the role of culture, to the extent of being accused as being ethnocentric. A good case to make is that unlike Westerners, most Asian cultures do not value Tact Maxim as more binding than Generosity Maxim; conversely, the Asians regard Modesty Maxim as more crucial than the Western counterparts do.

Another issue we can take with Leech's Politeness Principle is the number of maxims included. As in the case of Grice's Cooperative Principle, it is a tricky thing why just 6 instead of 8 or more maxims are listed out. One cannot help wondering if there is a limit to the list. After all, the more we include, the less generalizability the theory has.

Recent developments in politeness research are often termed as "the second-wave" as opposed to the "first wave" that characterizes Leech's approach (Kádár & Haugh, 2013). Specifically, the new paradigm of politeness research no longer takes politeness as the property of certain linguistic units, but rather as something that emerges from the interlocutor's evaluation. Also, there is an upsurge of interest in the investigation of impoliteness, the other side of the "politeness" coin, which early researchers significantly overlooked. Methodologically, recent studies place almost exclusive emphasis on the emic perspective as opposed to the etic perspective; in other words, researchers count on the participants' response instead of their own judgment as analysts. As a consequence, they stress the use of naturally occurring data that are often meticulously transcribed so that conversational traces such as long pauses, high pitches, laughter, overlaps, repairs and the like become meaningful evidence in the judgment of politeness.

6.6 Summary

To conclude this brief and incomplete introduction to pragmatics, we may maintain that language used in context is not just to reflect or represent the world; rather, its use has an effect on it. When we use language to perform speech acts, we are concerned with three major aspects: what we utter, what we intend to do, and what we expect to bring about. Also, speech acts are typed in terms of the kind of things performed via language use. When it comes to conversational interaction, we find that it is not so much of a mess as it seems to be. Instead, conversational behavior is principle-governed. People cooperate in order to communicate with each other and take advantage of the presumption of cooperativeness in order to convey implicit meanings. Finally, language use is socially constrained or motivated. In order to be polite, language users deliberately give up direct or economical ways of speaking but resort to a variety of more or less conventionalized interpersonal strategies. The choice of the strategies is not only socially but also culturally variable, by and large.

Further Readings

Culpeper, J. & Haugh, M. 2014. *Pragmatics and the English Language*. Basingstoke: Palgrave MacMillan.
Huang, Yan 2007. *Pragmatics*. Oxford: Oxford University Press.
Kádár, D. & Haugh, M. 2013. *Understanding Politeness*. Cambridge University Press, Cambridge.
Leech, G. 1983. *Principles of Pragmatics*. London: Longman.
Mey, J. 1991/2001. *Pragmatics: An introduction*. 北京：外语教学与研究出版社.
Yule, G. 1996/2000. *Pragmatics*. 上海：上海外语教育出版社.
陈新仁，2009，《新编语用学教程》。北京：外语教学与研究出版社。
何自然，陈新仁，2004，《当代语用学》。北京：外语教学与研究出版社。

Questions and Exercises

1. Define the following terms.
    deixis   speech act   indirect speech act
    performatives   constatives   locution
    illocution   perlocution   felicity conditions
    conversational implicature   Cooperative Principle   Politeness Principle
2. How is pragmatics defined from the perspective of context?
3. How is pragmatics defined from the perspective of speaker meaning?
4. How are syntax and semantics related to pragmatics?
5. Discuss with your peers why the following utterances (Levinson, 1983:7) are pragmatically problematic.
    a. ?? As everyone knows, the earth please revolves around the sun.
    b. ?? Aristotle was Greek, but I don't believe it.
    c. ?? I order you not to obey this order.
    d. ?? I hereby sing.
6. Context plays a crucial role in the production and comprehension of utterances. Think of a couple of contexts in which the following utterances may be interpreted differently.
    a. It's the taste.
    b. Boys will be boys.
7. Collect some data to prove that perlocutionary acts may sometimes fail to obtain the effect or outcome intended by the speaker. Explain what may have led to the failure.
8. Compare the following two ways of speaking. Why is the first option more in line with the Manner Maxim? In what context is the second option likely to be heard?
    a. Open the door.
    b. Walk up to the door, put the key into the lock, turn the key clockwise twice and push.

Chapter 6
Pragmatics: The Use of Language in Context

9. Collect more examples to illustrate how conversational implicature is generated through the flouting of conversational maxims.
10. How do you tell the difference between implicature and presupposition?
11. Explain the degree of politeness or impoliteness of the following utterances according to the Politeness Principle.
    a. Lend me your car.
    b. Could you possibly lend me your car?
    c. You can lend me your car.
    d. Have another sandwich.
    e. How stupid of you!
    f. How clever of you!
    g. I absolutely disagree with your plan.
    h. I'm pleased to hear that your cat died.
    i. I'm terribly sorry to hear about your cat.

Chapter 7

Discourse Analysis: Language Above the Sentence

7.1 Introduction

Discourse analysis is a relatively new area of study in linguistics. The term "discourse analysis" was first used by Zellig Harris in 1952. Increasingly in the humanities and social sciences there has been a "turn to discourse", a new interest in the role played by language in social life and a new emphasis on meaning making. Schiffrin (1994: 5) points out that discourse analysis is "one of the most vast, but also one of the least defined, areas in linguistics", because "our understanding of discourse is based on scholarship from academic disciplines that are very different from one another". Accordingly, discourse analysis can be regarded as a "hybrid" field of enquiry.

7.2 What is Discourse Analysis

The word "**discourse**" comes originally from Latin *discursus*, denoting "conversation" or "speech". In modern linguistics, discourse is regarded as a unit of language in use, and it is usually larger than the unit of sentence or utterance. Sometimes a short utterance used in a given communicative situation like "Fire!" or "Help!" may be called a discourse, but generally a discourse is a continuous stretch of language which can be as short as a question-answer sequence or a paragraph, or as long as an entire article or novel.

There is no agreement among linguists as to the use of the term *discourse*. Consequently, a distinction has sometimes been made between *discourse* and *text* by some linguists who use the former to refer to oral production and the latter to written language. This has in turn led to the emergence of the two terms *discourse analysis* and *text linguistics*. However, many linguists do not make a distinction between *discourse* and *text*, and the two terms are very often used interchangeably in linguistic analysis.

Then what is meant by "discourse analysis"? A good starting point is the definition given by Stubbs (1983: 1), who refers to discourse analysis as "the linguistic analysis of naturally occurring connected speech or written discourse" or as "attempts to study the organization of language above the sentence or above the clause". In other words, discourse analysis studies how sentences in spoken and written language form larger meaningful units such as paragraphs, conversations, interviews, etc. " (Richards et al., 2002). Discourse analysis not only describes linguistic forms, but also considers the relationship between language and the social and cultural contexts in which it is used, as well as the ways that the use of language presents different views of the world and different understandings (Paltridge, 2006: 2). To sum up, discourse analysis is concerned with (a) language use beyond the boundaries of a sentence or utterance, (b) the interrelationships between language and the social and cultural contexts, and (c) the interactive or dialogic properties of everyday communication.

7.3 Cohesion

According to Halliday and Hasan (1976: 2), a text has **texture**, which distinguishes it from something that is not a text. So one of the key issues in discourse analysis is to find exactly what it is that makes some texts hang together. One major resource for texture is **cohesion** in discourse, which refers to the relationship between items in a text, especially those surface-structure features which link different elements of a text. The basis for cohesion is semantic. That is, words and sentences are linked together because of meaning.

Cohesive devices include grammatical devices such as reference, ellipsis, substitution and conjunction, and lexical devices such as reiteration and collocation (Halliday & Hasan 1976; Halliday 1994). We will look at each of these devices in turn in the following sections.

7.3.1 Reference

What characterizes **reference** as a cohesive device is the specific nature of the information that is signaled for retrieval. To interpret the meaning of a given linguistic element, the reader has to refer to something else that appears in the text. For example:

(1) Tom: How do you like my new Mercedes Vito?

Mary: *It* is a nice van, *which* I'm also thinking of buying.

We need to look back in the text in order to figure out that *it* and *which* in Mary's turn refer to the *new Mercedes Vito*.

Reference may be classified according to where the relevant information is. Sometimes the presumed identities are to be found outside the verbal text, in the situation of speaking. Let us imagine we are in the middle of a lecture. Suddenly there is a loud crash outside the classroom, and the teacher asks:

"What is *that*?" Here the teacher is referring to something the audience can sense in the real world. The reference realized by the pronoun *that* in this context is called **exophoric reference**, because the referent is in the situational context.

The most obvious place to look for a presumed identity, however, is the surrounding text. This is referred to as **endophoric reference**, and it can be either forward (cataphoric) and backward (anaphoric). **Anaphoric reference** is backward reference to an antecedent that is introduced earlier in the discourse, as the use of the pronoun *it* in example (1). Similarly, in "John *kissed* Mary *because he loved her*", the two pronouns *he* and *her* refer backward to *John* and *Mary* respectively. **Cataphoric reference** is forward reference to a noun phrase or clause that will be mentioned later in the text, like the demonstrative *this* in the following example:

(2) In brief, the soon widely held assumption was *this*: man could understand the universe because it was natural and he was rational.

There are three main kinds of reference: personal reference, demonstrative reference and comparative reference. **Personal reference** is reference through the category of person, including personal pronouns, possessive determiners and possessive pronouns. The first and second persons (*I*, *you*, etc.) are deictic in nature; their meaning is defined in the act of speaking. The third person forms can also be used exophorically; but more commonly, they are anaphoric, referring back to a previously mentioned item, as exemplified earlier. Here is another example, where *he* refers back to *the dog*.

(3) The dog got in the garbage. *He* got sick from eating the stale bread.

The second kind of reference, realized by **demonstratives**, such as *this/that*, *these/those*, may be either exophoric or endophoric. Also included in this group are *here/there* and *now/then*. The basic sense of demonstratives is one of proximity, spatial or temporal, from the point of view of the speaker. *This/these* and *here/now* normally point to something nearby, while *that/those* and *there/then* pick out something further away. For example:

(4) He merely laughed and said that she was imagining things. *This* typical male reaction resulted in a row.

(5) In the final year, a number of special option courses allow specialization in areas of particular interest to the student. *These* normally include Syntax, Semantics and Pragmatics, Second Language Acquisition, Experimental Phonetics...

(6) He later made the unusual switch to the army. *There* he had a brilliant career.

The third type of reference is **comparative reference**. Any comparison presumes some standard of reference in the preceding text. Two types of comparison can be distinguished: general and particular. In general comparison, two things are said to be the same, similar or different. Such comparison expressions include: (a) Identity: *same, equal, identical(ly), just as*; (b) Similarity: *similar(ly), additional, such, so, likewise*; and (c) Difference: *other, different(ly), otherwise, else*. For example:

(7) Two men were killed by lethal injection in Texas this year, even though there were 17 when they committed their offences and *another* 65 juveniles are on death row ... "*Such* executions are rare worldwide," the report says.

(8) In our homes we associate the small screen with entertainment. We expect to enjoy the experience of viewing. Learners bring the *same* expectations to the experience of viewing video in the classroom.

In particular comparison, two things are compared with respect to a specific quantity or quality. Particular comparison is realized by comparative degrees like *more, fewer, less, further, bigger, better, more/less* + adjective or adverb. Ordinal numbers are also included in this group, since for example, *the third* only makes sense as being compared with the previously mentioned *first* and *second*.

7.3.2 Substitution

In order to avoid repeating the same word several times in one paragraph, it is replaced, most often by *one, do* or *so*. Three types of **substitution** are distinguished:

- **Nominal substitution**: realized by the substitutes *one, ones* and *same*, which can substitute only for a nominal group.
- **Verbal substitution**: realized by the substitute *do*, which can only substitute for a verbal group.
- **Clausal substitution**: realized by the substitutes *so* and *not*, which may substitute for a clause.

(9) I thought I'd finished with the toughest assignments. They didn't tell me about this *one*.

(10) I want to read this document. You can sign it after I've *done so*.

(11) Tom has created the best web directory. I told you *so* a long time ago.

In all these examples, a substitute form marks the place where earlier elements need to be brought in, thus creating cohesion.

7.3.3 Ellipsis

According to Thompson (1996: 148), "**ellipsis** is the set of resources by which full repetition of a clause or clause element can be avoided, and by which it can be signaled to readers that they should repeat the wording from a previous clause (or, in some cases, from their own knowledge)". Ellipsis is very similar to substitution; it is omission of a noun, verb, or clause on the assumption that it is understood from the linguistic context. Like substitution, we can also identify three types of ellipsis: nominal, verbal, and clausal. For example:

(12) **Nominal ellipsis**
    A: How many apples would you have?
    B: I'd have two < >.

(13) **Verbal ellipsis**
    A: Has he sold his collection yet?
    B: Well, he has < > some of the paintings; I'm not sure about the rest.

(14) **Clausal ellipsis**
    A: Are you coming to the party tonight?
    B: Yes. < > [full ellipsis]
    A: Why is he so angry?
    B: I don't know why < >. [partial ellipsis]

We can see that ellipsis works anaphorically by leaving out something mentioned earlier, whereas substitution works by substituting a "holding device" in the place of earlier elements. By way of comparison, let us look at the following example:

(15) A: Will we make it on time?
    B: (a) Yes, *we will make it on time* (repeated form).
       (b) I think *so* (substitution of *we will make it on time* by *so*).
       (c) If we hurry (ellipsis: omission of *we will make it on time*).

With substitution and ellipsis, the intended meanings can be reconstructed from the preceding discourse and from world knowledge.

7.3.4 Conjunction

According to Halliday and Hasan (1976: 226), "conjunctive elements are cohesive not in themselves but indirectly, by virtue of their specific meanings", and "they express certain meanings which presuppose the presence of other components in the discourse".

There have been several classifications of these **conjunctions**. Following Halliday and Hasan (1976), we classify them into four categories here: additive, adversative, causal and temporal. For example:

(16) For the whole day he climbed up the steep mountainside, almost without stopping.
    (a) *And* in all this time he met no one. (additive)

(b) *Yet* he was hardly aware of being tired. (adversative)
(c) *So* by night time the valley was far below him. (causal)
(d) *Then*, as dusk fell, he sat down to rest. (temporal)

Apart from a small set of conjunctions (*and*, *or*, *nor*, *but*, *yet*, *so*, *then*, etc.), conjunctive elements also include conjunctive adjuncts (*nevertheless*, *therefore*, *on the other hand*, *anyway*, *as a matter of fact*, etc.). The devices which create conjunction constitute cohesive bonds between sections of text.

7.3.5 Lexical Cohesion

Lexical cohesion is cohesion resulting from the selective use of vocabulary. Speakers and writers can create cohesion in discourse through the choice of lexical items that are related in some way to those that have gone before. Two types of lexical cohesion are differentiated, namely, reiteration and collocation.

7.3.5.1 Reiteration

Reiteration adopts various forms, particularly repetition, synonymy, hyponymy and antonymy. The first technique for achieving lexical cohesion through reiteration is simply the repeated use of the same word or phrase. For example:

(17) Four-twenty *blackbirds*, baked in a pie ... When the pie was opened, the *blackbirds* began to sing.

Here the second occurrence of *blackbirds* harks back to the first.

Repetition helps to cognitively reinforce key ideas and new terms. The danger of overusing repetition is that it often results in a text which drones on in a monotone. To avoid monotony, we can vary the modifiers associated with the key term or use synonyms. The writer can simply use a different word that has the same meaning in the given context. Sometimes a synonym may require a different sentence structure than the original word, as in the following pair.

(18) a. The package *arrived*.
b. The package *reached* us.

Antonymy can also help create lexical cohesion in discourse, e.g. *fell asleep* and *woke up* in example (19).

(19) He *fell asleep*. What *woke* him up was a loud crash.

Another device for achieving lexical cohesion is hyponymy, which is a relationship existing between specific and general lexical items. The basic organization of hyponymy is hierarchical. For example, *table* and *chair* are co-hyponyms and are linked by their common inclusion under a superordinate *furniture* in whose class they belong.

In achieving lexical cohesion, hyponymy involves climbing the ladder of generalization, as it were. Take, for example, the word *aspirin*. If we consider the terms that could refer to *aspirin* from the most specific to the least, we might construct a progression like this: *aspirin—pain reliever—drug—stuff* or *thing*. In a text, we can refer to an item by a class or group to which it belongs instead of exact repetition (such as *pain reliever* or *drug* in the case of *aspirin*). We can also refer to an item by abstract generic terms which simply distinguish between people, animals, objects, facts, and the like. So example (17) above can also be rephrased as (20):

(20) Four-twenty *blackbirds*, baked in a pie ... When the pie was opened, the *birds/creatures* began to sing.

7.3.5.2 Collocation

The other type of lexical cohesion is **collocation**. According to Halliday and Hasan (1976: 284), collocation is a type of lexical cohesion that is achieved through the association of lexical items that regularly co-occur. While we can typically find a semantic basis for collocation, the relationship is at the same time a direct association between the words.

Lexical items are grouped into lexical sets as a series of semantically related options from which a coherent text can be constructed. Thus, *chemistry*, *lion*, and *realism* would be unlikely to co-occur in a lexical set whereas *thirst*, *drink*, *beer* would be more likely to. Of course, lexical items in collocation may enter into many different kinds of semantic relations with each other, as in the following example:

(21) People have *cleared forests*, *drained swamps*, and *dammed rivers* to clear the way for *agriculture* and *industry*.

7.4 Coherence

A text or a discourse is not just a concatenation of clauses; it forms a unified, coherent whole. **Coherence** is the relationship which links the meaning of utterances or sentences in a discourse. These links may be based on the language users' knowledge of the world, the inferences they make, and assumptions they hold, and the functions language is used to perform. For example:

(22) A: That's the telephone.
　　 B: I'm in the bath.
　　 A: O.K.
　　　　　(Widdowson, 1999: 28)

How do we understand the dialogue in (22) as a coherent discourse? Based on our knowledge of the world, we know that this dialogue most probably occurs

Chapter 7
Discourse Analysis: Language Above the Sentence

in a home. A's first utterance would be a request, which can be interpreted as *Can you answer the phone, please?* B's utterance would be recognized as a reply to A's request and as an excuse for not complying with A's request. A's second utterance would be interpreted as an acceptance of B's excuse and as an undertaking to answer the phone.

It seems that coherence is more complicated than cohesion. In a stretch of discourse like a paragraph, cohesive devices alone may not warrant coherence. Generally a paragraph has coherence if it is a series of sentences that develop a main idea (Richards et al. 1985: 45). Let us look at the following examples:

(23) Resources are commonly divided into two broad categories. Some are classified as renewable, which means that they can be replenished over relatively short time spans. Common examples are plants and animals for food, natural fibers for clothing, and forest products for lumber and paper. Energy from flowing water, wind, and the sun are also considered renewable. By contrast, many other basic resources are classified as non-renewable. Important metals such as iron, aluminum, and copper fall into this category, so do our most important fuels: oil, natural gas, and coal.

(24) By contrast, many other basic resources are classified as non-renewable. Important metals such as iron, aluminum, and copper fall into this category, so do our most important fuels: oil, natural gas, and coal. Resources are commonly divided into two broad categories. Energy from flowing water, wind, and the sun are also considered renewable. Some are classified as renewable, which means that they can be replenished over relatively short time spans. Common examples are plants and animals for food, natural fibers for clothing, and forest products for lumber and paper.

It is easy to see that the sentences in example (23) fit together to make a coherent text, whereas it is difficult to make sense of the connections between the sentences in example (24).

If we examine the text in (23) closely, we can see some of the cohesive devices that help to link the sentences together. For example, the words *some* and *they* in the second sentence refer back to *resources* and *some (resources)* respectively, and the words *other* in the fifth sentence and *this* in the last sentence have a similar function. The conjunctive expressions *also* and *by contrast* both presuppose the presence of other related components in the discourse. Then there are the repetitions of the words *resources* and *category*. All these devices help to create a coherent text.

In example (24), however, the order of the sentences has been rearranged. The cohesive devices are still there, but cohesive devices alone cannot ensure the coherence of the text since the ideas are not logically presented. The first sentence begins with *by contrast* and gives us the feeling that we are in the middle of a text and that we have missed a component in the discourse. The conjunctive word *also* cannot show the additive relation between the sentences any more. Most of the referring items do not work properly either since it is hard to find out what they refer to in the discourse.

The above analysis also serves to highlight an important distinction between cohesion and coherence. As Thompson (1996: 147) points out, cohesion refers to the linguistic devices of the text, and is thus a textual phenomenon: we can point to features of the text which serve a cohesive function. Coherence, on the other hand, is in the mind of the writer and reader: it is a mental phenomenon and cannot be identified or quantified in the same way as cohesion. In other words, coherence refers to establishing logical and functional connections between the ideas and concepts presented, and has a lot to do with mental processes of understanding. Cohesive devices, on the other hand, highlight the surface-structure connections between elements of discourse. Coherence takes precedence; if ideas are not coherent, there is no text.

Although the existence of cohesive devices does not guarantee that a text will be coherent, they facilitate text processing by rhetorically signaling the relationships between concepts in the text, highlighting the connections for the addressee and making the connections more verbally explicit.

Of course, in a communicative event, both the sender and receiver of a message normally have the implicit agreement that the message being communicated is coherent. Receivers generate inferences on the basis of background knowledge and discourse constraints. Much of the background knowledge is experiential; hence, it involves common procedures and activities, social interactions, and spatial settings. For instance, a narrative usually describes a setting, an action sequence with a conflict and plot, and an outcome. Thus patternings in texts also contribute to their coherence, as it is thanks to patterns that writing is structured in a way that enables readers to easily access the received message with prior knowledge.

7.5 The Structure of Discourse

Apart from the study of cohesion and coherence, discourse analysts are also interested in the organization of discourse, especially the sequential structure of conversations and patternings in written discourse. Moreover, the way messages are presented also contributes to the structure of discourse, to which we now turn.

Chapter 7
Discourse Analysis: Language Above the Sentence

7.5.1 Thematic Structure and Information Structure

In English, the clause is organized textually into two simultaneous message lines, one of Theme +Rheme, and one of Given + New. The former is the **thematic structure** of a clause, and the latter is the **information structure** of a clause. Thematic structure is speaker-oriented and includes the division of what is said into **Theme**, i. e. the point of departure of the message, and **Rheme**, i. e. the element about the Theme. Information structure is listener-oriented and includes the division of what is said into units of information, with one unit being already known or predictable and the other unit being new or unpredictable.

7.5.1.1 Theme and Rheme

The study of thematic structure can be traced back to the linguistic analysis named **functional sentence perspective** by the Prague School. Functional sentence perspective refers to an analysis of utterances or texts in terms of the information they contain, the role of each utterance part being evaluated for its semantic contribution to the whole. In this framework of linguistic analysis, the various elements of an utterance is thought to have varying degrees of **communicative dynamism**, viewed as the degree to which an element of an utterance contributes to the achievement of a communicative goal. That is, different parts of an utterance contribute differently to the total communicative effect. The Theme of an utterance contributes little to the meaning, because it reflects only what has already been communicated, and is considered to have the lowest degree of communicative dynamism. By contrast, the Rheme is considered to have the highest degree of communicative dynamism, containing new information which advances the communicative process.

The notion of Theme was first clearly articulated by Mathesius in 1939 and has been developed by members of the Prague School since then. Influenced by the work of Mathesius and others, Halliday integrated the notion into the systemic functional model.

Before introducing Halliday's definition of Theme in systemic functional linguistics, let us look at the following clauses.

(25) a. The chef is preparing dinner in the kitchen.
  b. Dinner is being prepared in the kitchen.
  c. In the kitchen the chef is preparing dinner.

It is easy to see here that, although the wording has not changed too much, each of the three clauses starts the message from a different point, that is, a different Theme is chosen for each clause.

The structuring of the clause can help us understand how information is conveyed. Writers put in clauses the Theme first and this orients the reader to what is about to be communicated. It is easy to think of a different context in which each clause in example (25) might be appropriate.

According to Halliday (1994: 37), Theme is "the element which serves as the point of departure of the message; it is that with which the clause is concerned". In English, this element always takes the first position of a clause. The remainder of the message is called Rheme. Thus, as a message unit, a clause takes the thematic structure of Theme ^ Rheme. The following shows how Theme can be identified in different types of clauses:

The chef	is preparing dinner in the kitchen.
What	are you doing here?
Would you	like a cup of tea?
Don't disturb	me while I'm preparing dinner.
Theme	**Rheme**

The Themes in the above clauses are simple themes. A simple theme consists of just one structural element, and that element is represented by just one unit—one nominal group, adverbial group or prepositional phrase.

A clause may have more than one Theme, as in *But surely the course doesn't start till next week*. In this case, we have a multiple Theme, and the typical ordering of elements in a multiple Theme is textual ^ interpersonal ^ experiential.

But	surely	the course	doesn't start till next week
textual	**interpersonal**	**experiential**	**Rheme**
Theme			

7.5.1.2 Thematic Progression

The notion of **thematic progression** concerns the ways that texts develop the ideas they present. More specifically, it concerns where Themes come from and how they relate to other Themes and Rhemes of the text. Daneš (1974) suggests that Theme has two functions: (a) connecting back and linking in to the previous discourse, maintaining a coherent point of view; (b) serving as a point of departure for the further development of the discourse. A number of typical patterns of thematic progression have been identified (Daneš, 1974), which include 1) linear thematic progression, 2) Theme iteration, and 3) progression with derived Themes.

In **linear thematic progression**, the content of the Theme of a second clause (Theme 2) derives from the content of the previous Rheme (Rheme 1), the content of Theme 3 derives from Rheme 2, and so on, as in example (26) below.

$$
\begin{array}{l}
T1 - R1 \\
\quad \downarrow \\
\quad T2\ (=R1) - R2 \\
\qquad \downarrow \\
\qquad T3\ (=R2) - R3
\end{array}
$$

(26) Yesterday, I met a person from New York. He told me a very interesting story. This story reminded me of my own experience of travelling alone in a forest.

Theme iteration is also called the continuous theme pattern, in which the same Theme enters into relation with a number of different Rhemes. As a result, the Themes in the text constitute a chain of co-referential items which extends through a sequence of clauses, as in example (27).

$$
\begin{array}{l}
T1 - R1 \\
\ \downarrow \\
T2\ (=T1) - R2 \\
\ \downarrow \\
T3\ (=T1) - R3
\end{array}
$$

(27) The cat is valued by humans for its companionship and its ability to hunt vermin, snakes and scorpions. It has been associated with humans for at least 9,500 years. The cat is known to hunt over 1,000 species for food. It can be trained to obey simple commands. Individual cats have also been known to learn on their own to manipulate simple mechanisms, such as doorknobs...

In the third type of thematic progression, **progression with derived Themes**, the text as a whole concerns a single general notion, and the Themes of the clauses all derive from that general notion, but are not identical to one another, as in example (28).

$$
\begin{array}{l}
T1 - R1 \\
\ \downarrow \\
T2 - R2 \\
\ \downarrow \\
T3 - R3
\end{array}
$$

(28) (We all helped John in one way or another.) Mary brought food and water. Jack gave him some money. Tom cooked meals for him...

7.5.1.3 Given and New

Speakers usually begin clauses by referring to the information known by the listener and then add the new information. New information, which is the focus of the message, usually comes at the end of the clause. Therefore, **Given** is often conflated with Theme, and **New** with Rheme. In fact, in Mathesius' (1939) formulation, Theme is described as 1) "that which is known or at least obvious in the given situation" and 2) that "from which the speaker proceeds". This view is usually called "the combining approach".

Halliday (1994: 299), however, takes a "separating approach" and points out that, Given + New and Theme + Rheme are different. The Theme is what I, the speaker, choose to take as my point of departure. The Given is what you, the listener, already know about or have accessible to you. Theme + Rheme is speaker-oriented; that is, it presents the information from the speaker's angle. Given + New is listener-oriented; that is, it presents information from the hearer's angle (Halliday, 1994: 299). The Theme and New are realized in quite different ways: the Theme by first position in the clause; the New prosodically, by greatest pitch movement in the tone group. Thematic structure and information structure are also closely related. As Halliday (1994: 299) puts it, other things being equal, a speaker will choose the Theme from within what is Given and locate the focus, the climax of the New, somewhere within the Rheme.

Most systemic functional linguists adopt the separating approach, arguing that a constituent with the function of Theme does not necessarily have the function of Given as well. Halliday (1994: 298) points out that one form of "newness" that is frequent in dialogue is contrastive emphasis, as in the following clauses:

(29) **You** can go if you like. **I'm** not going.

Similarly, in "The technology is not wrong. We have not learned how to use it", we would tend to assume that the emphasis is on the last lexical item of each clause, but it is possible to signal the contrast between *technology* and *we* by stress and intonation as "The **technology** is not wrong. **We** have not learned how to use it".

Speakers can also exploit other resources to shift the information structure of a clause, for example, by using predicated Theme and the marked version of thematic equatives:

(30) It's not the technology which is wrong. It is we who have not learned how to use it.

(31) That's why he has finally resigned.

As Halliday (1994: 300) states, within any given context, "the speaker can exploit the potential that the situation defines, using thematic and information structure to produce an astonishing variety of rhetorical effects".

7.5.2 The Structure of Conversations

Attempts have been made in conversation analysis to uncover the structural properties of talk in terms of sequential development. One area of investigation is **turn-taking**. It is revealed that conversation is a rule-oriented activity where two or more people take turns at speaking; that is, people tend to obey a rule of one-speaker-at-a-time. Typically, the roles of speaker and listener in conversation change constantly, and conversation is regarded as a sequence of conversational turns. Several features of talk are related to this preference, including when speakers choose to begin their turns.

On most occasions, participants wait until the current speaker indicates that he or she has finished, usually by signaling a completion point, called the **transition relevance place**, which is the recognizable end of a turn unit. Speakers can select which participant will speak next or mark the transition relevance place by naming, or by asking a question, or by changing the pitch of speech, or by pausing at the end of a completed syntactic structure like a phrase or a sentence.

If the current speaker selects the next speaker, he or she usually also selects the type of next utterance by producing the first part of an **adjacency pair**, for example, a question which constrains the selected speaker to produce an appropriate answer. An adjacency pair is a two-turn sequence of adjacent utterances by successive speakers, in which the first utterance sets up an expectation for the second, such as question-answer and greeting-greeting. For example:

(32) A: What's your name?
    B: John.
(33) A: Hello.
    B: Hello.

It can be seen from (32) and (33) that an adjacency pair is a sequence of two utterances that are ordered as a **first pair part** and a **second pair part**. Adjacency pairs are the fundamental structural units in conversation. They are not only important for the management of turn-taking during conversation, but are also used for opening and closing conversation, for example, the greeting-greeting sequence (e. g. *Hi there-Hello*) and the farewell-farewell sequence (e. g. *Bye then-Bye*).

As the first part sets up expectation for the second, certain potential second parts to a first part of an adjacency pair are structurally more likely than others. This structural likelihood is called **preference**, which is a socially determined structural pattern and not a personal wish. **Preference organization** divides potential second parts to **preferred** and **dispreferred** ones. The preferred is the unmarked (i. e. usual) and structurally expected turn, while the dispreferred is the marked (i. e. unusual) and structurally unexpected turn. The following table indicates the preference organization of some typical adjacency pairs:

First Pair Part	Second Pair Part	
	Preferred	Dispreferred
assessment	agree	disagree
blame	denial	admission
invitation/Offer	acceptance	refuse/decline
proposal	agree	disagree
question	expected answer	unexpected answer or non-answer
request	acceptance	refusal

As preferred seconds are unmarked, they usually occur as structurally simpler turns, while dispreferred seconds are marked by various kinds of structural complexity and tend to be avoided. Thus, dispreferred seconds are typically delivered: (a) after some significant delay; (b) with some prefaces marking their dispreferred status, often with the particle *well*; (c) with some account of why the preferred second cannot be performed (Levinson, 1983/2001: 307). This difference can be illustrated by the following examples from Yule (1996/2000), in which the second part of (34) is preferred, while that of (35) is dispreferred.

(34) A: Can you help me?
B: Sure.
(35) A: Come over for some coffee later.
B: Oh-eh-I'd love to-but you see-I-I'm supposed to get this finished-you know.

To avoid potentially embarrassing or annoying situations such as a possible rejection of an invitation or offer, participants in conversation draw attention to, or prepare the ground for, the kind of turn they are going to take next. The utterances which do this are known as **pre-sequences** (or "opening sequences"). Well-known kinds of pre-sequences include pre-invitation, pre-request and pre-announcement. For example:

(36) pre-invitation { A: Are you free tonight?
B: Yes.
invitation { A: Come over for some coffee then.
B: Ok. Thanks.

Sometimes, when the speaker produces a first part of an intended adjacency pair, it may not immediately receive its second part. There are cases of **insertion sequences**, that is, one adjacency pair occurring inside another. This pattern is illustrated in (37) from Levinson (1983/2001: 304).

(37) A: May I have a bottle of Mich?　(Q1)
　　　B: Are you twenty one?　　　　　(Q2)
　　　A: No.　　　　　　　　　　　　 (A2)
　　　B: No.　　　　　　　　　　　　 (A1)

The sequence in (37) takes the form of Q1-Q2-A2-A1 instead of Q1-A1-Q2-A2. That is, after speaker A produces a first pair part (Q1), speaker B produces not a second pair part (A1) but another first pair part (Q2). Thus, the answer to Q1 will not be provided until Q2 is answered, hence the insertion sequence Q2-A2.

7.5.3　Patterns in Written Discourse

Textual patterns in written discourse help create coherence, as they help us process the information in text. Some of the common patterns in written discourses include claim-counterclaim, problem-solution, question-answer and general-specific statement arrangements (Hoey, 1983). For example:

(38) Most people like to take a camera with them when they travel abroad. But all airports nowadays have X-ray security screening and X-rays can damage film. One solution to this problem is to purchase a specially designed lead-lined pouch. These are cheap and can protect film from all but the strongest X-rays. (McCarthy, 1991: 30)

This is a very common text pattern, which is referred to as the **problem-solution pattern**. Many texts can be treated as conforming to the pattern **Situation ⌒ Problem ⌒ Response ⌒ Evaluation/Result** with recursion on Response—that is, a Response may itself cause a new Problem, requiring a new Response, etc.

Another common textual pattern is the **claim-counterclaim** (or "**hypothetical-real**") **pattern**, where a series of claims and contrasting counterclaims are presented in relation to a given issue. It is also found that some signaling items, such as *claim*, *assert*, *expect*, *state*, *truth*, *false*, *in fact*, *in reality*, characteristically cluster round the elements of such patterns (McCarthy, 1991: 80). For example:

(39) The engineers expected that the earthquake would have caused damage to their underground tunnel. It did; it was at least the magnitude of 6 on the Richter Scale.

The **general-specific pattern** is another frequently occurring arrangement of texts, and it has two variations. In the first one, a general statement is followed by a series of specific statements, ultimately summarized by one more general remark. Alternatively, a general statement at the beginning might be followed by a specific statement, and then several increasingly more specific statements, and finally a return to the general idea (McCarthy, 1991: 158). For example:

(40) Maps and architects' models, although both are types of iconic model, are very different in a number of important respects. For example, a map will only contain those features which are of interest to the person using the map, while architects' models, on the other hand, will be limited to include only those features which are of interest to the person considering employing the architect.

Recognizing these patterns will certainly help us understand the "gist" of the text, since as we read a text, we retain much less than the word-by-word presentation. In our minds, we summarize and organize what we read into macrostructures. These textual patterns reduce the amount of complex information, creating a more generalized or global meaning that has been derived from the individual sentences.

7.6 Critical Discourse Analysis

Unlike traditional discourse analysis, critical discourse analysis (CDA) is distinctive for its overt socio-political stance, and it is sometimes referred to as "discourse analysis with an attitude". The origin of CDA can be traced back to critical linguistics (CL), a social approach to linguistics developed at the University of East Anglia during the 1970s. Viewing language as a social practice, CL aims to explore the linguistic constitution of social processes, especially in the production and reproduction of social inequality and power abuse. Ideology is believed to play a key role during this process, because it contributes to the naturalization and maintenance of social dominance. CL thus seeks to examine how underlying ideologies and unequal power relations are embedded and reproduced in certain discursive patterns and strategies, such as the choice of words, over-lexicalization, predication, membership categorization, transitivity, transformation, modality, presupposition, and so on.

For example, in lexical analysis, it is believed that the choice of particular words often carries important ideological meanings, as can be witnessed in the following analysis of news reports about the 1991 Gulf War against Iraq (cited in Richardson, 2007: 47—48).

(41) **They have**   **We have**
    a war machine   Army, Navy and Air force
    Censorship   Reporting restrictions
    Propaganda   Press briefings

Discourse Analysis: Language Above the Sentence

They	**We**
Destroy	Suppress
Kill	Eliminate
Their men are	**Our men are**
Troops	Boys
Hordes	Lads

Another aspect is **over-lexicalization**, which refers to the existence of an excess of quasi-synonymous terms for entities that are a particular preoccupation or problem in the culture's discourse. For example, women and their attributes tend to be overlexicalized, as in Examples (42) and (43) below.

(42) brazen hussies, sugar-dipped cuties, girl friend, a wonderful dancer, make-up girl, clever girl, another of those magical personalities

(43) high heels, exquisite figure, hair falling round her shoulders, dainty feet, golden tresses, prettiest little face and laughing eyes

These words represent women from an explicit sexual angle, thus contributing to the reproduction of sexual stereotypes towards women.

We may also focus on **Transitivity**, a key concept in systemic functional grammar. It is concerned with the conceptualization of our experiences into a manageable set of processes (including material, relational, mental, verbal, behavioral, and existential) as well as the participants and circumstances involved in these processes (Halliday, 1994). The choice of one process over the others usually carries important ideological meanings, which can be illustrated as follows.

(44) The police shot dead the man. (Material process)

The man was dead. (Relational process)

As the above examples show, the material process represents the event as an action, with its actor (the police) and the goal (the man). It suggests that the police was responsible for the death of the man. However, the relational process only represents the event as a state, which only foregrounds the death of the man but backgrounds the cause.

In order to expose the opaque as well as transparent relationships between language and society, CDA has to draw insights from both linguistic and social theories and develop an approach that can bring together both fields. CDA is multidisciplinary or interdisciplinary in nature, and what CDA contributes is the theorization of the relationship between social and linguistic aspects of language use. Linguistically, CDA lays its foundation primarily on systemic functional linguistics, but other linguistic theories like pragmatics, corpus linguistics, and cognitive linguistics, and argumentation theories have also been incorporated into CDA studies to yield illuminating linguistic analyses.

Philosophically, CDA has been influenced by social theories of Jürgen Habermas, Michael Foucault, Karl Marx, and so on. Important concepts in socio-political theories have been borrowed and further developed in CDA, such as power, ideology, manipulation, hegemony, and legitimacy. This gives rise to a number of sub-disciplines that propose different analytic frameworks to combine linguistic and social analyses. Among them, the most influential are Teun A. van Dijk's socio-cognitive approach, Norman Fairclough's socio-dialectical approach, Ruth Wodak's discourse-historical approach.

Despiteits diverse analytic framework and multifarious applications in different fields, three general objectives and theoretical claims can be identified for CDA (Bloor & Bloor, 2007: 12):

Three main objectives:
- To analyze discourse practices that reflect or construct social problems
- To investigate how ideologies can become frozen in language and find ways to break the ice
- To increase awareness of how to apply these objectives to specific cases of injustice, prejudice, and misuse of power

Three theoretical aims:
- To demonstrate the significance of language in the social relation of power
- To investigate how meaning is created in the context
- To investigate the role of speaker/writer *purpose* and authorial *stance* in the construction of discourse

7.7 Conclusion

As a conclusion, some brief connections need to be made to new developments in the field, particularly to **multimodal discourse analysis** (MDA). Apart from linguistic devices, discourse analysts have turned their attention to other semiotic devices in discourse. Pioneering work on the interaction between the verbal and visual in texts and discourse, as well as on the meaning of sounds and images, has led to the emergence of multimodal discourse analysis, which has become a very exciting research frontier (Martin & Rose, 2007).

Further Reading

Bloor, M. & Bloor, T. 2007. *The Practice of Critical Discourse Analysis: An Introduction*. London: Arnold.
Brown, G. & Yule, G. 1983/2000. *Discourse Analysis*. 北京:外语教学与研究出版社.
Coulthard, M. 1985. *An Introduction to Discourse Analysis*. London: Longman.
Halliday, M. A. K. 1994. *An Introduction to Functional Grammar*. London: Arnold.

Chapter 7
Discourse Analysis: Language Above the Sentence

Halliday, M. A. K. & Hasan, R. 1976/2001. *Cohesion in English*. 北京:外语教学与研究出版社.

McCarthy, M. 1991. *Discourse Analysis for Language Teachers*. Cambridge: Cambridge University Press.

胡壮麟,1994,《语篇的衔接与连贯》。上海:上海外语教育出版社。

黄国文,2001,《语篇分析的理论与实践——广告语篇研究》。上海:上海外语教育出版社。

Questions and Exercises

1. Define the following terms.

discourse analysis	cohesion	coherence
communicative dynamism	thematic structure	thematic progression
information structure	turn-taking	adjacency pair
preference organization	pre-sequence	insertion sequence
critical discourse analysis		

2. What is the relationship between cohesion and coherence?
3. What are the major types of cohesive devices?
4. Identify the cohesive devices in the following passage.

   Yet if our agriculture-based life depends on the soil, it is equally true that soil depends on life, its very origins and the maintenance of its true nature being intimately related to living plants and animals. For soil is in part a creation of life, born of a marvelous interaction of life and nonlife long eons ago. The parent materials were gathered together as volcanoes poured them out in fiery streams, as waters running over the bare rocks of the continents wore away even the hardest granite, and as chisels of frost and ice split and shattered the rocks. Then living things began to work their creative magic and little by little these inert materials became soil.

5. Here isa text in which cohesive devices are mishandled. Identify the misused cohesive devices and discuss how they are misused.

   The Story of Women is based on the true story of a woman in Nazi occupied France during the war. Because of having an ineffectual husband and two children to care for, she starts doing abortions which were illegal in France at the time. She does the first one as a favor for a friend and then eventually starts doing them for money which vastly improves her family's living conditions. Since this is a true story, it has a tragic yet triumphant ending.

6. The following is an incoherent text. In what sense is this text incoherent?

   The river is full of pollutants. The pollutants include sewage and industrial wastes. The industrial wastes come from Gopher Chemical. Gopher Chemical makes paper products. The paper products come from the forests of Oregon. The Oregon forests are suffering from drought. The drought may be the result of global warming. Global warming changes seasonal weather patterns.

7. How are thematic structure and information structure related?
8. The following text is about the importance of Governments. Discuss how the information flow in the text can be improved.

   I think Governments are necessary because if there weren't any there wouldn't be any law: people would be killing themselves. They help keep our economic system in order for certain things.

If there wasn't any Federal Government there wouldn't be anyone to fix up any problems that occur in the community. It's the same with the State Government—if the State Government didn't exist there wouldn't be anyone to look after the schools; vandalism and fighting would occur every day. The local Government is important to look after rubbish, because otherwise everyone would have diseases.

Chapter 8

Historical Linguistics: Language Through Time

8.1 Introduction

It is an indisputable fact that all languages have been constantly changing through time. Essentially, modern linguistics has centered around two dimensions to deal with language change: the synchronic dimension and the diachronic dimension. The synchronic dimension has dominantly been applied to describe and explain differences or variations within one language in different places and among different groups at the same time. The synchronic dimension is usually the topic of sociolinguistics, which will be discussed in Chapter 10. This chapter will focus on the diachronic dimension of language change. Those who study language from this latter point of view are working in the field of **historical linguistics** (Poole, 2000: 123). To put it more specifically, **historical linguistics** is the study of the developments in languages in the course of time, of the ways in which languages change from period to period, and of the causes and results of such changes, both outside the languages and within them (Robins, 2000: 5).

8.2 When Language Changes

Although language change does not take place overnight, certain changes are noticeable because they usually conflate with a certain historical period or major social changes caused by wars, invasions and other upheavals. The development of the English language is a case in point. Generally speaking, the historical development of English is divided into three major periods: Old English (OE), Middle English (ME), and Modern English (ModE).

In about the year 449 AD, the Germanic tribes of Angles, Saxons and Jutes from northern Europe invaded Britain and became the founders of the English nation. Their language, with the Germanic language as the source, is called *Englisc*, the name derived from the first tribe, the Angles. It had a vocabulary inherited almost entirely from Germanic or formed by compounding or derivation from Germanic elements (Dension, 1993: 9). From this early variety of *Englisc*, many of the most basic terms in the English language came into being: *mann* ("man"), *cild* ("child"), *mete* ("food"), *etan* ("eat"), *drincan* ("drink") and *feohtan* ("fight"). From the sixth to the eighth centuries AD, the Anglo-Saxons were converted to Christianity, and a number of terms, mainly to do with religion, philosophy and medicine, were borrowed into English from Latin, the language of religion. The origins of the modern words *angel*, *bishop*, *candle*, *church*, *martyr*, *priest* and *school* all date from that period. From the eighth century to the tenth century AD, the Vikings from northern Europe invaded England and brought words such as *give*, *law*, *leg*, *skin*, *sky*, *take* and *they* from their language, Old Norse (Yule, 2000: 218).

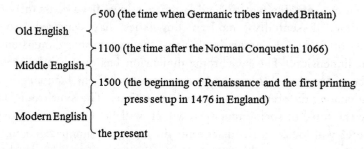

In the year of 1066 AD, the Norman French conquered the whole of England, bringing French speakers into the ruling class and then pushing French to the position as the "prestige language" for the next two hundred years. This language was used by the nobility, the government, the law and civilized behavior, providing the source of such modern terms as *army*, *court*, *defense*, *prison* and *tax* (Yule, 2000: 219). Yet the language of the peasants remained English.

By the end of the ME period, when English had once again become the first language of all classes, the bulk of OE lexis had become obsolete, and some ten thousand French words had been incorporated into English, maybe 75% surviving into ModE (Baugh & Cable, 2001:174).

During the early ModE period, which coincided with the Renaissance period, English borrowed enormous lexical resources from the classical languages of Latin and Greek. And, later on as the British Empire expanded, the range of lexical influence widened to ever more exotic source languages (Dension, 1993: 13).

The types of borrowed words noted above are examples of external changes in English, and the internal changes overlap with the historical periods described above. According to Fennell (2005: 2), the year 500 AD marks the branching off of English from other Germanic dialects; the year 1100 AD marks the period in which English lost the vast majority of its inflections, signaling the change from a language that relied upon morphological marking of

Chapter 8
Historical Linguistics: Language Through Time

grammatical roles to one that relied on word order to maintain basic grammatical relations; and the year 1500 AD marks the end of major French influence on the language and the time when the use of English was established in all communicative contexts. Thus, those internal changes will be elaborated below at the phonological, lexical, semantic and grammatical levels.

8.3 How Language Changes

The change of the English language with the passage of time is so dramatic that today people can hardly read OE or ME without special study. In general, the differences among OE, ME and ModE involve sound, lexicon and grammar, as discussed below.

8.3.1 Phonological Change

The principle that sound change is normally regular is a very fruitful basis for examining the phonological history of a language. The majority of sound changes can be understood in terms of the movements of the vocal organs during speech, and sometimes more particularly in terms of a tendency to reduce articulatory effort (Trask, 2000: 70, 96).

8.3.1.1 Phonemic Change
8.3.1.1.1 Vowel Change

One of the most obvious differences between ModE and the English spoken in earlier periods is in the quality of the vowel sounds (Yule, 2000: 219). Sometimes a language experiences a wholesale shift in a large part of its phonological system. This happened to the long vowels of English in the fifteenth and sixteenth centuries AD, each vowel becoming closer, the highest becoming diphthongs as in the words *wife* and *house* (respectively changed from *wayf* /wiːf/ and *haws* /huːs/ in OE). We call this shift the Great Vowel Shift (Poole, 2000: 127), and the specific changes may be diagrammed as follows (Robins, 2000: 342).

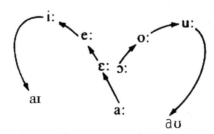

In ME, the vowels in nearly all unstressed syllabic inflections were reduced to [ɒ], spelled ⟨e⟩ (Dension, 1993: 12). The general obscuring of unstressed syllables is a most significant sound change (to be elaborated further in 8.3.3), since it is one of the fundamental causes of the loss of inflections (Fennell, 2005: 99).

8.3.1.1.2 Consonant Change

Consonants are produced with an obstruction of the air-stream, and tend to be less stable over time than vowels in most languages. Two fairly common processes are **assimilation** and **lenition.**

Assimilation is the process by which two sounds that occur close together in speech become more alike. This sort of change is easy to understand: moving the speech organs all over the place requires an effort, and making nearby sounds more similar reduces the amount of movement required, and hence the amount of effort (Trask, 2000: 53). Instances can be found in words such as *irregular*, *impossible* and *illegal*, in which the negative prefixes *im-* and *il-* should be "*in-* based" in accordance with etymology.

Under the influence of neighboring vowels, consonants may also be weakened. This weakening or **lenition**, can change a voiceless consonant into a voiced one and a plosive into a fricative (Poole, 2000: 126). Instances of [h] in native English words generally derive from the lenition of an earlier *[k]: such words as *head*, *heart*, *help*, *hill* and *he* all began with [k] in a remote ancestral form of English, but this [k] was lenited first to [x] and then to [h], and the modern lenition of [h] to zero merely completes a process of lenition stretching over several thousand years (Trask, 2000: 59).

8.3.1.2 Whole-segment Change

Certain phonological changes are somewhat unusual in that they involve, not just changes in the nature of segments, but a change in the number or ordering of segments, and these are referred to as whole-segment processes (Trask, 2000: 66). The change known as **metathesis** involves a reversal in position of two adjoining sounds. The following are examples from OE:

| acsian→ask | bridd →bird | brinnan →beornan (burn) |
| frist→first | hros →horse | waeps →wasp |

(Yule, 2000: 220).

8.3.2 Lexical Change

As defined by Freeborn (2000: F23), lexical change refers to new words being needed in the vocabulary to refer to new things or concepts, with other words dropping out when they no longer have any use in society. Lexical change may also involve semantic change, that is, change in the meaning of words. Thus, lexical change mainly consists of addition of new words, loss of words and change in the meaning of words.

8.3.2.1 Addition of New Words

The conditions of life for individuals in society, their artifacts, customs, and forms of organization are constantly changing. Accordingly, many words in languages and the situations in which they are employed are equally liable to change in the course of time (Robins, 2000: 343). Floods of new words constantly need to be added to the word-stock to reflect these developments. **Etymology**, which is the study of the history of individual words, shows that while the majority of words in a language are **native words**, there may also be **loan words** or **borrowed words** from another language. Native words are those that can be traced back to the earliest form of the language in question. In English, native words are words of Anglo-Saxon origin, such as *full*, *hand*, *wind*, *red*. Loan words are those that are borrowed or imported from another language, such as *myth*, *career*, *formula*, *genius*. Apart from borrowing, many new words are added to a language through word-formation. The following processes are quite pervasive in the addition of new words in the evolution of English.

8.3.2.1.1 Compounding and Affixing

According to Fennell (2005: 77—8), new words in OE were mainly formed on the basis of **compounding** and **affixing**. Many words were formed through compounding, e.g. *blod* + *read* ("blood-red"); *Engla* ("Angles") + *land* = *England*. Affixing covers suffixing and prefixing in OE, the former usually used to transform parts of speech while the latter generally used to change the semantic force. A suffix like *-dom* could create an abstract noun from another noun or adjective: *wis* + *dom* ("wisdom"). The perfective prefix *ge-* was most often used to form past participles: *ceosan* ("to choose"), *gecoren* ("chosen"); *findan* ("to find"), *gefunden* ("found"). It could also be used to change the meaning of a word: *hatan* ("to call"), *gehatan* ("to promise").

In modern English, new words are added not only through compounding and affixing, but also by means of coinage, conversion, blending, backformation and abbreviation. All these word-formation processes are discussed in Chapter 3.

8.3.2.1.2 Reanalysis and Metanalysis

Reanalysis means that a word which historically has one particular morphological structure, is perceived by speakers as having a second, quite different structure. The Latin word *minimum* consisted in Latin of the morphemes *min-* ("little", also found in *minor* and *minus*) and *-im-* ("most"), plus an inflectional ending; however, thanks to the influence of the unrelated *miniature*, English speakers have apparently reanalyzed both words as consisting of a prefix *mini-* ("very small") plus something incomprehensible, leading to the creation of *miniskirt* and all the newer words which have followed it (Trask, 2000: 102).

The history of English provides some nice examples of reanalysis involving nothing more than the movement of a morpheme boundary, a type of change impressively called **metanalysis**. Forms like *a napron* and *an ewt* were apparently misheard as *an apron* and *a newt*, producing the modern forms. Other similar instances are *adder* (the English former word: *naddre*), *umpire* (*noumpere*) and *nickname* (*ekename*) (Trask, 2000: 103).

8.3.2.1.3 Analogical Creation

Analogical creation is the replacement of an irregular or suppletive form within a grammatical paradigm by a new form modeled on the forms of the majority of members of the class to which the word in question belongs. The virtual replacement of *kine* by *cows* as the plural of *cow* is an example of analogical creation, and so are the more modern regular past tense forms *helped*, *climbed*, and *snowed*, for the earlier *holp*, *clomb*, and *snew* (Robins, 2000: 359). Analogical creation is quite persuasive in accounting for the process of cultural transmission to be discussed in 8.4.2.

8.3.2.2 Loss of Words

In the course of time, some words pass out of current vocabulary as the particular sorts of objects or ways of behaving to which they refer become obsolete. One need only think in English of the former specialized vocabulary, now largely vanished, which relates to obsolete sports such as *falconry* (Robins, 2000: 343). Such examples abound in almost every language.

8.3.2.3 Semantic Change

Semantic change refers to changes in the meanings of words. There are mainly three processes of semantic change: broadening, narrowing and meaning shifts (Fromkin & Rodman 1983: 297).

Broadening and **narrowing** are changes in the scope of word meaning. That is, some words widen the range of their application or meaning, while other words have their contextual application reduced in scope. Broadening is a process by which a word with a specialized meaning is generalized to cover a broader or less definite concept or meaning. For example, the original meaning of *carry* is "transport by cart", but now it means "transport by any means". Narrowing is the opposite of broadening, a process by which words with a general meaning become restricted in use and express a narrow or specialized meaning. For example, the word *girl* used to mean "a young person", but in modern English it refers to a young female person. More examples of broadening and narrowing are provided below:

Broadening:
dog (*docga* OE)	one particular breed of dog	→all breeds of dogs
bird (*brid* ME)	young bird	→all birds irrespective of age
holiday (*holy day*)	a religious feast	→the very general break from work

Narrowing:
hound (*hund* OE)	any kind of dog	→a specific breed of dog
meat (*mete* OE)	any kind of food	→edible food from animals
deer (*dēor* ME)	any beast, animal	→one species of animal

Meaning shift is a process by which a word that used to denote one thing is used to mean something else. For example, the word *coach*, originally denoting a horse-drawn vehicle, now denotes a long-distance bus or a railway vehicle. Meaning shifts also include **transference of meaning**, that is, change from the literal meaning to the figurative meaning of words. For example, in expressions like *the foot of a mountain*, *the bed of a river* and *the eye of a needle*, we use *foot*, *bed* and *eye* in a metaphorical way. Other types of meaning shifts include **elevation** and **degradation**. Elevation of meaning is a process by which a word changes from a derogatory sense to an appreciative sense. For example, the word *nice* originally meant "ignorant" and *fond* simply meant "foolish". Degradation of meaning is a process by which a word of appreciative meaning falls into pejorative use. For example, the word *silly* used to mean "happy" and *cunning* originally meant "skillful".

8.3.3 Grammatical Change

The most fundamental feature that distinguishes Old English from the language of today is its grammar (Baugh & Cable, 2001: 54). Modern English is an analytic language while Old English is a synthetic language. The major difference is that a synthetic language is one that indicates the relation of words in a sentence largely by means of inflections, but an analytic language makes extensive use of prepositions, auxiliary verbs, and depends on word order to show other relationships. In OE, the order of words in a clause was more variable than that of ModE, and there were many more inflections on nouns, adjectives and verbs (Freeborn, 2000: 66). The grammatical changes of English such as those in number, gender, case and tense mainly took place at its morphological level, while syntactic changes such as those in word order are the consequence of the loss of rich inflections in English. The most sweeping morphological change during the evolution of English is the progressive decay of inflections. OE, ME and ModE can be called the periods of full, reduced and zero inflections, respectively because, during most of the OE period the endings of the noun, the adjective, and the verb are preserved more or less unimpaired, while during the ME period the inflections become greatly reduced, and finally by the ModE period, a large part of the original inflectional system had disappeared entirely (Dension, 1993: 12; Baugh & Cable, 2001: 50).

The loss of inflections in the case system of Old English is a good example of grammatical change. Case is the grammatical feature that marks functions of the subject, object, or possession in a clause. In OE, nouns showed a four-term case contrast, for which the Latinate terms nominative (subject), accusative (direct object), genitive (possessive) and dative (indirect object) are conventionally used, and the case-ending system can be illustrated by the following:

CASE	MODERN ENGLISH	OE SINGULAR	OE PLURAL
nominative	stone/stones	stān	stānas
genitive	stone's/stones'	stānes	stāna
dative	stone/stones	stāne	stānum
accusative	stone/stones	stān	stānas

(Fromkin & Rodman, 1983: 290)

The ME period is the beginning of the loss of most of the inflections of OE, mainly through the weakening and dropping of the final unstressed vowels. For example, when the vowel was dropped in the plural form of *stones* [stɔːnəs], it became [stɒwnz], and when the "weak" syllables representing case endings in the forms of the singular, genitive plural, and dative plural were dropped, English lost much of its case system (ibid).

The loss of inflections marks a transition of English from a synthetic to an analytic language, and thus led to a greater reliance on word order. Word order in OE was more variable than that of ModE: word order was not as fixed or rigid in OE as it is in ModE (Fennell, 2005: 59). Both the orders *subject-object-verb* ("*hē hine geseah*": "he saw him") and *object-subject-verb* ("*him man ne sealde*": "no man gave [any] to him") are possible (Yule, 2000: 221). Word order in an OE sentence was not so crucial because OE is so highly inflected. The doer of the action and the object of the action were revealed unambiguously by various case endings, which makes the sentence meaning perfectly clear.

It can be said that changes in sound, lexicon and grammar do not operate separately or independently of each other, but they are interacting and interdependent. One change is often integrated or incorporated into the other changes. And, it is the complex interrelationships among them that have shaped the whole process of the language change. As is shown above, the dropping of the final unstressed vowels led to the loss of inflections of OE, and this in turn led to a greater reliance on word order.

8.4 Why Language Changes

No change described above has happened overnight, but has constantly and gradually taken place. Many changes are difficult to discern while they are in progress. The causes of language change are many and various, and only some of them are reasonably well understood at present (Trask, 2000: 12). Two broad categories of factors contribute to language change: external and internal factors.

8.4.1 External Causes

External causes of linguistic changes are the contacts between the speakers of different languages: the sort that occurs when a language is imposed on a people by conquest or political or cultural domination, or when cultural and other factors produce a high degree of bilingualism between adjacent speech areas (Robins, 2000: 340). The significant influence of Norman French on the English language from the eleventh century AD supports this proposition. It can be said that any dramatic social change caused by wars, invasions and other upheavals can possibly bring about correspondent changes in language.

8.4.2 Internal Causes

According to Yule (2000: 222), the most pervasive source of change seems to be in the continual process of cultural transmission (in particular, the transmission of speech habits from one generation to another). Each new generation has to find a way of using the language of the previous generation. In this unending process whereby each new language-user has to "recreate" for him- or herself the language of the community, there is an unavoidable propensity to pick up some elements exactly and others only approximately. There is also the occasional desire to be different.

In the process of cultural transmission, some underlying physiological factors can also play a vital role, mainly marked by least effort. For sound change, one key motivator is ease of articulation. There is a tendency for intervocalic voiceless plosives to be subjected to lenition because producing a voiced fricative between vowels requires less physiological change than does the production of a voiceless plosive (Poole, 2000: 130). For grammatical change, it is not difficult to see that the principle of least effort works for widespread simplification of the grammatical categories in the English language, exemplified by substantial losses of gender, case and tense distinctions.

8.5 Summary

In this chapter we have focused on language change in the diachronic dimension, namely from the historical perspective of change. We draw the conclusion that English has gradually and continuously shifted from a synthetic language to an analytic language in the course of time, marked by interrelated and interdependent changes at all levels, including the general obscuring of unstressed syllables, the progressive decay of inflections and the rigidity of word order. And, this shift may be mainly caused by major social changes and contacts, and by cultural transmission and least effort.

Further Readings

Baugh, A. C. & Cable, T. 2001. *A History of the English Language* (Fourth Edition). 北京：外语教学与研究出版社.

Lehmann, W. P. 2002. *Historical Linguistics: An introduction*. 北京：外语教学与研究出版社.

Schendl, H. 2001/2003. *Historical Linguistics*. 上海：上海外语教育出版社.

Trask, R. L. 2000. *Historical Linguistics*. 北京：外语教学与研究出版社.

李赋宁,1991,《英语史》. 北京：商务印书馆.

Questions and Exercises

1. Define the following terms

historical linguistics	Great Vowel Shift	lenition
metathesis	etymology	reanalysis
analogical creation	synthetic language	analytic language

2. How are the historical developments of the English language generally divided? What are the main features that characterize each period?
3. Can you apply the theory of reanalysis to explain how *cheeseburger*, *chickenburger* and *vegeburger* are derived from the word *hamburger*? Can you find more examples of reanalysis in English?
4. Use one or two examples to show how the grammatical case is changed in the course of the historical evolution of English.
5. Use one or two examples to illustrate how changes in sound, lexicon and grammar are integrated or interrelated.
6. What are the semantic processes in the changes of word meanings?
7. Among the phonological, lexical and grammatical levels of language change, which level do you believe undergoes the fastest change and which level the slowest change? Can you account for these changes?

Chapter 8
Historical Linguistics: Language Through Time

8. In the English language, some names of animals are generally known by the Germanic terms and the resultant meats by the French terms. Which of the following words are derived from OE and which from Norman French? Can you trace the reason for this differentiated origin?

   calf, pork, mutton, ox, veal, swine, beef, sheep

9. Give examples to account for the causes for language change.

Chapter 9

Stylistics: Language and Literature

9.1 Introduction

Stylistics can be roughly defined as "the study of style" (Wales, 1989: 437). However, it has been defined in different ways. Leech (1969: 1) regards it as the "study of the use of language in literature" and Widdowson (1975: 3) defines it as "the study of literary discourse from a linguistic orientation". No one would deny that stylistics is oriented toward literary texts, but it may also involve non-literary texts as indicated in the following definition: a branch of modern linguistics devoted to the detailed analysis of literary style, or of linguistic choices made by speakers and writers in non-literary contexts (Baldick, 1991). Therefore, it is safe to say that stylistics is the study of the use of language in literary and non-literary texts, with literary texts as its primary concern. Some key aspects of stylistics can be summarized as follows:

- The use of linguistics (the study of language) to approach literary texts
- The discussion of texts according to objective criteria rather than according purely to subjective and impressionistic values
- Emphasis on the aesthetic properties of language (for example, the way rhyme can give pleasure)

(Thornborrow & Wareing, 2000: 4)

Thus, more specifically, stylistics is concerned with the choices that are available to a writer or speaker and the reasons why particular forms and expressions are used rather than others, especially the effect of the particular choices on the reader or hearer.

9.2 Important Views on Style

In linguistics, **style** is associated with characteristics or particular ways of language use. The study of style has a long history. As part of a discipline, style was first presumably involved in classical rhetoric (McArthur, 1992), the art of good speaking in the time of Aristotle. Style in classical rhetoric is mainly concerned with how the arguments in persuasion or public speaking can be dressed up into effective language. With the passage of time, the term "style" has been associated with many different meanings. Style may refer to the language habits of one person (Shakespeare's style) or of a group of people at a given time (the eighteenth century style). It may also refer to the characteristics of language use in a particular genre (style of advertising discourse). Sometimes, style refers to the effectiveness of language use (lucid style, plain style, pompous style). As a result of these different interpretations, stylisticians have come up with many different views and definitions. In conducting stylistic analysis, the same text can be analyzed in different ways because styliticians may hold different views on style. These different views determine how a text is analyzed, especially what aspects of the text will be the focus of analysis. Thus, we can summarize the mainstream views on style as the conceptual frameworks for stylistic analysis.

9.2.1 Style as Deviation

According to this view, style is regarded as **deviation** or **deviance**, i. e. departure from what is normal. The phrase *a grief ago* from a poem by Dylan Thomas is a good example. Generally, we use a noun indicating time in the expression "a ... ago", such as *a moment ago*, *a month ago*, and the word to fill the slot is normally a countable noun. In this phrase, *grief* does not meet the conventional requirement. However, as it occurs in a poem, where a novel expression is allowed, it is acceptable. Besides, it expresses an idea in a beautifully succinct way. Since grief means a feeling of great sadness, and any feeling has to last for some time, it is not difficult to figure out the message. That is, something terribly sad has happened, and the speaker of the poem may have experienced grief repeatedly so that he can measure time in terms of it. As the phrase *a grief ago* represents a special twist on the conventional expression "a ... ago", it will leave a deep impression on the reader. Such departure is doubtless delightful, but the view of style as deviation tends to undervalue all non-deviant language.

9.2.2 Style as Choice

This view implies the concept of "style as variation". That is, style consists of saying the same thing in different ways. Here are five sentences roughly conveying the same message:
(1) Smokers are requested to occupy rear seats.
(2) Smokers please sit at the back.
(3) If you smoke, sit at the back.
(4) Smokers must sit at the back.
(5) Smokers at the back.

Since there are different ways of saying the same thing, the key to language use is to make the best choice. Thus, a speaker or writer consistently chooses certain words or structures over others available in the language system. The view that style is choice is a broader view. It may in some way subsume the view of style as deviance, for deviance is only one aspect of the language of literature (Traugott & Pratt, 1980).

9.2.3 Style as Foregrounding

The view of style as **foregrounding** appears to be a compromise between the two views discussed above. According to this view, style consists of choices of both the deviant features and those linguistic phenomena which are not deviant, but nevertheless striking. This view emphasizes two major types of choices, i.e. choices that are deviant and those that are overregular, for they both produce foregrounding. Deviation produces foregrounding by breaking the rules or norms of everyday language. **Overregularity** produces foregrounding by means of uniformity of choice within the language system (e.g. rhythmic patterns, rhyming patterns and parallelism) in order to draw readers' attention. Deviation can occur at all levels of language: phonological, graphological, lexical, syntactic, semantic and textual, whereas overregularity exists mainly at the phonological and syntactic levels of language.

9.3 Stylistic Analysis

Stylisticians approach style by means of **stylistic analysis**, which is generally concerned with the uniqueness of a text; that is, what it is that is peculiar to the uses of language in a literary text for delivering the message. Short (1984: 15) points out that stylistic analysis involves three logically ordered parts: description, interpretation and evaluation. Description is logically prior to interpretation because a reasonably convincing interpretation of a literary text is only derived from a careful and systematic examination of its language. Interpretation is also logically prior to evaluation because evaluation is impossible without a proper understanding of the text. Following this three-part analytical procedure, stylistic analysis can be carried out at different linguistic levels: phonological, graphological, lexical, syntactic, semantic and pragmatic.

9.3.1 Phonological Analysis

Phonological devices have a role to play in contributing to stylistic effects. Proper use of speech sounds is pleasant to the ear and helps with the conveyance of ideas, thoughts, and feelings. Poor sound effect will certainly

Chapter 9
Stylistics: Language and Literature

lead to negative stylistic effects. Phonological devices that bring about stylistic effects include sound patternings—alliteration, assonance, consonance, onomatopoeia, rhyming patterns and rhythmic patterns, most of which are instances of overregularity. In poems, phonological devices not only add to the musical quality of poems, but also function to make poetic texts more organized.

9.3.1.1 Alliteration

Alliteration is the repetition of the initial consonant cluster in stressed syllables. It is the main stressed syllable of a word that carries the alliteration, not necessarily its initial syllable, as in *common occurrence*. Here are more examples:

(6) Every one then called, "Call the barber," but none *stirred* a *step*. (Henry Fielding, *Tom Jones*)

(7) The fair *breeze blew*, the white *foam flew*,
The *furrow followed free*;
We were the first that ever burst
Into that *silent sea*. (Samuel Taylor Coleridge, *The Rime of the Ancient Mariner*)

9.3.1.2 Assonance

Assonance is the repetition of identical vowels or diphthongs in stressed syllables. For example:

(8) I arise from *dreams* of *thee*
In the first *sweet sleep* of night... (P. B. Shelley)

9.3.1.3 Consonance

Consonance is the repetition of the final consonant cluster in stressed syllables. For example:

(9) Nothing lovelier than that lonely *call*,
Bare and singular, like a *gull*,
And three notes or four, then that was *all*.
It drew up from the quiet like a *well*,
Waited, sang, and vanishing, was *still*. (John Swan, *In Her Song She Is Alone*)

9.3.1.4 Onomatopoeia

Onomatopoeia is originally a means of word formation by which new words are created in imitation of the natural sounds, e. g. *buzz*, *cuckoo*, *tick* (of a clock). In a broad sense, onomatopoeia may refer to the recurrence of sounds that suggests certain natural sounds, emphasizing the meaning conveyed. Here are two examples.

(10) the *murmur* of innumerable bees

(11) with beaded *bubble* winking at the brim

The first is by Tennyson to mime the noise made by the bees. The second was used by Keats when he wrote of wine.

9.3.1.5 Rhyme

Rhyme is defined in *The Concise Oxford Dictionary* (Ninth Edition) as identity of sound between words or the endings of words, esp. in verse. There are one-syllable rhymes, also known as **masculine rhymes** (e. g. *foe-toe*, *light-bright*), two-syllable rhymes, also known as **feminine rhymes** (e. g. *buffer-rougher*, *liquor-quicker*), and poly-syllabic rhymes (e. g. *tenderly-slenderly*).

Rhyme-scheme refers to the pattern of rhyme arrangement, which is marked by small letters. For example, ababcdcdefef indicates rhyming every other line. In the following couplet the lines rhyme in pairs.

(12) What is this life if, full of care,   a
     We have no time to stand and stare!   a
     No time to stand beneath the boughs,   b
     And stare as long as sheep and cows.   b
     No time to see, when woods we pass,   c
     Where squirrels hide their nuts in grass.   c
     Not time to see, in broad daylight,   d
     Streams full of stars, like skies at night.   d

(W. H. Davies, *Leisure*)

Rhyme is pleasant in itself. More importantly, it suggests order, and it also may be related to meaning, for it brings two words together, often implying a relationship. Rhyme actually serves as a cohesive device for a poem, binding lines which are closely associated in content. For example:

(13) For I have known them all already, known them all—
     Have known the evenings, mornings, afternoons,
     I have measured out my life with coffee spoons.

Here, *afternoons* and *spoons* not only rhyme with each other, but the two words are logically relevant in that people spend their afternoons drinking coffee, hence coffee spoons.

9.3.1.6 Rhythmic Patterns

In English verse, **rhythmic patterning** is usually analysed in terms of **meter**. As English verse is based on stress, the meter is the more or less regular pattern of stressed and unstressed syllables in a line of poetry. The meter of a poem is determined by the **foot** that appears most regularly in the lines. The foot is the unit of stressed and unstressed syllables (Stress is indicated by the mark /; lack of stress by v). The repetition of feet produces a regular pattern throughout the poem, called **metrical pattern**. There are four major types of foot: Iamb, Trochee, Anapaest, and Dactyl.

Iamb or **iambic foot** alternates stressed and unstressed syllables, beginning with an unstressed syllable, e. g.

   v / v / v / v /
(14) In eve|ry cry |of eve|ry man
   v / v / v / v /
  In eve|ry in|fant's cry |of fear (W. Blake)

Trochee or **trochaic foot** alternates stressed and unstressed syllables, beginning with a stressed syllable, e. g.

   / v | / v | / v | / v
(15) Let her | live to | earn her | dinner. (J. M. Synge)

Anapaest or **anapaestic foot** has two unstressed syllables alternating with one stressed syllable, beginning with an unstressed syllable, e. g.

   v v / v v / v v / v v /
(16) There are man|y who say | that a dog | has his day. (Dylan Thomas)

Dactyl or **dactylic foot** alternates one stressed syllable and two unstressed syllables, beginning with a stressed syllable, e. g.

   / v v / v v / v v /
(17) Sing me a |song of a | lad that is | gone (R. L. Stevenson)

There are different types of dmeters, depending on the number of feet included in verse lines. Thus, **monometer** consists of one foot; **dimeter**, two feet; **trimeter**, three feet; **tetrameter**, four feet; **pentameter**, five feet, and so on. We can describe the metrical pattern of a poem in terms of the type of foot and the number of foot in the poem. Example (14) is written in iambic tetrameter, and example (16) is written in anapaestic tetrameter.

9.3.2 Graphological Analysis

Graphology in linguistics refers to the encoding of meaning through visual symbols, such as the shape of the text, the type of print, capitalization, punctuation, and so on. The graphological aspect of language may speak a lot. Given a particular shape, a text helps highlight the message to convey. Design of the shape of a text in an unconventional way results in graghological deviation, which may suggest a certain literary theme. In the following poem, the lines are arranged in such a way that it is shaped like a Christmas tree.

(18)   A Christmas Tree
                  Star
              If you are
           A love compassionate,
       You will walk with us this year,
    We face a glacial distance, who are here
                 Huddled
              At your feet
                                    (W. S. Burford)

Another example is concerned with the concept of loneliness. The poem is so arranged that it looks like a falling leave, vividly and visually bringing home to the reader the main idea.

(19) l (a
     le
     af
     fa
     ll
     s)
     one
     l
     iness
    (e. e. cummings)

9.3.3 Lexical Analysis

A common view of style is that it concerns the careful choice of the right word. As the famous British author Jonathan Swift (1667—1745) put it, "proper words in proper places make the true definition of a style". Toolan (1996: 162) made a similar comment: word-choice (or lexis, or what used to be called "diction") is central to whatever is distinctive about a particular literary text. Not for nothing did Coleridge talk about prose as words in their best order and poetry as "the best words in the best order". He then reformulated this observation as "the best words in the best order relative to particular purposes at a particular sociocultural moment". In a sense, we may say that the study of style is the study of the choice of words or expressions.

Many figures of speech are actually a matter of word choice. One example is **pun**, which is generally known as play on words for humorous effects. It depends on the sameness or similarity of sound and a disparity of meaning and in many cases it makes use of a homonym. The title of Hemingway's *A Farewell to Arms* involves punning on the word *arms*, because it is a homograph, meaning "weapon" or "upper limbs of a person" or "embrace".

Chapter 9
Stylistics: Language and Literature

Other types of figure of speech like metaphor, metonymy and synecdoche also involve word choice. As such figures of speech have more to do with meaning, they are often treated at the semantic level of stylistic analysis.

A lot of factors are involved in the choice of words. Choices can be made among synonymous words, because synonyms are not always equivalent. They usually differ in their fine shades of meaning within a general framework. They may differ in emotional coloring. A *small* village is different from a *little* one in that the former presents an objective description of the size of the village while the latter contains an extra meaning of fondness. Synonyms may also differ in degree of formality. Words derived from Old English are usually informal whereas those of Greek, Latin, or French origins are formal. For example, you say *rodent operative* instead of *rat catcher* in a formal situation. A relevant difference lies in length. Those informal words are mostly monosyllabic while those formal ones are polysyllabic, including three or more syllables, e.g. *ask/interrogate*. Then, synonyms may differ in terms of reflected meaning, in which case, people turn to euphemisms to avoid taboo meanings or undesirable associations. For example, you say *excrement* to avoid a taboo word. Synonyms may differ in emphasis, as when you answer *right* when you might have said *yes*. Apart from differences between synonyms, words also differ in terms of specificity of meaning. Choices can be made between words with generic and specific meanings, or between hyponyms and superordinates. For instance, you may refer to the same vehicle as a *car* or a *Benz*; the former is more general and the latter, more specific.

9.3.4 Syntactic Analysis
9.3.4.1 Sentence Types

Rhetorically, sentences fall into four categories: loose, periodic, balanced, and mixed. A **loose sentence**, also called routine sentence, is a type of sentence in which the independent clause comes first, followed by dependent grammatical units such as phrases and clauses. A **periodic sentence** is one in which the main idea is held in suspense till the end of the sentence and which is not grammatically complete until the end is reached. A **balanced sentence** expresses parallel ideas in parallel structure. A **mixed sentence** is a loose-periodic sentence. For example:

(20) I was born in the year 1632, in the city of York, of a good family, my father being a foreigner. (loose)

(21) (Cleanliness is a great virtue.) But when it is carried to such an extent that you cannot find your books and papers which you left carefully arranged on your table, it becomes a bore. (periodic)

(22) Crafty men condemn studies, simple men admire them, and wise men use them. (balanced)

(23) Owing to the inability of the newly arrived student to make himself understood in any language but his own, he decided not to venture far from home during the first few days of his stay in the country. (mixed)

Of the various types of sentences, it is impossible and unfair to say which is preferable. The choice of a sentence type depends on the subject matter, on the intention of the writer, on the tone of writing, and especially on the position of that particular sentence in the paragraph and even on its position in the whole text. The stylistic analysis of sentence types may provide information about whether a certain type of text tends to employ one particular type of sentence, or whether a certain type of sentence predominates in a specific text. For example, a loose sentence is very appropriate in an easy, somewhat familiar style. However, a great number of them may give the impression of carelessness and lack of finish. A periodic sentence in which the main thought is not complete until the end of the sentence is by itself more effective than a loose sentence. By ascending to the climax at the end, a periodic sentence gains in dignity and strength, but when used extensively it renders the style stiff and formal. Short simple sentences usually provide intense clarity. They are most effective when used after a long sentence to summarize what has been said, or to provide transition between two or more ideas. Here is a case in point:

(24) So President John Adams saw one newspaper editor after another thrown into jail, or subjected to heavy fines, for criticizing the administration; and the country came to believe that he was, if not actually a tyrant yet, on the way of becoming one. *That finished him.*

9.3.4.2 Sentence-related Figures of Speech

At the syntactic level, stylistic effects are not only achieved through the choice of sentence types, but also through the use of sentence-related figures of speech, or overregular patterns at the syntactic level.

- **Repetition**: the case of copying a previous unit in a text, which is employed to emphasize a statement or to express a strong emotion. A case in point is the repetition of *I have a dream* in Martin Luther King's famous speech "I Have a Dream".
- **Climax repetition**: repetition of at least three items in an increasingly important way, e.g.

(25) A smile would come into Mr. Pickwick's face: a smile extended into a laugh; the laugh into a roar, and the roar became general.

- **Parallelism**: a figure of speech which expresses parallel ideas in the same or similar grammatical structure. It often results in linguistic brevity, structural balance and pleasant rhythm, e. g.

(26) I came, I saw, I conquered. (Julius Caesar)

    When two parallel ideas indicate contrast, it is called **antithesis**, e. g.

(27) Not that I love Caesar less, but that I love Rome more. (Shakespeare, *Julius Caesar*)

- **Climax**: the arrangement of a series of ideas which go from the least important to the most important with steady strengthening of emotion and tone, e. g.

(28) Some books are to be tasted, others to be swallowed, and some few to be chewed and digested.

- **Anticlimax**: a figure of speech in which a series of ideas are arranged in such a way that they go from the most important to the least important with steady weakening of emotion and tone. It is usually employed for jocular and humorous effect, e. g.

(29) He lost his empire, his family, and his fountain pen.

9.3.5 Semantic Analysis

Semantic analysis in stylistics mainly focuses on semantic deviation, that is, linguistic effects involving something odd in the cognitive meaning of a certain linguistic unit (Leech, 1969: 131). Semantic deviation mainly involves figurative language that comes in varied forms, and we will discuss some of the most frequent meaning-related categories: transference, contradiction and deception.

9.3.5.1 Transference

Transference of meaning is the process whereby a word denoting one thing changes to refer to a different but related thing. It is a process of changing from the literal meaning of a word to the figurative meaning. As semantic deviation, it very often involves literary absurdity. Typical transference in literature includes such traditional figures of speech as metaphor, synecdoche, metonymy and transferred epithet.

Metaphor as a figure of speech is an implied comparison between two things of unlike nature that yet have something in common. Metaphor is a device for seeing something in terms of something else. Taken literally, a metaphor is a category error, a semantic contradiction, which asserts or implies "A is non-A". For example, *Men are wolves*. A complete metaphor has three components: tenor, vehicle, and ground. In the case of *Men are wolves*, the tenor is the first term or principal subject, *men*, the vehicle is the second term, *wolves*, and the ground refers to their shared element. Here are more examples.

(30) He has the *microwave* smile that warms another person without heat.

(31) A policeman waved me out of the *snake* of traffic and flagged me out to a stop.

In a broad sense, especially in cognitive linguistics, language is regarded as metaphorical. Nietzsche (1873) asserted that any apparently literal concept is "merely the residue of a metaphor". As will be discussed in Chapter 13, metaphor is pervasive in everyday life, not just in language but in thought and action.

Synecdoche is a figure of substitution taking two inverse forms: substituting the part for the whole or the whole for the part. "Many *hands* (people) make light work" and "*Australia* beat *Canada*" are typical examples. In cognitive linguistics, synecdoche is subsumed under metonymy (See Chapter 13).

Metonymy is a figure of speech which designates something by the name of something associated with it. It has to do with the substitution of the name of one thing for that of another. Metonymy differs from metaphor in that metaphor expresses association through comparison, metonymy through contiguity and possession. For example:

(32) The *pen* is mightier than the *sword*.

(33) She sets a good *table*.

(34) He took to the *bottle*.

Transferred epithet is a figure where an epithet (an adjective or descriptive phrase) is transferred from the noun it usually modifies to another noun to which it does not really belong. Transferred epithets are very often regarded as conventionalized metaphors (Leech, 1969; Ungerer & Schmid, 2008). For example:

(35) No footmarks could be found on the *virgin* snow.

(36) He passed many an *anxious* hour in the train.

(37) I spoke to them in *hesitant* French.

9.3.5.2 Contradiction

Contradiction is a type of semantic deviation which conveys self-conflicting ideas. Contradiction can achieve stylistic effects because it appears absurd but makes sense in literary texts. There are two kinds of contradiction: paradox and oxymoron.

Paradox is a statement which is apparently absurd or self-contradictory but actually reasonable and logical, e.g.

(38) More haste, less speed.

(39) Everybody's business is nobody's business.

(40) My only love sprung from my only hate. (Shakespeare, *Romeo and Juliet*)

Oxymoron is a figurative device in which apparently contradictory terms appear in conjunction. It is a condensed or compressed form of paradox, e. g.

(41) Good night, good night! Parting is such *sweet sorrow*. (Shakespeare, *Romeo and Juliet*)

(42) To live a life half dead, a *living death*. (John Milton)

(43) *Speaking silence, dumb confession,*
   Passion's birth, and infant's play. (Robert Burns, *To a Kiss*)

The following are the common forms of oxymoron:

adj + noun: *a living death, tearful joy*
adj + adj: *cold pleasant manner, poor rich guys*
adv + adj: *dully bright, mercifully fatal*
verb + adv: *hasten slowly, shine darkly*
noun + noun: *a love-hate relationship*

9.3.5.3 Deception

Deception, also known as honest deception, is a type of semantic deviation involving the deliberate use of overstatement, understatement and irony, each of which misrepresents the truth in some way.

Overstatement, or **hyperbole**, is the deliberate use of exaggeration to achieve emphasis, e. g.

(44) Belinda smiled, and *all the world was gay*.

(45) For she was beautiful—*her beauty made
   The bright world dim*, and everything beside
   Seemed like the fleeting images of a shade. (P. B. Shelley)

(46) Hamlet: I loved Ophelia: *forty thousand brothers could not, with all their quantity of love, make up my sum.* (Shakespeare, *Hamlet*)

Understatement is a figure which deliberately expresses an idea too weakly. It is the opposite of hyperbole in that it describes something in a way that makes it seem less important than it really is. It consists of two sub-types: **litotes** and **meiosis**. Litotes means understatement by the use of negatives, e. g.

(47) He was a man of *no mean wealth*.

(48) The face *wasn't a bad one*; it had what they called charm.

(49) I hope my labors *have not been fruitless*.

Meiosis refers to understatement without the use of a negative construction, involving the use of words like *a bit, rather, almost, kind of, something of*, e. g.

(50) Money is *kind of tight*. But I can manage.

(51) My daughter got a passing grade for History. But her score *could be better*.

Irony is a figure of speech which takes the form of saying the contrary of what one means, or saying one thing but meaning the opposite. For example:

(52) Robbing a widow of her savings was certainly a noble act.

(53) Blessed are the young, for they shall inherit the national debt.

(54) "Generally speaking," said Miss Murdstone, "I don't like boys. How d'ye do, boy?" Under these *encouraging* circumstances, I replied that I was very well, and that I hoped that she was the same, with such an indifferent grace that Miss Murdstone disposed of me in two words, "Wants manner!" (Charles Dickens, *David Copperfield*)

9.3.6 Pragmatic Analysis

The study of language in use has been prosperous in the past four decades or so, offering fresh insights into linguistic studies. Our pragmatic analysis here is based on three important topics of pragmatics: speech act, turn-taking and conversational implicature.

9.3.6.1 Speech Acts

As has been mentioned in Chapter 6, the basic idea of Speech Act Theory is that speech, or language use in general, is a way of doing things; that is, or to say something is to do something. As Searle (1969) puts it, the unit of linguistic communication is not the symbol, word or sentence, but rather the production of the symbol or word or sentence in the performance of the speech act.

In the stylistic analysis of literary texts, especially dialogues or dramatic discourse, it is important to identify speech acts and the ways characters respond to them. Characters may produce speech acts which are appropriate to their status within the play, relative to other characters, or ones which appear inappropriate, which mark either a misapprehension on the part of the character about their status, or a change in their status (Thornborrow & Wareing, 2001: 136). In addition to analyzing what speech acts characters use, we also need to consider how they perform their speech acts (Culpeper, 2001: 236). The following extract is from Shakespeare's *Richard III*. The analysis is based on Culpeper (2001: 236).

(55) 1) Buckingham   My lord, I have considered in my mind
                                 The late request that you did sound me in.
    2) Richard   Well, let that rest. Dorset is fled to Richmond.
    3) Buckingham   I hear the news, my lord.

Chapter 9
Stylistics: Language and Literature

4) Richard	Stanley, he is your wife's son. Well, look unto it.
5) Buckingham	My lord, I claim the gift, my due by promise,
	For which your honour and your faith is pawn'd:
	Th'earldom of Hereford, and the moveables
	Which you have promised I shall possess.
6) Richard	Stanley, look to your wife; if she convey
	Letters to Richmond, you shall answer it.
7) Buckingham	What says your Highness to my just demand?
8) Richard	I do remember me, Henry the Sixth
	Did prophesy that Richmond should be King,
	When Richmond was a little peevish boy.
	A king ... perhaps ... perhaps-
9) Buckingham	My lord!
10) Richard	How chance the prophet could not, at that time,
	Have told me—I being by—that I should kill him?
11) Buckingham	My lord, your promise for the earldom-
12) Richard	Richmond! When last I was at Exeter,
	The mayor in courtesy show'd me the castle,
	And call'd it Rougemont, at which name I started,
	Because a bard of Ireland told me once
	I should not live long after I saw "Richmond".
13) Buckingham	My lord-
14) Richard	Ay- what's o'clock?
15) Buckingham	I am thus told to put your Grace in mind
	Of what you promis'd me.
16) Richard	Well. But what's o'clock?
17) Buckingham	Upon the stroke of ten.
18) Richard	Well, let it strike.
19) Buckingham	Why let it strike?
20) Richard	Because that like a jack thou keep'st the stroke
	Betwixt thy begging and my mediation.
	I am not in the giving vein today.
21) Buckingham	May it please you to resolve me in my suit?
22) Richard	Thou troublest me; I am not in the vein.

(Shakespeare, *Richard III*)

Prior to this extract, Richard requests Buckingham's help in plotting the death of Hastings, in return for which Buckingham is promised the Earldom of Hereford and the possessions of the late king when Richard ascends to the throne. In this extract, Buckingham is claiming the promised things after fulfilling his part of the bargain. At the beginning, Buckingham introduces his request for the title and wealth very indirectly. This is because Richard is the more powerful participant and so Buckingham must soften the imposition of his request with indirectness. As Richard ignores his request by talking about another topic and engaging Stanley, Buckingham is more direct: *I claim the gift*. This is more than a straightforward request and this request is justifiable because the gift is his due by promise and it is Richard who has made the promise. Buckingham's next utterance (turn 7) becomes an indirect request couched as a question. Interestingly, Buckingham describes the speech act he has been trying to perform as a *demand*, suggesting that he sees it as stronger than a request, and made from a position of moral power. It can be said that Buckingham's conversational behaviour is characterised as the speech act of *begging*, implying that the "request" is made from a position of complete powerlessness. As Culpeper (2001: 237) puts it, analyzing how characters perform their speech acts tells us much about their goals, how they perceive interpersonal relationships, and how they manage the social context.

9.3.6.2 Turn-taking

In a conversation, the participants usually take turns in speaking. That is, the speaker and the listener constantly change their roles. How one takes his or her turn may vary from case to case. Most conversations go on in a good order, with each participant having a turn to speak. Sometimes, however, as in a quarrel, the speaker might be interrupted. In formal situations like debates and conferences, only the chairperson controls the turns of speaking. According to Culpeper (2001: 173), we need to take into account the following aspects in describing conversation in literary texts:

- The way in which talk is distributed between participants: More specifically, we can look at the number of conversational contributions or turns for each participant, the length of each turn, and the total volume of talk for each participant.
- The way in which speakers alternate (that is, the transitions between turns), which includes (a) self-selection: speakers may either self-select-spontaneously grab the conversational floor, (b) turn allocation: speakers may have a turn allocated to them by another speaker, who may ask them a question or somehow signal that now it is their turn to speak, (c) interruption: speakers may also butt in without waiting for the other speaker to finish his or her turn, (d) turn overlap: speakers overlap particularly at the end of one turn and the beginning of another.
- The way in which topics are introduced, maintained and changed: Topic management is related to power distribution, as well as to

attitudes, degrees of involvement in the interaction, and so on.

It can be said that patterns of turn-taking have much to do with conversational power and the relationship between participants. As Short (1996: 206—207) puts it, "all other things being equal, powerful speakers in conversation have the most turns, have the longest turns, initiate conversational exchanges, controls what is talked about, who talks when, and interrupt others". Short provides the following framework for the analysis of turn-taking:

	Powerful Speakers	Powerless Speakers
Who has most turns?	X	
Who has the least?		X
Who has the longest turns?	X	
Who has the shortest?		X
Who initiates conversational exchanges?	X	
Who responds?		X
Who controls the conversation topic?	X	
Who follows the topic of others?		X
Who interrupts?	X	
Who is interrupted?		X
Who uses terms of address not marked for respect (e.g. first name only)?	X	
Who uses terms of address marked for respect (e.g. title + last name)?		X
Who allocates turns to others?	X	

(Short, 1996: 206)

Now let's have a look at Culpeper's (2001) analysis of the conversation in example (55) to see what turn-taking can reveal about the characters and their relationships in literary texts. This conversation consists of 22 turns, with each participant having an equal share of turns. However, it is Richard who dominates the conversation, speaking 50.9% more words than Buckingham. This is understandable because Buckingham is making a request from a position of complete powerlessness. Although Buckingham is socially less powerful, he is morally more powerful than Richard, because Richard has made the promise and the request is justifiable. Therefore, Buckingham actually speaks 29 words more than Richard in the first third (turns 1-7), where he is making his just claim for the promised title and wealth. In the second third (turns 8-13), Richard swamps Buckingham with unilateral talk about another topic, the rebel Richmond, and Richards thus speaks 75 words more than Buckingham. In the final third (turns 14-22), Richard changes tactics and engages Buckingham in a topic of his own choosing, resulting in a distribution of words that is much more balanced—Richard speaks only 9 more words than Buckingham. In terms of the allocation of turns, Richard dominates the conversation by denying Buckingham speaking rights. Thus, Buckingham has no choice but to self-select, which can be shown in turns 5, 7, 9, 11 and 13, and he even interrupted Richard in turn 9. We can also notice that Richard interrupts Buckingham twice (turns 12 and 14) in the conversation. Richard controls not only turn allocation but also the conversational topic. At the beginning, when Buckingham introduces his claim for the title and wealth, Richard immediately commands him to drop this topic (*Well, let it rest.*) and introduces a different topic of his own (*Dorset is fled to Richmond.*). Although Buckingham reintroduces the topic of his claim several times, Richard explicitly ignores this topic and succeeds in bringing out a topic of his own. The terms of address used by the two characters are also revealing. Buckingham's choices are all marked for respect: *My lord* (6 times), *your Highness*, and *your Grace*. Richard avoids using forms of address until his final two turns, where he addresses Buckingham using the second person pronoun *thou*. This stark contrast suggests that while Buckingham acknowledges Richard's higher social status and tries to soften the imposition of his request through the choice of polite forms of address, Richard makes it plain that Buckingham is in no position to request anything of him.

9.3.6.3 Conversational Implicature

Implicature is what is intended by the speaker in saying something. In literary discourse, conversational implicature is generated by flouting the conversational maxims of the Cooperative Principle. Flouts of conversational maxims are intended to portray characters and their relationships and to indicate the relation between the reader and the author. In the following extract from *Wuthering Heights*, Nelly Dean and Isabella are talking about Heathcliff:

(56) "Hush, hush! He's a human being," I said. "Be more charitable; there are worse men than he is yet!"

"He's not a human being," she retorted, "and he has no claim on my charity. I gave him my heart, and he took and pinched it to death, and flung it back to me."

In this example, according to Leech and Short (2001: 297), when Nelly

Chapter 9
Stylistics: Language and Literature

Dean calls Heathcliff a "human being" she flouts the maxim of quantity by stating what is self-evidently true and therefore redundant. The implicature is that he deserves to be treated with the sympathy and consideration that human beings usually afford to each other. Isabella flouts the maxim of quality by uttering that Heathcliff is not a human being, and that he has torn out her heart and killed it. The implicature is that she has been seriously ill-treated by her husband and that her resentment towards him is really deep.

Further Readings

Leech G. N. & Short, M. H. 1981/2001. *Style in Fiction*. 北京:外语教学与研究出版社.

Thornborrow, J. & Wareing, S. 2000. *Patterns in Language: Stylistics for Students of Language and Literature*. 北京:外语教学与研究出版社.

Widdowson, H. G. 1992. *Practical Stylistics*. Oxford: Oxford University Press.

Wright, L. & Hope, J. 2000. *Stylistics: A Practical Coursebook*. 北京:外语教学与研究出版社.

王守元,2000,《英语文体学要略》。济南:山东大学出版社。

王佐良、丁往道(主编),1987,《英语文体学引论》。北京:外语教学与研究出版社。

Questions and Exercises

1. Define the following terms.

foregrounding	alliteration	assonance
consonance	onomatopoeia	prosody
rhyme-scheme	meter	metrical pattern
parallelism	anticlimax	semantic deviation
transference of meaning	metonymy	transferred epithet
paradox	oxymoron	overstatement understatement irony

2. What is your understanding of style?
3. What is your definition of stylistics? What issues do you think stylistics tries to address?
4. Name three major views on style and make a comment on each.
5. How do you conduct stylistic analysis from a linguistic point of view?
6. Discuss the stylistic effects of phonological devices in the following:
    a. Clean and Clear (brand of a cosmetic product)
    b. Magnetic, Magnificent Meryl (1982 best actress in the U. S.)
    c. Sea, sun, sand, seclusion—and Spain (an ad)
    d. Military glory is a bubble blown from blood.
7. Analyze the semantic deviation involved in each of the following:
    a. I'm parked two blocks away in an illegal parking zone. (Clue: what is parked?)
    b. He crashed down on a *protesting* chair.
    c. *Lazy* clouds drifted across the sky.
    d. The child is father of the man.
    e. "How you shot the goat and frightened the tiger to death," said Miss Mebbin, with her *disagreeably pleasant laugh*.
    f. It is a *crime* to stay inside on such a beautiful day.
    g. She *cried her eyes out*.

h. I *didn't half like* that.
   i. It gave me *no small pleasure* to receive a letter form you.
   j. One million dollars! Don't you think that's *a little* steep (unreasonable)?
   k. This hard-working boy seldom reads more than an hour per week.
8. Comment on the following jokes according to your knowledge of style.
   1) A: You know what my father always calls me?
      B: No. What?
      A: He always calls me Johnny.
      B: Why's that?
      A: It's my name.
   2) A: Would you call me a taxi, please.
      B: Okay. You're a taxi.
   3) A: Who was that lady I saw you with last night?
      B: That was no lady. That was my wife.
9. Compare and comment on the following three versions of a passage in terms of their stylistic effects.
   A. Where the wind blew free and there was nothing to break the light of the sun, I was born. Where there were no enclosures and where everything drew a free breath, I was born.
   B. I was born where there were no enclosures and there was nothing to break the light of the sun. I was born upon the prairie, where the wind blew free and where everything drew a free breath.
   C. I was born upon the prairie; I was born where the wind blew free; and I was born where there was nothing to break the light of the sun. I was born where there were no enclosures; and I was born where everything drew a free breath.
10. Analyze the stylistic effect of the four lines of Tennyson's *The Brook* from a phonological perspective.
    I chatter over stony ways,
    In little sharps and trebles,
    I bubble into eddying bays,
    I babble on the pebbles.
11. Make a stylistic comment on the following poem by William Wordsworth.
    The coco is crowing,
    The stream is flowing,
    The small birds twitter,
    The lake doth glitter,
    The green field sleeps in the sun;
    The oldest and youngest
    Are at work with the strongest;
    The cattle are grazing;
    There are forty feeding like one!

    Like an army defeated
    The snow hath retreated,
    And now doth fare ill
    On the top of the bare hill;

Chapter 9

Stylistics: Language and Literature

  The Ploughboy is whooping—anon—anon;
  There's joy in the mountains;
  There's life in the fountains;
  Small clouds are sailing,
  Blue sky prevailing;
  The rain is over and gone!

12. Find a dramatic discourse and make a stylistic comment on it with reference to the speech acts and turn-takings in it.

Chapter 10

Sociolinguistics: Language and Society

10.1 Introduction

Sociolinguistics is the study of language in relation to society. The relationship between language and society has long been a concern of modern linguists. However, serious studies of sociolinguistics did not begin until the mid of the twentieth century. Many findings and achievements of sociolinguists in the past decades have revealed the great efforts that have been made by sociolinguists in their attempts to define the inter-relationships between language and society. There have been generally two kinds of sociolinguistic study, one that emphasizes the understanding of social structure through the study of language, a sociolinguistic study of society and one that investigates the relation between language and society with the goal of a better understanding of the structure of language and of how language functions in communication, a sociolinguistic study of language. The former is also called the sociology of language, that is, the study of society in relation to language. The latter is often regarded as the central concern of sociolinguistics, that is, the study of language in relation to society. Therefore, our concern in this chapter is mainly about the latter, i. e. how the various social factors such as region, ethnic group, social class, gender, age, etc. affect the use of language. We will also introduce some basic concepts which are usually discussed in the sociology of language, such as diglossia, bilingualism and code-switching, which are linguistic features that serve to characterize particular social arrangements.

10.2 The Relations Between Language and Society

We are all familiar with one phenomenon in our daily life, technically called **phatic communion**: communication between people which is not intended to seek or convey information but has the social function of establishing or maintaining social contact. Usually, when we meet familiar people, we may comment on the weather or enquire about health as a way of maintaining social contact. This kind of communication also takes place between strangers who

Chapter 10
Sociolinguistics: Language and Society

meet for the first time. When two Englishmen who have never met before come face to face in a railway compartment, they may start talking about the weather. The conversation on the neutral topic like weather may not be something that the Englishmen are interested in, but it does play an important social function that is often fulfilled by language—easing the embarrassing situation people might encounter in the company of someone you are not acquainted with (Trudgill, 1974: 13).

Furthermore, in the process of conversing, we may find out certain things about each other quite easily, not so much from what the speaker says as from how he says it, for whenever we speak we cannot avoid giving our listeners clues about our origins and the sort of person we are. For example, our accent and our speech generally show where we are from and what sort of social background we have.

Thus, as far as the social functions of language are concerned, the above two aspects of language behaviour are reflections of the fact that there exists a close inter-relationship between language and society: first, the phatic function of language in establishing and maintaining social relationship; and second, the role played by language in conveying information about the speaker.

Apart from the social functions of language, two views of the possible relationships between language and society hold sway in sociolinguistics (cf. Wardhaugh, 1986: 10). One is that social structure may either influence or determine linguistic structure and/or behaviour. Firstly, as has been mentioned above, the way we speak and the varieties of language we use reflect such matters as our regional, social, or ethnic origin and possibly even our age and sex. The age-grading phenomenon is a case in point. That is, people at different age levels may speak differently. Young children speak differently from older children and, in turn, children speak differently from mature adults. Secondly, particular ways of speaking, choices of words, and even rules for conversing are determined by certain social requirements. Hudson (1980/2000: 119) maintains that society controls our speech in two ways: by providing a set of norms and by providing the motivation for adhering to these norms, and for putting effort into speech (as into social interaction in general). **Ethnography of communication**, the study of the place of language in culture and society, is mainly concerned with rules of speaking, the ways in which speakers associate particular modes of speaking, topics, or message forms, with particular settings and activities. For example, we are required to respond when someone else greets us; when someone else is talking we are required to keep more or less silent (but not totally so). It is rewarding to follow the norms because social relationship is properly maintained and communication is made efficient. Thirdly, the values of a society can also have an effect on its language. For example, what words belong to taboo are determined by the values of a society. This also explains the reason why people tend to use euphemisms in certain situations.

A second possible relationship is that linguistic structure and/or behaviour may either influence or determine social structure. This is the view behind the Sapir-Whorf hypothesis (see Chapter 11) and the claims of Bernstein (1972). Bernstein made a distinction between **restricted code** and **elaborated code**. The restricted code was an example of the speech patterns used by the working-class and was thought to be used in relatively informal situations, stressing the speaker's membership of a group, relying on context for its meaningfulness, and lacking stylistic range. Linguistically, the restricted code is signaled by a high proportion of personal pronouns, particularly *you* and *they*, by tag-questions soliciting the agreement of the listener, and so on. The elaborated code was the language style used by the middle and upper classes and was said to be used in relatively formal, educated situations, permitting people to be reasonably creative in their expression and to use a range of linguistic alternatives. The elaborated code is said to be characterized linguistically by the use of a relatively high proportion of subordinate clauses, passive verbs, adjectives, uncommon adverbs and conjunctions and the pronoun *I*. Bernstein claimed that the lower achievement of working-class children than middle-class and upper-class children in schools was caused by the fact that working-class children had less access to the elaborated code than the upper-class and middle-class children. As schooling is conducted primarily in the elaborated code, working-class children's restricted code prevents them from taking an active part in classroom discussion.

10.3 Speech Community and Speech Variety

Language is more than an abstract system; it is also a means of communication by which people can identify themselves by the way they use their language. This is because varieties of language exist among the speakers of different regional, social, political and cultural backgrounds. People do not have to be very observant in order to find that the language spoken by people vary from place to place, profession to profession, ethnic group to ethnic group. This linguistic diversity of the language users is a manifestation of the social factors such as age, sex, ancestry, ethnic group, and geographic location, etc.

The term **speech community**, also called **linguistic community**, is widely used by sociolinguists to refer to a community based on language. Speech community is viewed differently by different scholars. The simplest definition of the term is given by Lyons (1970: 326), who defines it as "all the people who use a given language". A similar definition is offered by Hockett (1958: 8), namely, "the whole set of people who communicate with each other, either directly or indirectly, via the common language". Here, the criterion of communication within the community is added, so that if two communities both speak the same language but had no contact with each other at all, they would count as different speech communities. Though linguists define the term differently, they all seem to agree that people in the same speech community tend to share certain linguistic patterns or norms that can distinguish them from those of other communities. Therefore, we can define the term speech community simply as a group of people who share a set of language varieties and a set of norms for using them in their linguistic communication.

The difference of speech communities gives rise to the difference in language use, and thus exhibits people's social identity. It should be noted that speech communities may overlap. For example, a child may identify groups on the basis of sex, age, geography, and race, and each grouping may contribute something to the particular combination of linguistic items which they select as their own language.

The members of a speech community have at least one speech variety in common, and share norms about the selection of varieties. In bilingual and multilingual communities, people would usually have more than one speech variety in common. In any speech community there is hardly any speaker who sticks to one style of speaking all the time. A competent native speaker of a language is in possession of a variety of ways in using the language. The totality of linguistic varieties possessed by an individual constitutes his **verbal or linguistic repertoire**.

Speech varies with the users of language and the purposes of language use. Thus, **speech variety** can be classified with respect to the user and use. The speech variety which is defined according to the characteristics of the user (region, class, sex, etc.) is called **dialect**, e. g. regional dialects and social dialects. The speech variety which is defined according to the use of language in social situations (i. e. nature of activity in which language is functioning) is called **register**, e. g. lawyers' language, scientific language, business language. Dialect is a **dialectal variety** that can be said to be saying the same thing differently, while register is a **diatypic variety** which can be said to be saying different things. Therefore, dialects tend to differ in some words, grammar and pronunciation, but not in semantics. Registers, however, tend to differ in semantics and therefore words and grammar, but rarely in pronunciation.

10.4　Dialect

As mentioned above, a dialect is a variety of alanguage which is defined according to the characteristics of the user of the language, such as region, social class, age, sex, ethnic background, and so on. A dialect is often associated with a particular **accent**, a particular way of speaking which tells the listener something about the speaker's background. Dialects can be classified into regional dialect and social dialect, but apart from these two broad categories, there are also dialectal varieties called idiolect and temporal dialect. **Idiolect** is the language system of an individual as expressed by the way he or she speaks or writes within the overall system of a particular language. It is the features of speech or writing which distinguish one individual from others, such as voice quality, speech rhythm, diction, and other stylistic features. **Temporal dialect** is the variety of language associated with a particular period of time, such as Old English and Modern English. Furthermore, a distinction is often made between standard and non-standard dialects according to the range of intelligibility.

10.4.1　Regional Dialect

It is generally believed that when people are separated from each other geographically, dialectal diversity develops, and the greater the geographical distance between two dialects the more dissimilar they are linguistically. For instance, those regional varieties of British English which are most unlike the speech of London are undoubtedly those of the north-east of Scotland.

A **regional dialect** refers to the language variety used in a geographical region. A regional dialect differs from language in that the former is considered a distinct variety, yet not distinct enough from other dialects of the language to be regarded as a different language.

Dialectologists have found that regional dialect boundaries often coincide with geographical boundaries, such as mountains, swamps or rivers. For example, all local-dialect speakers in the areas of Britain north of the river Humber (between Lincolnshire and Yorkshire) still have a monophthong in words like *house* ("*hoose*" [hu:s]), whereas speakers south of the river have had some kind of [haus]-type diphthong for several hundred years (Trudgill, 1974).

Dialect differences increase proportionately to the degree of communicative isolation between the groups. Communicative isolation refers to a situation two or three hundred years ago, or in the old times. Although there was some contact through commerce and migration, the real contact was rare. Today the isolation is less likely pronounced because of the mass media, internet, and travel by jet, but even within one country, regionalisms still persist. There is no evidence that any dialect adjustment occurs due to the mass media or internet.

The difference between regional dialects is often phonological, as illustrated in the examples mentioned earlier. The difference, however, could also be morphological and syntactic. For example, a particular number of words may be used in a regional dialect. The dragonfly is referred to in most of Virginia as *snake doctor*, in Southwestern Pennsylvania as *snake feeder*, in eastern North Carolina as *mosquito hawk*, in New England as (*devil's*) *darning needle*, in coastal New Jersey as *spindle*, in northern California as *ear sewer*, and so on.

10.4.2 Social Dialect

Social dialect, or sociolect, refers to a variety of language associated with a particular social group, such as a particular social class, or ethnic group, or those based on age, gender and occupation. Speakers of a sociolect usually share a similar social background.

10.4.2.1 Language and Social Class

Linguists have known for a long time that different dialects and accents are related to the differences of social class background. One typical instance is the regional features in the speech of people from a lower social class. In Britain, for example, conservative and rural dialects—old-fashioned varieties associated usually with groups lowest in the social hierarchy—are typical styles of English that bear strong social class identity. In between Norfolk and Suffolk as well as between Cornwall and Aberdeen, there exist a whole series of different dialects which gradually merge into one another. This series is referred to as a **dialect continuum**—a large number of different but not usually distinct non-standard dialects connected by a chain of similarity, but with the dialects at the either end of the chain being very dissimilar (Trudgill, 1974: 40). At the other end of the social scale, however, the situation is very different. Speakers of the highest social class employ the dialect called standard English, which is only slightly different in different parts of the country, and their speech tends to be closer to Received Pronunciation.

This difference between social classes can be observed from different aspects of language. At the lexical level, for example, there is in the standard English dialect a word *scarecrow* signifying a humanoid object farmers place in fields to scare off birds. Linguists have found a far greater degree of regional variation in the most localized regional English dialects of the lower class people. In these local dialects, corresponding to *scarecrow*, there exist *bogle*, *fly-crow*, *mawpin*, *mawkin*, *birdscarer*, and several others.

The same kind of pattern is also found with grammatical differences which exhibit social class difference. For instance, there are two possibilities in the negation of the sentence *I can eat anything* in standard English, i. e. either *I can't eat anything* or *I can eat nothing*. But there exists a third possibility in non-standard English, i. e. *I can't eat nothing*. As is reported by Trudgill (1974), the third possibility is most frequently found in the speech of the lowest working class, but is rarely found in the speech of the upper middle class.

Class difference can also be found in terms of accent. For example, there exists a distinctive variation in the accent of the speakers in Great Britain where Received Pronunciation is closely associated with people of high social classes, and the most localized accent is found among the lowest social classes.

10.4.2.2 Language and Sex

Research suggests that men and women use language in different ways. In some cases the differences are quite small, but in others, the differences may be quite large, overtly noticed. For example, it is often believed that men tend to use more taboo words than women, and besides, women consistently use language forms which more closely approach those of the standard variety or prestige accent than those used by men (Trudgill, 1974). Women are also reported to use words of exaggeration (*stunning*, *fantastic*, *lovely*, *divine*, *adorable*, *cute*, *wonderful*, *such*) and qualifiers and intensifiers (*simply gorgeous*, *terribly nice*, *absolutely beautiful*, *perfectly charming*, *awfully pretty*, *so marvelous*) more frequently than men do. Research also suggests that women's speech is characterized by the frequent use of interrogatives, tag questions and other tentative forms, and the frequent use of indirect request or command, while men tend to be more competitive and assertive in their speech and are more likely to interrupt.

Gender varieties arise because language, as a social phenomenon, is closely related to social attitudes. Men and women are socially different in that society lays down different social roles for them and expects different behavior patterns from them. Language simply reflects this social fact. Not only do men and women speak differently, as we have demonstrated, but also women's speech is (socially) "better" than men's speech. This is a reflection of the fact that, generally speaking, more "correct" social behavior is expected of women. Gender varieties, then, are the result of different social attitudes towards the behavior of men and women, and of the attitudes men and women themselves have towards language as a social symbol.

10.4.2.3 Language and Ethnic Group

It is generally believed that linguistic difference exists among people of different racial or ethnic backgrounds. Ethnic difference may give rise to ethnic dialects, which are dialectal varieties associated with different ethnic groups. One frequently discussed ethnic variety of the English language is English spoken by the black people in America, often called **"Black English"** or **"Black English Vernacular (BEV)"**. These terms are generally used to refer to the non-standard English spoken by lower class blacks in the urban ghettoes of the northern USA and elsewhere.

Black English is mainly characterized by its phonological and grammatical variations. The most frequently cited characteristics of the phonological features include:

- Many black speakers do not have postvocalic /r/ in *cart* or *car*.
- Black speakers do not have /θ/, as in *thing*, or /ð/, as in *that*. In initial positions, they may be merged with /t/ (rarely) and /d/ respectively, so that *this* is *dis*.
- The present participle is usually /ɪn/, not /ɪŋ/, so that *walking* is pronounced /wɔːkɪn/.
- Black speakers tend to simplify final consonant clusters in words like *lost*, *west*, *desk*, *end*, or *cold* (where both consonants are either voiced or voiceless), where another consonant follows: *los' time*, *wes' coast*.
- Often word-final /l/ is deleted, so that *cool* is pronounced /kuː/.

The following are some of the most frequently discussed grammatical features of Black English:

- The lack of the verb inflection *-s*: Black English does not have the verb inflection *-s* in third-person singular present-tense forms, so that forms such as *he go*, *it come*, *she run* are usual.
- The absence of the copula— the verb *to be*—in the present tense: So one can find the following type of sentences:
  She real nice.
  They out there.
  I leaving.
- The "invariant *be*": the use of the form *be* as a finite verb form to indicate "habitual aspect". For example:
  He usually be around.
  Sometimes she be fighting.
  She be nice and happy.
  They sometimes be incomplete.
- Multiple negation: Multiple negation is fundamental to Black English

syntax, so that *I didn't eat nothing* is used to mean *I didn't eat anything* or *I ate nothing*.

10.4.3 Standard Dialect

Sometimes, a dialect gains status and becomes the standard variety of a country, i.e. the standard dialect or language. A **standard dialect** refers to a special variety of language that has no connection with a particular region or social class. That is to say, a standard dialect enjoys a wide range of intelligibility. This variety of language is often referred to as the standard language. Command of the standard language is the goal of formal language instruction. Because of its function as the public means of communication, it is subject to extensive codification (especially in grammar, vocabulary, pronunciation, and spelling), which is controlled, and passed on via the public media and institutions, but above all, through the school systems.

With its codified grammar, vocabulary, spelling, and pronunciation, standard dialect becomes the dialect of a language that wins literary and cultural supremacy over the others and gains some kind of institutional support from government administration and news media, and also from individuals who write grammars and books on correct usage.

Any speech or writing which differs in pronunciation, vocabulary, or grammar from the standard variety of the language is referred to as a **non-standard dialect** or **variety**. Non-standard varieties are usually used in specific speech communities and thus do not enjoy a wide range of intelligibility nor have the same social functions as the standard variety. However, non-standard varieties have valuable functions in intimate settings and for individual group identity. One typical example of non-standard varieties of language is the so-called **vernacular**, i.e. the language or dialect of a speech community, such as black English vernacular and pidgin languages, often associated with everyday, casual, or intimate speech, as distinct from the standard language.

10.5 Register

Register refers to the functional variety of language that is defined according to its use in a context of situation. People participating in recurrent communication situations tend to use similar vocabularies and ways of speaking. For example, a physician may use technical terms when he is talking with his fellow physicians, but he may use ordinary vocabulary when he is talking to his patients. When talking about salt, a chemist may use "NaCl" in writing, but he may use the word *salt* before a preschool child.

According to systemic functional grammar, register is determined by the

three variables of the context of situation: field, tenor and mode (Halliday, 1978).
- **Field of discourse**: what the language is being used to talk about, which includes what is happening, the nature of the social action that is taking place and what the participants are engaged in. Field is the linguistic reflection of the role of the language use with a definite purpose in a situation. Grammatical features tend to be determined by the field of discourse. Technical English, for example, are field-restricted.
- **Tenor of discourse**: who is taking part, the role relationships between the language users in a particular situation (e. g. teacher-pupil, parent-child).
- **Mode of discourse**: what role language is playing in the interaction, which includes channel (e. g. written, spoken, written-to-be-spoken) as well as rhetorical mode (e. g. persuasive, rhetorical, expository, didactic, etc.).

Thus, "parent praising child in speech" and "employer blaming employee in writing" are different registers in that they are associated with different fields (praising vs. blaming), tenor (parent-child vs. employer-employee) and mode (speech vs. writing). As a result, the use of language will be different in the two registers.

10.6 Language Contact and Contact Languages

Language contact occurs when speakers of different languages interact, especially when at least one of the languages is influenced by the contact. Any language which is created through contact between two or more languages is a **contact language**, e. g. a pidgin or creole. Contact languages arise from a basic need that people speaking different languages have to find a common system of communication. Such a system is often called a lingua franca. All contact languages are lingua francas, although not all lingua francas are contact languages.

10.6.1 Lingua Franca

Lingua franca is the general term for a language that serves as a means of communication between groups of people who speak different native languages. A lingua franca can be any of the following four types of language:
- a trade language, like Swahili in East Africa;
- an international language, like English, or the native language of one of the groups;

- a contact language, like a pidgin or creole;
- an auxiliary language, like Esperanto.

The term "lingua franca" is from Italian, meaning "Frankish tongue". It originated in the Mediterranean region in the Middle Ages among crusaders and traders of different language backgrounds. Nowadays, English is the world's most common lingua franca.

10.6.2 Pidgin

A **pidgin** is a contact language which develops as a common means of communication when groups of people who speak different languages come into contact and communicate with one another. A pidgin is not the native language of any speech community. It simply arises in situations like foreign trade, where speakers of different languages cannot understand each other's native language. In such situations, the structure and vocabulary of the individual native languages are reduced in order to bring about general mutual understanding. Gradually, a functional mixed language develops and is learned along with one's native language. Linguistically, pidgins are characterized by a limited vocabulary, a greater use of paraphrase and metaphor, a simplified phonological system, and a reduced morphology and syntax.

The term "pidgin" is said to come from the English language word *business*, as pronounced in the pidgin English which developed in China. One example of pidgin is Tok Pisin in Papua New Guinea.

10.6.3 Creole

A **creole** is a pidgin language that has become the native language of a group of speakers. That is to say, a pidgin becomes a creole when it has acquired native speakers. The process by which a pidgin turns into a creole is called **creolization**. However, not every pidgin becomes a creole, i. e. undergoes the process of creolization. Pidgins acquire native speakers, and thus become creolized, by being spoken by couples who have children and rear them together. As creolization involves the expansion of the vocabulary and the grammatical system, creoles are characterized by a complex grammar and vocabulary in comparison with pidgins. Creoles are usually classified according to the language from which most of their vocabulary comes. For example, Jamaican Creole and Hawaiian Creole are English-based creoles because most of their vocabulary comes from the English language.

10.7 Choosing a Code

We are often faced with the problem of code selection in daily communication. "Code" here is used as a neutral term referring to a language or a variety of a language. Code choice is an important aspect of linguistic communication because few people are single-code speakers. A **polyglot**, for example, can speak many languages, and most people are able to use several varieties of a language. Whenever we speak, we have to select a particular language or language variety for a given situation. This is not only the case in bilingual or multilingual situations, but also in diglossic situations where two distinct codes have clear functional differences. Moreover, speakers can and will switch, as the occasion arises, from one code to another.

10.7.1 Diglossia

The term **"diglossia"** was first used by Charles Ferguson in the late 1950s referring to a particular kind of language situation where two distinct varieties of a language exist side by side throughout the speech community, and each of the two varieties is assigned definite social functions. The two linguistic varieties in a diglossia situation are considered by the speakers to be discrete, and comprise a standardized **High variety** and **Low variety** which is also standardized but may be subject to geographical differentiation. In Switzerland, for example, Standard German is the High variety, while Swiss German is the Low variety. The two varieties have overt recognition in the speech community, and each is used for different purposes. In a diglossic situation, the High variety, which is the prestige variety, is used in government, media, education, serious literature and religious services. The Low variety, which lacks prestige, is used in conversation with family and friends, "folk" literature, and other relatively informal settings.

10.7.2 Bilingualism

Bilingualism is the use of at least two languages either by an individual or by a group of speakers. A bilingual situation is easily found in many countries of continental Europe such as Holland, Belgium, France, Germany and Switzerland, where two languages are used side by side. In Belgium, French and Flemish Dutch are both recognized as official languages. Canada is the country where both French and English are recognized as official languages. Other countries and regions in the world which are bilingual include Australia, Singapore, Pakistan, and parts of the United States. As the result of immigration, it is reported, over 50 percent of people in the United States speak another foreign language at home.

Sometimes, the term **"multilingualism"** is also used to mean the use of two or more languages, but very often it is used in contrast with "bilingualism", meaning the use of more than two languages.

10.7.3 Code-switching

Code switching is the switch made by a speaker or writer from one language or language variety to another. A person may start speaking one language and then change to another. A speaker may also switch from the standard variety to a regional dialect, or from the occupational variety to the domestic variety. Code-switching can occur between sentences or within a single sentence, involving words or phrases or even parts of words.

Two types of code-switching are usually identified: **situational code-switching** and **metaphorical code-switching**. Situational code-switching takes place when language users change languages according to the situations of language use, involving no topic change: they speak one language in one situation and another in a different one. Metaphorical code-switching takes place when a change in the language used is required by a change of topic.

Situational code-switching assumes a direct relationship between language and the social situation. For example, everyone in the village of Sauris, in northern Italy, spoke German within the family, Saurian (a dialect of Italian) informally within the village, and standard Italian to outsiders and in more formal village settings (school, church, work). Each individual could expect to switch codes several times a day according to the social situations (Denison, 1971).

Metaphorical code-switching, on the other hand, is not related to change in social situations. Rather it is associated with how speakers employ particular languages to convey information that goes beyond their actual words, especially to define social situations. Speakers change codes in order to redefine the situation: formal to informal, official to personal, serious to humorous, and politeness to solidarity. For example, at the community administration office, clerks may use both standard and dialect expressions, depending on whether they are talking about official affairs or not. Likewise, when residents step up to a clerk's desk, greeting and inquiries about family affairs tend to be exchanged in the dialect, while the business part of the transaction is carried on in the standard variety (Hudson, 1980/2000).

There are various reasons for code-switching. Firstly, code-switching a word or phrase from one language into another language can facilitate communication because it is easier or more convenient to use the word or phrase in another language, especially it is right in the mind of the speaker at the moment of speaking. Secondly, code-switching is a means of maintaining speaker or group identity, and it helps relationship-building, creates a sense of belonging or reinforces solidarity among a group of people. Thirdly, code-switching is a means of defining or signalling social situations, as discussed above.

Chapter 10
Sociolinguistics: Language and Society

Further Readings

Fasold, R. 2001. *The Sociolinguistics of Language*. 北京:外语教学与研究出版社.
Hudson, R. A. 1980/2000. *Siociolinguistics*. 北京:外语教学与研究出版社.
Trudgill, P. 1974. *Sociolinguistics: An Introduction to Language and Society*. Harmondsworth: Penguin.
Wardhaugh, R. 1986/2000. *An Introduction to Sociolinguistics*. 北京:外语教学与研究出版社.
祝畹瑾,1992,《社会语言学概论》。长沙:湖南教育出版社。

Questions and Exercises

1. Define the following terms:

sociolinguistics	phatic communion	ethnography of communication
restricted code	elaborated code	speech variety
speech community	linguistic repertoire	register
dialect	accent	idiolect
temporal dialect	regional dialect	social dialect
dialect continuum	standard language	vernacular
field of discourse	tenor of discourse	mode of discourse
contact language	language contact	pidgin
creole	lingua franca	diglossia
bilingualism	polyglot	

2. How is language related to society?
3. To what extent is Bernstein's claim about the relationship between social class and language code justified?
4. How does speech vary according to its user?
5. How does speech vary according to its use?
6. What is register? Illustrate it with an example of your own.
7. Explain briefly bilingualism and diglossia.
8. Why do people switch codes? What is the major difference between situational code-switching and metaphorical code-switching?

Chapter 11

Intercultural Communication: Language and Culture

11.1 Introduction

Culture determines and shapes every aspect of human life, and language is no exception. All of the human linguistic activities, ranging from the acquisition of the mother tongue, daily greetings and forms of address, to verbal communication between people of different linguistic and social background, are inevitably embedded within specific cultural settings, and are therefore subject to the profound influence of cultural elements. From a different perspective, some researchers also argue for a "reversed effect" for human language on its culture, in the sense that our language also influences, if not determines, the way we perceive the world, interpret our experiences, and organize our ideas. In a word, language and culture are intrinsically connected to each other, and their interaction could be manifest in many aspects.

11.2 Definitions of Culture

Any attempt at defining a general and evasive concept such as culture would definitely be troublesome. It is said that there have been more than 150 definitions of culture, made by different researchers, from different perspectives, and for different purposes. Below are just a few of them.
- Culture may be defined as what a society does and thinks. (Sapir, 1921)
- What really binds men together is their culture—the ideas and standards they have in common. (Benedict, 1935)
- Culture is man's medium; there is not one aspect of human life that is not touched and altered by culture. This means personality, how people express themselves, including shows of emotion, the way they think, how they move, how problems are solved, how their cities are planned and laid out, how transportation systems function and are organized, as well as how economic and government systems are put together and function. (Hall, 1959)

Chapter 11
Intercultural Communication: Language and Culture

- Culture might be defined as the ideas, customs, skills, arts, and tools that characterize a given group of people in a given period of time. But culture is more than the sum of its parts. (Brown, 1994)
- Culture refers to the total way of life of particular groups of people. It includes everything that a group of people thinks, says, does, and makes. (Kohls, 1979)

As can be seen from the above examples, there could be as many definitions as researchers. It is difficult, if not impossible, to give an all-inclusive definition of such a general concept, yet we could still capture some essential features of culture from the above definitions. **Culture** is the total way of life of a particular group of people. It includes both the tangible and intangible aspects, ranging from an individual person's daily life to large-scale institutional or societal organizations and abstract norms, values, and mindsets in general. Besides, the boundary of the concept may also vary from subject to subject: it either refers to the general behavioral patterns of a race (the Western culture) or a nation (the American culture), or those of a community (the folk culture of Hong Kong) or even a small group (the corporate culture). The scope of definition is determined by the purpose and target of specific research.

11.3 The Relationship Between Language and Culture

Culture is maintained by three different means. The first is cultural artifact, which includes concrete objects such as food, dress, building, and means of transportation, to name but a few. The second means includes various forms of documents and literature, such as legal documents, historical documents, and literary works. The third means is verbal communication, including folklores, local operas, language games, and so on. It is plain to see that language plays a very important role in cultural construction and maintenance. People rely heavily on their language in sharing their emotion, exchanging their views, improving their knowledge and asserting their value systems.

However, some linguists, sociologists and anthropologists hold that language is more than a container of cultural contents. Rather, it plays a more active and determining role in molding the culture of its speakers. According to this role, people of different language systems not only possess different communicative tools, but also perceive, interpret and understand the world differently. Simply language also influences, if not shapes, our culture, and this is what we usually term as "linguistic relativity", which will be discussed in Section 11.6.

All in all, language and culture are closely intertwined. Language definitely reflects its culture; at the same time, language also plays a crucial role in the construction of the shared view of reality held by speakers of a common language. Altogether there are three major ways in which language helps shape our culture. First of all, language allows people to name the objects and events in the physical and social world. Second, particular cultures have unique ways of speaking and communication. Third, each language has some covert grammatical categories which may influence or even determine the way of thinking of its speakers. The following sections will be devoted to a more detailed discussion of the above three aspects.

11.4 Naming the World Through Language

Language enables us to attach verbal labels to objects and events around so that we can understand, remember, and talk about these objects and events later. What is important is that no two languages share exactly the same inventory of labels. Instead, different cultures will invent and develop their own vocabulary according to their own concerns and interest. For example, Eskimos are said to have hundreds of different words to refer to snow in different states, whereas the English language has only one. If an Englishman wants to describe snow with greater subtlety, he has to add some modifications, such as *heavy snow*, *drifting snow*, etc. Similar cases abound. Some Arabic languages have a lot of words for camel, and the Hawaiian local dialect has a lot of words for rain. All these cases indicate that the language system is closely related to its culture, and reflects its speakers' primary concern in their daily life.

11.4.1 Color Terms

An often-quoted example of cultural difference in lexis is color terms. While human beings are similar in their physiological ability to distinguish the colors and hues on the spectrum, their categorization and linguistic labeling of the colors may be different. For English-speaking people, the basic color terms are *red*, *yellow*, *orange*, *blue*, *green*, and *purple*. Chinese people, however, would readily recognize seven colors named "chi" (red), "cheng" (orange), "huang" (yellow), "lü" (green), "qing" (dark blue), "lan" (blue), and "zi" (purple), with a more subtle distinction between different shades of blue.

Not all languages have such a rich repertoire of color terms as in Chinese or English. Some languages only distinguish two colors: *black* and *white*, or more precisely, dark colors and light colors. Some languages have three color terms, and interestingly, the third color is always *red*. If a language has a

Chapter 11
Intercultural Communication: Language and Culture

fourth or fifth color term, more often than not that would be either *yellow* or *green*. In other words, some color terms, such as *red*, *blue*, *green* or *yellow*, are more readily accepted into the vocabulary of a language than others, such as *brown*, *pink* or *purple*. What is more, variations in color terms across cultures are not totally random; instead, they seem to follow certain predictable patterns, which might be related to the experiential or cognitive features of human beings. Studies in this aspect provide interesting and unequivocal evidence for the universal patterns observed among human cultures.

11.4.2 Kinship Terms

Languages not only reflect human experiences and perceptions of the natural environment, but also mirror the complex human society in itself. People of different cultures organize and maintain their communities and societies in different ways, and such differences are manifest in their language systems too.

Kinship terms would be a good case in point. While family is a universal human institution, the way people address their family members and relatives may not be the same. For example, native-speakers of English would be quite confused by the following Chinese kinship terms, as there are no ready equivalents in their mother tongue.

叔叔、伯伯、舅舅、姨父、姑父
姨母、舅母、姑母、婶婶、伯母
小姨子、小叔子、小舅子、姐夫、妹夫、大嫂、小姑
表兄、表弟、堂兄、堂弟
岳父、岳母、公公、婆婆
连襟、妯娌

Similarly, a Chinese learner of English would find the word *cousin* too evasive and unspecific. Such a difference in kinship terms would naturally cause great difficulty in translating some classic literary works, such as the following line：

林黛玉的母亲是贾宝玉的姑母，贾宝玉的母亲是林黛玉的舅母，又是薛宝钗的姨母。

Underlying the complex Chinese kinship terminology is the meticulous classification and arrangement of family members, which is a result of the long-lasting value about the traditional Chinese family. Respect for the senior, differentiated role and status for male and female, and the idea about the blood-related members as "insiders" and the marriage-related ones as "outsiders"—all these values typical of Chinese culture would help to explain why Chinese people would take the trouble to make all these subtle distinctions in kinship terms.

11.4.3 Culture-loaded Words

Even though both English and Chinese have the color term *red* ("hong"), there is no guarantee that the equivalent color terms always have exactly the same meaning or connotation across cultures. For example, an Englishman may be confused by the Chinese phrase "yan hong" (red eyes,眼红), since in his language a jealous person is supposed to be green-eyed rather than red-eyed. Similarly, a Chinese student might not consider "red tapes" as something troublesome and unpleasant, as the color of red is usually associated with luck or success in Chinese culture. The meanings of words, therefore, are multi-layered. While dictionaries usually offer us the conceptual or denotative meaning of a word, its associative or connotative meanings are often manifest in idiomatic expressions or set phrases, and are more greatly influenced by the cultural factors inherent in the language. Words carrying cultural connotations or expressing culture-specific meanings are called **culture-loaded words**, or **culturally-loaded words**.

Culture-loaded words have aroused great interest among language researchers and learners. Apart from color terms that carry cultural connotations, some animal words also contain culture-specific meanings. For example, the word *dog* in such English idioms as *a lucky dog* and *love me, love my dog* has a more pleasant connotation than its Chinese equivalent "gou" in Chinese phrases such as "gou yao Lü Dongbin"(狗咬吕洞宾)or "gou tui zi" (狗腿子). Another example is *bull* in English, which also carries quite different connotations from its Chinese equivalent "niu". While a *bull-headed* person in English is usually stubborn, a "niu ren"(牛人)in Chinese is however very successful and admirable. Animal names which carry culture-specific connotations also include *crane* as in "he fa tong yan"(鹤发童颜)and *horse* as in "long ma jing shen"(龙马精神). Another case worth mentioning is the difference between the Chinese word "long"(龙)and the English word *dragon*. While this legendary animal enjoys an almost sacred position in Chinese culture, it is usually deemed a fierce monster in most Western cultures. Some Chinese researchers have also pointed out that the Chinese "long" and dragon are in fact different imaginary animals, not even equivalent in their denotative meanings, let alone their connotations.

Culture-loaded words are not only fun facts for language learners, but also tricky traps in cross-cultural understanding, especially in translation. Consider the classic description of a pair of beautiful hands in traditional Chinese language:"zhi ruo xue cong gen"(指若削葱根)—Could it be directly translated into English as "the fingers are like peeled green onion shoots"? Even though the foreign readers could finally figure out what "peeled green onion shoots" look like, they might still wonder why such fingers are beautiful, as they may have quite different values about female beauty from ours.

11.5 Communicative Patterns Across Cultures

Cultural influences on language go beyond the word level, and permeate every aspect of our language use. On the one hand, culture teaches us how to address people when we meet them, how to strike a conversation, how to maintain a friendly chat, and how to end a conversation in a natural and polite way. Culture also teaches us how to tell a story, how to give a lecture, how to make a bargain, and how to write an essay. On the other hand, culture may teach a man to speak assertively, while it may teach a woman to speak gently. American students are taught to "put the most important thing first" in essay writing, while Chinese students are taught to "save the best for the last" in delaying their arguments until in the final paragraph. All in all, cultural differences are shown not only in the language system per se, but also in the way we use our languages in various social contexts.

11.5.1 Address Forms

Whenever people speak to one another, they have to choose the most appropriate way to address their interactants. The addressing options differ greatly across cultures.

When addressing a stranger, Chinese people often use such expressions as "lao daye" (aged uncle), "lao dama" (aged aunt) or "lao shifu" (aged master) to draw the stranger's sympathetic attention. But American people would simply use "Excuse me" in the similar circumstances.

American people usually use "Mr" or "Miss" in most formal cases, yet Chinese people would make more subtle distinctions. Suppose a person happens to be the head of a bureau ("ju" in Chinese), then he might be called "Li Ju" (Bureau Li) rather than "Li Xiansheng" (Mr Li). By the same token, a chief engineer would be called "Li Zong" (Chief Li), a head of a department, "Li Chu" (Department Li). Besides working titles, Chinese people also address others by their occupation, such as "Li Dao" (Director Li), "Li Jingli" (Manager Li), "Li Jiaolian" (Coach Li). In contrast, there are only a few cases in English where the occupation could be used as address forms, such as "Professor Li" and "Doctor Li", yet "Teacher Li" in English would sound very awkward as an address form.

Another feature incomparable in English is the use of "Lao" (old or senior) and "Xiao" (young or junior) in Chinese address forms, such as "Lao

Zhang" (Old Zhang) and "Xiao Zhang" (Young Zhang). In some cases the character "Lao" has become an indispensable component of the words, as in the case of "Lao Shi" (teacher) and "Lao Ban" (boss). American people, in contrast, seem much less concerned with the relative age or status of their addressee, and the simple form like "Mr Li" would be appropriate in most cases.

Another distinct feature of Chinese address forms is the frequent use of kinship terms. American children would be quite confused if asked to address their mothers' colleagues or friends as "aunt" or "uncle", yet it would be quite natural and easy for Chinese children to do so. Chinese prefer their children to address family guests or even strangers as if they were family members, such as "Auntie Zhang", "Uncle Wang" or "Sister Liu". A Chinese boy would politely call an 80-year-old lady "Grandma", though she might be a complete stranger to him.

11.5.2 Greetings

Greetings vary greatly from person to person, and from culture to culture. Someone will simply nod at others without saying a word, whereas someone might grasp the hand of an acquaintance, pumping, and talk for half an hour. Englishmen are widely known for their discussion of weather as a greeting to each other, and the American greeting "Hi!" has traveled virtually throughout the world as a universal greeting form.

Chinese greetings also have some unique and culture-specific features. A peculiar greeting once very common in Chinese daily greeting is "ni chi le ma?" (Have you got your meal?). It has served as a typical example of cultural difference between the East and the West, as in the Western cultures, such a question would be considered as an implicit invitation rather than a greeting. Without a doubt a foreigner visiting China would be quite perplexed, if not irritated, if someone asks him whether he has got a meal and simply passes by without any further comment.

Admittedly, such a greeting is now not very common even among Chinese. People now adopt more neutral and simpler forms of greeting such as "ni hao" (Hello) or "zao shang hao" (Good morning). Sometimes people would use some general comments like "You look terrific today" or "It is quite hot today" as greetings, which is very similar to Western practice. However, some Chinese greeting forms may still sound awkward or even intruding to foreigners. For example, it is very natural for a Chinese person to ask a friend "Where are you going?" or "Where have you been?" when they meet in street, even though he is not at all interested in the exact destination of his friend.

11.5.3 Giving and Accepting Compliments

Although human beings universally appreciate compliments, the actual delivering of and responses to verbal compliments are never universal. While some people openly and directly offer compliments to others, and accepts others' compliment with a satisfied smile, others prefer to withhold their emotion and exchange mutual appreciation in a more implicit and indirect manner. The following are some examples of giving and accepting compliments.

(1) A: Gee, you look gorgeous!
    B: Thanks, that's my favorite dress.
(2) A: That's a nice shot!
    B: I was just lucky.
(3) A: Your home is really nice!
    B: It is a bit small, though.
(4) A: That's a great hat you're wearing.
    B: Beauty lies in the eye that can find it.

As we can see from the above examples, people are very strategic in accepting compliments from others. The first case is a direct acknowledgement, echoing the other's positive opinion about oneself. Such an "honest" acceptance of accomplishment is often used between very close friends, or in rather informal situations. It is not usually regarded as the typical Chinese way of speaking, as we Chinese may find it a bit impolite and self-contented. The second case shows a different strategy, that is, instead of accepting the credit, the speaker gives it to a third party (the luck). This is a very modest hence preferred way in traditional Chinese culture. The third strategy is to deny the merits or to deprecate oneself. While others are commenting on the nice home, the hostess tactfully shows her modesty by emphasizing the drawback (limited size) of it. Similarly, a Chinese girl being praised for her new dress often responds by deliberately deprecating the dress in such words as "No, that's a very cheap one". Such a strategy might sound a bit strange to Americans, as the response is not overtly related to the compliment, and therefore sounds a bit irrelevant and abrupt. The fourth strategy, as shown above, is to positively appreciate others' compliments, which is quite rare in both American and Chinese cultures, yet relatively common among Arabic communities. Since different cultural groups attach differential importance to such values as sincerity, modesty and politeness, the verbal patterns of giving and accepting compliments are also different. For those cultures which emphasize interpersonal relationship and the virtue of modesty, it is preferred to respond to the compliment in an indirect, even seemingly negative, way. In contrast, in those cultures which highlight such values as sincerity and personal achievement, compliments might be accepted and responded to in a more direct and positive manner.

11.5.4 High Context Versus Low Context

Language use is inextricably connected with the context, which includes not only the physical settings such as the time, place and surroundings of the communicative act, but also the social and psychological settings such as the topics and background of the interaction, as well as the relations of the people involved. In some cases, the information contained in the context may be as much as that actually conveyed through language. For example, when seeing a friend wearing an anxious look and passing by in a great haste, we would wonder what is wrong with him — Has he lost something important, or is he involved in some unexpected troubles? There is no need to strike a conversation and ask some questions, as we can infer most of the message from the way he walked and looked, as well as our world knowledge about human nature in general. In a word, context also conveys meanings of an event.

Some researchers find that cultural groups also differ greatly in their reliance on context in meaning exchanges: some depend more on contexts while others more on actual words being said or written. An important distinction is then made between **high-context** (HC) and **low-context** (LC) cultures. In an HC culture, most of the information is in the context, be it the physical setting of the event or psychological setting shared by its people. In this case, very little information is actually contained or transmitted through the verbal messages. In contrast, an LC culture relies heavily on explicit messages, and is not much concerned with the context of the event. It should be made clear that most cultures can be positioned along a scale indicating their relative ranking on the HC-LC dimension. Specifically, American, German and Swiss cultures are more towards the LC end, whereas most Asian, African American, and Latin American cultures are more towards the HC end.

It has been suggested that an HC culture usually possesses homogeneous experiences and a steady history, and such a rich shared pool of common knowledge allows its people to communicate in a quite implicit way. Most information has already been provided through contextual factors such as the surroundings, gestures, facial expressions, and even silence. An LC culture is just the opposite. The less homogeneous social background makes it necessary for its people to be specific and explicit with verbal messages, as they do not have a shared common experience to rely on for mutual understanding. Such an HC-LC difference is manifest in many aspects of communication. While Asian people tend to use indirect and implicit expressions out of politeness or respect,

American people usually expect direct and explicit messages, or in their words, "Spell it out!" By the same token, American people would require explicit utterances like "I love you" or "I apologize" as a clear statement of affection or apology. Asian people, however, would not care so much about the mere uttering of a few words. Deeds speak louder than words, as the proverb goes, and Asian people would tell whether a person is truly in love or sincerely regretful from the things he does, rather than the words he says.

11.6 Language and Thought: Sapir-Whorf Hypothesis

One of the essential issues in our discussion of the interaction between language and culture is the relationship between language and thought. While researchers generally deem language as a means of describing, storing and exchanging thoughts, some researchers look at this issue from a totally different perspective. To them, language is more than a mere container of ideas, or labels attached to the physical world. Rather, language will influence, if not determine, the formation of our ideas about the world, hence exerting a great effect on the way we perceive and understand the world. Such a position, usually called **Sapir-Whorf hypothesis**, has gained much attention as well as criticism ever since its proposal, and remains one of the most influential theories in this field.

Sapir-Whorf hypothesis is named after its two advocators, Edward Sapir (1884—1939) and Benjamin Whorf (1897—1941). These two American anthropologists and linguists had conducted in-depth studies on American Indian languages, which they found different from Indo-European languages. They further proclaimed that such a great difference in languages would affect the way people perceive and interpret the world around them. In other words, "the real world is to a large extent unconsciously built up on the language habit of the group" (Sapir, 1921). To them, language is not simply a device of reporting experience, but also, and more importantly, a way of defining experience for its speakers.

There are two versions of the hypothesis: a strong version and a weak one. The strong version asserts that language determines people's thoughts and actions, and therefore it is also called **linguistic determinism**. The weak version claims that different linguistic systems will exert relative influence on people's thoughts and actions, and therefore it is also known as **linguistic relativism**. Admittedly the strong version may be difficult to verify empirically. There are, however, quite a few examples to prove the validity of the weak version.

For example, American people often mistakenly assume the Upper Nile is in the north of Egypt while the Lower Nile is in the south. This is because American people are, consciously or unconsciously, under the guidance of the conventional words for direction in their mother tongue, English. Precisely, the north is usually deemed as "upper" while the south is "lower". Interestingly, the Chinese language follows a similar pattern, as we always use phrases like "bei shang" (going upper to the north) and "nan xia" (going lower to the south) rather than in the other way round. As the example indicates, language really directs the way we perceive the physical world, and further influences the way we understand it.

As another example, the language of English is very meticulous about time in that every sentence must be specific with the tense of the verb—*I eat it*, *I ate it*, or *I have eaten it*. The language system is especially concerned with the time of the verb: whether it is the present action, or the past, or the future. Likewise, the culture of English-speaking people is also preoccupied with time. They value punctuality, live in a fast pace, and, most typically, deem time as a precious resource to be spared, spent, saved, or wasted. In contrast, the Chinese language could be vague about the time of events. For example:

(5) 你吃鸡吗？

(6) 他读书。

The above two sentences are both ambiguous with regard to the tense. The first one could mean "Do you like chicken?" or "Will you eat the chicken?" And the specific meaning of it can only be determined with additional information provided in the context. Similarly, the second sentence could be interpreted as a general comment—"He loves reading", or a description of an action like "he is/was reading the book". Chinese culture is more concerned with the people engaged in events, rather than the events themselves. That is perhaps why most Chinese people are not very punctual for classes, lectures and meetings, and do not take time commitment (appointments, deadlines, work schedules, etc.) as seriously as Americans and Germans do.

So far we have seen quite a few examples showing that, apart from some apparent differences in vocabulary, languages also differ in their adoption of different grammatical categories to classify, describe, and highlight different aspects of the speakers' experiences, hence exerting profound influence on their cultures. It is in this sense that Sapir-Whorf hypothesis has attracted much attention since its proposal, and remains an issue of much debate even today. All in all, researchers now generally subscribe to the general claim that the intimacy and interaction between language and culture is indeed undeniable.

11.7 Intercultural Communication

11.7.1 Intercultural Communication as a Field of Research

Culture exerts subtle and profound influence on every aspect of human life. Consequently, contacts across different cultures are bound to be full of obstacles. **Intercultural communication**, that is, communication between people from different cultures, is an emerging subject of research focusing on the potential stumbling blocks involved in cross-cultural encounters.

Intercultural communication is both old and new. As a practice it is almost as old as human society itself. The traveling nomads, conquering warriors and religious missionaries would often find themselves in a totally alien community with quite different customs and beliefs, and had to struggle for a better mutual understanding through linguistic, cultural or even military means. Cross-cultural encounters as such were largely limited to a small group of people for certain specified purposes. However, developments in communication and transportation technology in the past century have drastically changed the way people live. The inventions of jet planes and speedy trains make it possible for one person to travel across thousands of miles within one day. On the other hand, the computer and internet technology, television broadcasting and telephones allow direct and real-time communication between people separated by oceans and even continents. All these changes, together with the recent trend of globalization and economic restructuring, drastically enhanced the intensity and extent of cross-cultural contact in contemporary societies. To varying extents, everyone in today's world is involved in intercultural communication.

It is against this backdrop that intercultural communication emerges as an independent subject of research. As it focuses on the dynamic process of communication between people from different cultural backgrounds, this subject of research inevitably involves multiple disciplines, such as linguistics, cultural studies, communication, sociology, psychology, and anthropology. The primary research focus of this inter-disciplinary field of research covers such issues as cultural dimensions, communicative competence, cross-cultural perception and adaptation, as well as potential obstacles of intercultural communication.

11.7.2 Conquering Obstacles in Intercultural Communication

Barna (1994) has identified six major stumbling blocks in intercultural communication, including assumption of similarities, language differences, nonverbal misinterpretations, preconceptions and stereotypes, tendency to evaluate, and high anxiety. For most people, it takes insight, training, and even a change in mindset before progress can be made in this regard. Samovar et al. (1981) suggest several steps in improving intercultural communication. First, a person needs to know himself. Simple as it may sound, it is nevertheless crucial to improving intercultural communication. One needs to know himself, and then his own culture, and more importantly, he should be aware of the attitudes, potential prejudice and opinions that he carries around unknowingly. What is more, he also needs to know his communication style so as to get better prepared for the communication.

The second step for improving intercultural communication is to understand different languages. Remember that language is more than a tool of communication, and contains more than words, phrases and sentences. Language is the primary medium of our life style, ways of thinking, and patterns of communication. Knowing a different language is the most important step to bridge the communicative gap between different cultural backgrounds.

The third step is to develop empathy, that is, the ability to interpret and understand things from the point of view of others so as to better understand others' feelings and opinions. Self-centeredness, or in a general scope, ethnocentrism, might bias our view of other people and their culture, hence causing unnecessary obstacles in cultural encounters. For intercultural communication to be successful, we need to go beyond personal boundaries and try to learn about the experience of people who are not part of our culture.

11.7.3 Value Dimensions

Studies in intercultural communication are usually based on frameworks of cultural values which can be used in analyzing and contrasting different cultures. One framework that is especially influential was proposed by Hofstede (2001), who, through extensive survey studies, came up with four underlying value dimensions along which different countries could be positioned. The four dimensions are based on four very fundamental issues in human societies to which every society has to find its particular answers. They include 1) individualism-collectivism; 2) large-small power distance; 3) strong-weak uncertainty avoidance; 4) masculinity-femininity. A fifth value dimension, the long-term vs. short-term orientation, was later added by Hofstede to distinguish different cultural patterns in the East and the West. Hofstede found in his research that these five value dimensions could largely account for the cultural differences between the countries under investigation.

The first dimension is basically concerned with people's self-concept, as well as the different degrees of interconnection between individuals and the society. Individualism stands for a general preference for a loosely knit social structure, whereas collectivism stands for a preference for a tightly knit one in a society in which everyone cares for their membership to certain groups, such as a family or a company. Generally speaking, Asian countries are typically collectivist cultures, while USA and the European countries are individualistic cultures.

The second dimension concerns the issue of social inequality. A culture of large power distance tends to regard inequality as a fact of life. People in such countries generally accept hierarchical order in which everyone has his own position. In contrast, people in a small-power-distance culture strive for power equalization and demand justification if there is power inequality. This value dimension exerts a profound influence on the way people build their social institutions and organizations.

The third dimension, uncertainty avoidance, refers to the extent to which people in a society feel uncomfortable with uncertainty and ambiguity. In other words, it is concerned with the degree to which a given culture can tolerate and accommodate different, even deviant, opinions, behaviors, and practices. Strong uncertainty avoidance societies tend to make specific and rigid regulations for social practice, and are relatively less tolerant towards deviant persons and ideas. Weak uncertainty avoidance societies, however, could be more relaxed and tolerant. This value dimension is essentially related to different views toward the unforeseeable future: should we try to make predictions and plan for the future, or just let it happen?

The fourth value dimension is related to the way in which a society assigns social roles to the sexes. While some societies try to maximize social differentiation between the sexes by allocating sex-specific roles to men and women, some other societies strive for minimal social differentiation between the sexes. Generally speaking, masculine societies value achievement, heroism, assertiveness and material success. Feminine societies however emphasize relationships, modesty, caring for the weak and the quality of life. In different contexts they are also referred to as "performance society" and "welfare society" respectively.

The fifth value dimension is also known as Confucian dynamism because it is related to Confucianism. According to this dimension, cultural groups with the long-term orientation attach greater value to persistence, social status and social order, thrift, and a strong sense of shame. Those with the short-term orientation, on the other hand, are more concerned with such values as personal stability, face, and tradition. For example, in business organizations, cultures that rank high on long-term orientation (Japan, South Korea, China including Hong Kong and Taiwan) would most likely have employees who reflect a strong work ethic and show great respect to their employers. We would also expect individuals who are members of these cultures to value social order and long-range goals. Those cultures that rank low on the long-term orientation index (United States, Great Britain, Canada, Philippines), according to Hofstede, often do not place a high priority on status, try to postpone old age, are concerned with short-term results and immediate gratification of their needs.

Each of Hofstede's five dimensions provides insights into the influence of culture on the communication process. Cultures with similar configurations on the five dimensions would likely have similar communication patterns, and cultures that are very different from one another would probably behave dissimilarly.

11.8 Summary

Language and culture are intimately connected. Language serves as the container and carrier of culture. At the same time it is also the primary medium in which culture is constructed, changed and exchanged. In this chapter we have seen, from different angles and at different levels, how language exerts subtle yet profound influence on the shaping and shapes of human cultures, and how different linguistic systems as well as communicative patterns may pose great obstacle for intercultural communication and understanding. Language is far more than a self-contained system of arbitrary codes. Instead, it constitutes the majority of, if not the whole, human experiences and social lives. In this sense, modern linguists need to accommodate, among many other fields of study, cultural studies and intercultural communication in their agenda of research.

Further Readings

Dodd, C. H. 2006. *Dynamics of Intercultural Communication* (Fifth Edition). 上海:上海外语教育出版社.
Kramsch, C. 1998/2000. *Language and Culture*. 上海:上海外语教育出版社.
Samovar, L. A., Porter, R. E. & Stefani, L. A. 1981/2000. *Communication Between Cultures*. 北京:外语教学与研究出版社.
Scollon, R. & Scollon, S. W. 2000. *Intercultural Communication: A Discourse Approach*. 北京:外语教学与研究出版社.
贾玉新,1997,《跨文化交际学》。上海:上海外语教育出版社。
许力生,2004,《跨文化交际英语教程》。上海:上海外语教育出版社。

Chapter 11
Intercultural Communication: Language and Culture

Questions and Exercises

1. Define the following terms.

   culture culture-loaded words high-context culture
   low-context culture Sapir-Whorf hypothesis linguistic determinism
   linguistic relativism intercultural communication

2. How is language related to culture?
3. What do the different ways of naming the world tell us about the relationship between language and culture?
4. What do the different communicative patterns across cultures tell us about the relationship between language and culture? Do you think such differences can cause problems in intercultural communication?
5. To what extent do you agree with the distinction between high-context culture and low-context culture?
6. Translate the following phrases into English, and discuss the cultural meanings contained within.

   a) 眼红   b) 大红人   c) 开门红
   d) 红得发紫   e) 黄道吉日   f) 白字先生
   g) 一穷二白

7. Translate the following phrases into Chinese, and discuss the cultural meanings contained within.

   a) blue-eyed boy   b) green-eyed   c) a white lie
   d) a yellow journalism e) a red-letter day   f) in a brown study
   g) the red tapes

8. Conduct a small-scale survey on college students' use of address terms in their daily conversation. What are the most common terms to address their classmates? And teachers? Compare your findings and discuss the reasons for the observed variation in address forms.
9. What does Sapir-Whorf hypothesis tell us about the relation between language and thought?
10. To what extent do you agree with the strong version of the Sapir-Whorf hypothesis, that is, linguistic determinism? And to what extent do you agree with the weak version, namely linguistic relativism?
11. How to overcome obstacles caused by cultural difference in intercultural communication?
12. Identify the positions of China along the five value dimensions proposed by Hofstede. What about the positions of USA, Japan, and Germany? Compare your predictions with Hofstede's own findings.

Chapter 12

Psycholinguistics: Language and Psychology

12.1 Introduction

Psycholinguistics, which falls within the broader field of cognitive science, is the psychological study of language with emphasis on the cognitive processes of language use. It is mainly concerned with the following three areas: language comprehension, language production, and language acquisition. As an interdisciplinary branch of science, psycholinguistics draws upon insights from, in addition to psychology and linguistics, computer science, neuroscience, philosophy, artificial intelligence etc. Language comprehension is concerned with the ways we perceive and understand oral and written language; language production deals with the ways in which we produce an utterance to express our idea; language acquisition, also termed language development by most psychologists, involves the ways children acquire their language. As a point of departure, let us first have a very brief discussion of the biological foundations of language.

12.2 Language and the Brain: The Biological Foundations of Language

It is claimed by some scholars that different language skills are represented in different parts of the brain, and therefore damages to certain parts of the brain may cause losses of corresponding language abilities. Is this claim justifiable? Although we cannot do justice to this question due to limited space, we can at least gain some insights from the discussion in this section. Furthermore, our discussion of the biological foundations of language will shed light on language comprehension, production and acquisition.

12.2.1 Cerebral Lateralization and Language Functions

The brain is divided into the right and left hemispheres, which are connected by the corpus callosum. The two sides of the brain have almost equal capacities for all functions (like logical reasoning, imagery, artistic creation etc.) when the baby is born, although recent research has demonstrated that the left hemisphere is more sensitive to some aspects of language from birth. However, as the child grows up, **lateralization**, the tendency for a given psychological function to be served by one hemisphere, occurs. The right hemisphere performs functions such as pattern perception, facial recognition, and part-whole judgements, while the left hemisphere performs functions such as various language functions and logical reasoning. Furthermore, it is generally held that language functions are localized in different parts of the left hemisphere. For example, **Broca's area** is mainly responsible for speech production, while **Wernicke's area** primarily for language reception. Before lateralization, the human brain retains sufficient elasticity or flexibility in that functions performed by certain damaged parts can be compensated by other parts.

12.2.2 Evidence of Lateralization

Supports come from aphasia studies. Both **Broca's area** and **Wernicke's area** are located in the left hemisphere. The former refers to an area that is close to the motor cortex and part of the frontal lobe (in front of and just above the left ear), and the latter a region in the left temporal lobe near the auditory cortex (around and under the left ear). **Broca's aphasia** is a disorder that is characterized by an individual's inability to express him- or herself and the omission of functional words such as articles, conjunctions, and grammatical inflections. However, the individual's ability to comprehend language seems to be less impaired. In contrast, Wernicke's aphasia is associated with speech that is fluent but of no informational value and with comprehension problems. Studies of other types of aphasia also lend support to the view that language functions are localized in different areas in the brain.

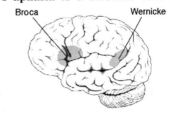

12.3 Language Comprehension

How do human beings comprehend language? This is one of the central issues in psycholinguistics. In order to have a better understanding of language comprehension, we need, first of all, to discuss briefly the mechanisms involved in language processing and the nature of our mental lexicon.

12.3.1 Human Information Processing System

The human information processing system is made up of sensory stores, working memory and permanent memory. **Sensory stores** are an imagined mechanism by means of which human beings take in a variety of information from the environment and keep it in a raw, unanalyzed form for a brief time. The sensory stores involved in language processing are visual and auditory stores for processing written and oral language respectively. **Working memory**, traditionally called **short-term memory**, is a temporary holding place where input from the sensory stores can be kept for further processing with the aid of input from the long-term memory. Short-term memory has a very limited capacity; it can hold around 7 ± 2 units of information (Miller, 1956). We prefer the term working memory to short-term memory because the former conveys a more dynamic view of the memory process: working memory has not only storage but processing functions as well. It is the very place where information from the environment and permanent memory is synthesized. **Permanent memory**, also termed **long-term memory**, is the place where various kinds of knowledge, including our knowledge of the world, rules of grammar, personal experiences, are kept. We use such knowledge for the interpretation of new experiences and for language comprehension. Within this warehouse of information, knowledge is stored in the form of either **semantic memory** or **episodic memory**. The former refers to knowledge of words, concepts, symbols and objects, and the latter traces of events that are specific to a time and place. Our knowledge of the vocabulary of a language is stored in our minds in the form of semantic memory. These two kinds of memories interact in our processing of information. Language processing is one specific kind of information processing.

We can use the terms discussed above to describe the process of language comprehension in the following way. First, when we hear/read a sentence, the sounds/written letters are stored in the auditory/visual store for around 2—4 seconds, a period that is long enough to recognize the auditory/visual pattern. In order to guarantee success of pattern recognition, we need to draw on information retrieved from permanent memory. Secondly, information is further processed in the working memory, which can only keep around 7 units of information (equal to about seven words). Therefore, we may improve processing efficiency and reduce storage burden by grouping the words into groups such as noun phrases and verb phrases. This process is called **parsing** in information processing theory, and **chunking** in psychology (Miller, 1956). The chunks thus formed are bigger and bigger until the whole sentence can be understood and a gist is extracted. Finally, the gist is stored in permanent memory. As we continue to receive input from the sensory stores, more sentences are processed. The gist that has already been stored in permanent memory is retrieved and integrated with the gist of succeeding sentences to form larger and larger units of meaning. In the process, permanent memory plays several important roles. Semantic memory contains information on speech sounds, written symbols (letters), and whole words that we retrieve during pattern recognition. It also contains other types of knowledge, especially knowledge about the rules of a language, meanings of words, sociolinguistic and pragmatic knowledge and general knowledge about the world, which are essential for comprehension at a higher level (Carroll, 2000).

There are two opposite views of information processing. One is **bottom-up processing** that assumes that processing proceeds from the lowest level to the highest level in such a way that higher levels of processing do not shed light on lower levels. For example, the identification of phonemes is not influenced by lexical, syntactic, or discourse levels. The other is **top-down processing** that posits that higher levels of processing may influence lower levels of processing. That is, on many occasions, information at various higher levels is used in lower levels of processing. For example, context at sentence or discourse level may influence word identification (Carroll, 2000; Haberlandt, 1994). The former is regarded as inadequate in accounting for how we understand language, whereas the latter is more plausible. When we read a text, various types of knowledge have a role in the comprehension process.

12.3.2 The Mental Lexicon

The **mental lexicon**, also called the internal lexicon, or simply lexicon, is a mental system, or a dictionary in the brain, which contains all the information a person knows about words. Vocabulary is the building blocks of any language; therefore, we need to know a great number of words in order to communicate our ideas effectively. However, what constitutes our word knowledge? How are the words organized in the brain to facilitate retrieval? How do we get access to words in the mental lexicon? These are the central concerns in this subsection.

12.3.2.1 What Constitutes Our Word Knowledge

First, the pronunciation of words is part of our word knowledge. We need to have an accurate representation of the pronunciation of words in the first place in order to have easy access to them in oral language comprehension and production. Correct representation is the necessary condition for correct production. That is why listening ability training should always precede speaking in foreign language teaching and learning. Secondly, syntactic knowledge is another part of our word knowledge. We need to know the syntactic category to which a word belongs and include syntactic categories in the lexical entries in our mental dictionary. Simply put, syntactic knowledge is the rules of how words can be combined to form larger units of language, such as phrases, clauses etc. The third type is morphological knowledge. We should know what morphemes (free or bound) are combined to form new words or grammatical forms. Finally, we should have knowledge of the meanings of words. Sense, reference, sense relations, denotation and connotation should all be included in the entries in our internal lexicon.

However, we insist that the aspects of meaning related to sociolinguistics and pragmatics, that is, meaning in language use, should also be included as part of our word knowledge. Such aspects are closely related to the culture of a language. For example, native speakers have no or little difficulty in understanding metaphors, but learners of English as a foreign language have great problems in this area. This may be explained in the following way: native speakers have already stored the figurative meanings of the words involved in a metaphor or the connections between concepts represented by the words involved in their mental dictionary, whereas non-native speakers do not have this knowledge (Liu & Shi, 2002). This is what some people call **metaphoric competence.**

12.3.2.2 How is the Mental Lexicon Organized

The mind is a warehouse that has limited storage space. How are the words of a language kept in the mind? Do we store them in the order we learned them? If the answer to the second question is "yes", then it is very difficult for us to retrieve them later on simply because we will get lost in the great mass of words without a clear knowledge of the relations among them. Actually, words in the mental lexicon should be stored in an organized way such that they form an interconnected network of concepts connected by various relations, known as **semantic network.** For example, hyponymy is a sense relation that provides a clear and reliable clue to the organization of some words.

To account for how words are organized in the internal lexicon, different theories are proposed. According to the **hierarchical network model,** some words are represented at higher nodes in the semantic network than others. It is somewhat like the classification of animals and plants in the world in biology. For example, the word *animal* is represented at a higher node than the word *bird*, but *bird* is represented at a higher node than *ostrich*. The features shared by members of a category are stored at the highest possible nodes in order to save storage space. For example, "can move around" is a feature common to all animals, so it is stored at the highest node with *animal*; the feature "has wings" is common to all birds, so it is kept with *bird*. However, the relationships between categories are not included in this model. Therefore, it is unable to capture the complexity of the mental lexicon.

However, according to **spreading activation models**, the organization is closer to a web of interconnected nodes, and activation spreads from one node to other nodes that have a shorter distance. In this network, information at conceptual, syntactic, and phonological levels is represented. Such a theory is different from the one discussed above in that it is not strictly hierarchical (Carroll, 2000; Haberlandt, 1994).

12.3.3 Sentence Comprehension

The study of language comprehension generally centers on two main areas: sentence comprehension and discourse comprehension. The main questions addressed in the study of sentence comprehension include: Do we use our syntactic, semantic, and pragmatic knowledge all at the same time while reading? Or do we use one kind of knowledge at different stages of comprehension?

Different theories, or models, have been proposed to account for the process of sentence comprehension. These include the modular theory, the interactive theory and the late assignment of syntax theory (LAST). Central to all of these theories are what functions syntactic analysis plays, how and when such analysis comes into play in the process of comprehension.

The modular theory assumes that comprehension is the result of many different modules with each devoted to a particular aspect of comprehension, and that syntactic analysis (parsing) is performed in the very beginning of the comprehension process and it is not influenced by higher-level contextual (semantic, pragmatic) information or by general world knowledge. Advocates of this theory posit that two strategies are used to carry out grammatical analysis. First, whenever possible, we prefer to attach new items to what immediately precedes. This is called **the late closure strategy**. For example:

(1) Tom told me that Mr. Smith had finished writing the book last week.

The adverbial phrase of time *last week* may be attached either to the main clause (*Tom told me*) or the subordinate clause (*Mr. Smith had finished...*). We prefer the latter. To illustrate this point, let us look at more examples:

(2) I placed the magazine Tom was reading in the reading room.

(3) Since Mary always jogs a mile seems like a very short distance to her.

Sentences such as (2) and (3) are **garden path sentences**. We tend to attach the elements such as *in the reading room* and *a mile* to the verbs preceding them. It seems that we were led down a garden path, but found out, at the end, that we took the wrong way. Then we have to correct our mistake by rereading the whole sentence. Such examples are considered as further evidence for the late closure strategy.

The second strategy is **the minimal attachment strategy**, which states that we prefer to attach a new item to the phrase going before. For example:

(4) John beat Tom and his brother reported this to the teacher.

When we hear or read this sentence, we prefer considering *and* as the noun phrase conjunction (John beat both Tom and his brother) rather than as a coordinate conjunction for the two clauses.

In contrast, **the interactive theory** insists that syntax and semantics interact in the course of comprehension. We simultaneously use all information available in the initial analysis of a sentence—syntactic, lexical, discourse, as well as nonlinguistic, contextual information. Research studies produced mixed results. However, up to now, we can conclude that syntactic analysis is influenced by both structural principles such as minimal attachment and late closure along with lexical and, to a lesser extent discourse factors. The two theories are not capable of explaining all the research results (Carroll, 2000; Townsend & Bever, 2001).

Dissatisfied with the above-mentioned theories, Townsend and Bever (2001) have proposed **the late assignment of syntax theory (LAST)** to explain the process of comprehension. According to this theory, language comprehension occurs in the following stages: 1) we form an initial meaning/form hypothesis on the basis of our learned knowledge of a language such as frequently used sentence patterns and function words. 2) Then we compare the resultant representation of the incoming sequence with the sentence representation produced by the application of grammatical rules of the language. If a perfect match is found, the sentence is understood. Otherwise, we go through the above process again. The former is pseudo-syntax, and the latter real syntax. Since real syntax has a role late during comprehension, this approach is called the late assignment of syntax theory. For example, function words elicit expectations of phrasal categories. Whenever we see the definite article *the*, we guess that what follows should be a noun phrase. As a matter of fact, we can use the same theory to explain sentence (6). The conjunction *and* is more frequently used to link up two nouns in a noun phrase than coordinate clauses. This model has more explanatory power than the previous models in that it takes into consideration information from various sources, including word order, structure and meaning. It captures the truth that we read everything twice most of the time and that reading is an integration of habits and rules. However, this theory does not explain how we use pragmatic

Chapter 12
Psycholinguistics: Language and Psychology

information in comprehension. Actually, the shared assumptions about communication may guide our comprehension.

12.3.4 Discourse Comprehension

For the past several decades, more and more attention has been directed to the study of discourse comprehension because discourse seems to be a more natural unit of language to investigate. Sentences in isolation are generally ambiguous. To understand discourse, we need to relate sentences in a logical way. Therefore, the central issue of discourse comprehension is how we establish coherence. To illustrate this point, let us look at the following passage:

(5) (f) And there is nothing wrong with their so doing. (h) And if something must be eliminated, it is sensible to throw out these extraneous things and stick to words. (a) Before we look at basic principles, it is necessary to interpose two brief statements. (g) But the great increase in our vocabulary in the past three decades compels all dictionaries to make more efficient use of their space. (b) The first of these is that a dictionary is concerned with words. (d) Some have tables of weights and measures on the flyleaves. (c) Some dictionaries give various kinds of other useful information. (e) Some list historical events and some, home remedies.

The passage is difficult to comprehend even if we understand every sentence. However, if we arrange them in the indicated alphabetical order, comprehension will be much easier for the reason that after rearrangement, the relationships between sentences in the passage are made salient. Such relationships are called the **local structure** or **microstructure** of a discourse, i.e. the logical or semantic connections between sentences at the local level of discourse. A discourse should also be organized at a higher macro-level if it consists of multiple paragraphs. The logical relationships between paragraphs, or the total arrangement of a discourse, are called the global structure or **macrostructure**. Both levels of structure contribute to the coherence of a text, i.e. the logical or semantic connections between different parts (usually sentences, paragraphs) of a text.

The most obvious clues for establishing coherence at the local level are the cohesive devices used in a text to connect sentences although such devices are not always reliable. The cohesive devices used in English include reference, conjunction, lexical repetition (including synonyms), hyponymy, ellipsis and so on (See Chapter 7). As for the establishment of coherence at the macro-level, other types of knowledge such as general world knowledge and knowledge of different genres are needed.

Written texts fall into the following four types: narration, argumentation, description, and exposition. Each type of writing has its own pattern of overall organization, which, to some extent, all writers should follow. Knowledge of this kind, if structured in some way, may be called a schema of that specific type of writing. Simply put, "a **schema** is a structure in semantic memory that specifies the general or expected arrangement of a body of information" (Carroll, 2000: 175). If such a schema is activated, comprehension can be facilitated because we, as comprehenders, can predict what will follow in the text. The genre that has received a great deal of research is narration. Researchers have formalized the original idea of schema into the concept of a **story grammar**, which is "a schema in semantic memory that identifies the typical or expected arrangement of events in a story" (Carroll, 2000: 177). Studies show that we use such schemata in comprehending and recalling a story.

As for general world knowledge, things are much more complicated. As a matter of fact, our schemata about the world are also activated in comprehension. However, schemata of this kind vary greatly from individual to individual, and it is too difficult for researchers to formalize them. The reason is that the formation of such schemata is determined by individuals' personal experiences, upbringing, education etc. However, schemata of this kind do play an important role in the process of reconstructing the global structure of a text.

12.4 Language Production

Language production is a much more difficult subject to study than language comprehension simply because the ideas leading to speech is too elusive to be investigated and we do not have the appropriate methodology for this purpose. What we know about language production is based on the study of slips of the tongue, the speech errors that are committed by speakers, and "practically anything one can say about speech production must be considered speculative, even by the standards current in psycholinguistics" (Fodor, Bever & Garrett, 1974: 434; Aitchison, 2000). This is the case even up to now.

We may distinguish four stages of production: conceptualization of an idea or a thought to be expressed, formulation of the thought into a linguistic plan, articulation of the plan and the monitoring of one's own speech. However, we have no way to know how the speaker conceptualizes the thoughts to be expressed. Therefore, our discussion of language production will begin with the second stage.

At the planning stage, we formulate our thought into a linguistic plan that is implemented at the succeeding stage of production. The **serial models** of linguistic planning assume that planning occurs step by step in six stages. 1) A meaning is generated on the basis of the thought conceptualized in the first stage of the whole production process; 2) a syntactic structure is selected; 3) a stress pattern is specified; 4) content words like nouns, verbs, and adjectives are inserted; 5) function words like conjunctions, articles, and prepositions are added; 6) the correct phonetic characteristics are specified according to the phonological rules of a language (Carroll, 2000). This is at best a plausible explanation of speech planning. At least we have some doubt about the separation of the insertion of content words and function words. However, there is indeed evidence that supports such a stage theory: speech errors generally occur at a certain stage specified above. For example:

(6) She's already *trunked two packs* (packed two trunks).

(7) An *anguage lacquisition* (a language acquisition)

In (6), the speech error occurs at stage 4 (wrong insertion of content words), while in (7), the phonetic characteristics are specified in a wrong way.

In contrast, the **parallel models** posit that multiple levels of processing take place simultaneously during language production. It is generally believed that language is represented in permanent memory at four levels (nodes): semantic, syntactic, morphological, and phonological. These representations work in parallel: the activation at one level may be spread to another level. While there is evidence to support such models, they cannot capture the complexity of language production either. It might be possible that both serial and parallel processes have a role to play in language production.

The unit of planning seems to be "a tone group, or phonetic clause, a short stretch of speech spoken with a single intonation contour" (Aitchison, 2000: 250). The evidence for this assertion is the fact that slips of the tongue usually occur within a single tone group rather than across clauses. For example:

(8) We forged this *congress... contract* in our own congress. (The speaker meant to say: We forged this contract in our congress.)

The third stage is the implementation of the linguistic plan. This information is sent from the brain to the organs involved in producing the desired speech sounds. The production of any speech sound is the coordination of all those organs involved. However, it should be noted that we never produce speech sounds in isolation in connected speech. Instead, the pronunciation of a speech sound is usually influenced by the surrounding sounds. That is, the shape of the vocal tract for any given sound often accommodates to the shape needed for surrounding sounds. This phenomenon is called **co-articulation** (See Chapter 2).

Another point that is worth considering is that speech planning and articulation to some extent overlap. That is to say, we begin to plan the next unit while still uttering the present one. The fact that we often pause within a clause rather than between clauses lends support to the above assertion.

The last stage of the production process is self-monitoring. From time to time, we interrupt our speech and correct ourselves. On detection of any error we have made, we repair the utterance by first indicating this through the use of editing expressions like *uh*, *sorry*, *I mean* and *oh*.

12.5　Language Acquisition

Language acquisition is the ground where different linguistic theories are tested. Noam Chomsky assumes that children acquire their first language effortlessly because they possess a special mechanism—language acquisition device (LAD), and it is difficult to acquire a second language for the reason that as they grow older, they have either lost or have no direct access to this device. In contrast, the behaviorist psychologist B. F. Skinner thinks that language learning is the formation of association between stimulus and response (i. e. formation of habits), and it is difficult to learn a second or foreign language because old habits get in the way of the formation of new habits (Skinner, 1957), suggesting that in order to learn a new language you have to give up the language you already have. Which view is more acceptable? As will be seen from the following discussion, neither of them is absolutely correct. In the following section, we are going to answer two major questions: How do children acquire their first language (L1)? How do both children and adults learn a second language (L2)? Before answering these questions, it is necessary to distinguish two terms: **acquisition** and **learning**. According to Krashen (1981), the former refers to the subconscious process of "picking up" a language through exposure (or immersion in the language environment), while the latter refers to the conscious process of studying it.

12.5.1　First Language, Second Language and Foreign Language

Many scholars (for example, Ellis, 1994; Brown, 2001; Larsen-Freeman & Long, 2000) hold a broader view of **second language**, which is any language acquired or learned after one has already had at least some knowledge of his native language and which includes what is called **foreign language** (FL). However, in this book we are going to adopt a narrower sense of second language to refer to language that is acquired and/or learned in the naturalistic setting after one has already had a relatively good command of his **first**

Chapter 12
Psycholinguistics: Language and Psychology

language.

On the basis of the above distinction, we can highlight the differences as follows. First language is one that a person is born and brought up with, and thus it plays a more important role in an individual's cognitive and social development (Goodman et al, 1987) because for the majority of very young children it is perhaps the only, or at least the most important means of communicating with others and of receiving information from the surrounding environments. Furthermore, children also depend heavily on their first language in order to achieve their purposes and to function well in society. In contrast, second language is less important than first language in that it does not play an equally important role in one's cognitive and social development. It is similar to first language in that learners generally have a more or less equally strong need to communicate in it (but it depends on the specific environment in which one lives and the personality of an individual), and that it is learned and/or acquired in the naturalistic setting and to a large extent through communication. Foreign language is quite different from the above two in that it is generally learned in a conscious way through formal instruction. Learners do not have the target language and cultural context that is necessary for acquisition to happen. Neither do they have the need to communicate in the foreign language. If it is true that children are completely socialized through their first language, they are only to a certain degree socialized through their second language. However, socialization through a foreign language is minimal. That is why it is very difficult, though not totally impossible, for learners of a second or foreign language to achieve native-like proficiency.

12.5.2 First Language Acquisition

It is now widely acknowledged that the learning of communication precedes the acquisition of language; the babbling sounds uttered by babies and considered to be meaningless, are in fact meaningful. Babies learn to communicate before they have a good command of any language (Gleason, 1997). No matter what cultures and language communities they are from, children around the world manage to become competent speakers of their first language in the first five years of life. Then how do children develop their first language (vocabulary, grammar, phonology, and morphology)?

12.5.2.1 Role of Input in First Language Acquisition

There are two opposing views concerning the role of input in language acquisition: one view (with B. F. Skinner as one of the representatives) holds that exposure to a language (frequency, quality, etc.) determines acquisition, while the other (represented by N. Chomsky) assumes that input plays only an insignificant role in the acquisition process, and that it only triggers off the LAD simply because the language received by the learner is generally grammatically ill-formed. The former provides only a partial explanation of the language acquisition process to the neglect of the learner's active involvement in it, and the latter is an underestimation of the importance of input in language acquisition.

Caregivers make formal adjustment to their speech, resulting in a special register of language called **caregiver talk** (also termed "baby-talk", "motherese", "caretaker talk" and "child-directed language [speech]") (Richards, Platt & Platt, 2000). Caregiver talk has characteristics of its own but is by no means "degenerate" (Miller & Chomsky, 1963). The input that children receive is both clearer and linguistically simpler than the speech addressed to adults. Caregivers modify their speech in order to (a) aid communication, (b) teach language, and (c) socialize the child. Caregivers seek to communicate with their children and this leads them to modify their speech in order to facilitate the exchange of meaning. The other two functions are the offshoots of the attempt to communicate (Ellis, 1994; Gleason, 1997).

12.5.2.2 Development of Speech Production

Speech production is generally preceded by a lengthy **silent period**, during which children are able to listen to people talk to them before they produce their first words. The average length of this period is around one year, but it varies from individual to individual, and sometimes it even lasts as long as two or three years. In the same period, babbling begins by about 6 to 7 months. It is the first attempt for very young children to communicate with others. There are different kinds of babbling to express different meanings (Gleason, 1997; Peccei, 2000).

Then around age one single word utterances begin to appear. The one-word utterances are used sometimes to name things that are present in the current situation, and sometimes to express other meanings. Toward the end of the one-word stage, young children tend more frequently to use one-word utterances to express whole statements. Such single word utterances are also termed **holophrases** by linguists.

Around age two and usually after they have acquired around 50 words, children begin to combine words into sentences. This is the beginning of the two-word stage. Children's language of this phase is characterized by the dropping of elements that contribute little information to the utterances. These elements include endings on verbs like -ed in *stopped* and -ing in *doing*, function words like articles, prepositions, copula and auxiliary verbs. Therefore, children's language at this stage is called **telegraphic speech**.

Chapter 12
Psycholinguistics: Language and Psychology

At around three to four years of age, three to four-word stages begin. Language used by children at these stages is still telegraphic in nature, with function words and endings on verbs omitted. However, what is worth pointing out is that the stages generally overlap and there are individual differences in the acquisition of certain linguistic features.

12.5.2.3 Developmental Patterns: Orders and Sequences

The development of children's language to a large extent depend on the development of their cognitive abilities. The stages in which certain features of a language are developed are called **developmental orders**. Generally speaking, children follow the following order in their development of the English language: present progressive -*ing*, preposition *in*, preposition *on*, plural -*s*, past irregular, possessive -'*s*, uncontractible copula *be*, article *a/the*, past regular -*ed*, third person regular -*s*, third person irregular, uncontractible auxiliary *be*, contractible copula *be*, and contractible auxiliary *be* (Carroll, 2000). The orders of development can be summarized as follows: the more meaningful features of the language that are cognitively less demanding are acquired earlier than those that bear little meaning and that are cognitively more demanding.

When it comes to the acquisition of a certain feature, children also follow a certain order. This is called **sequence** of development. For example, the acquisition of negative forms occurs also in stages. A case in point is the development of English negatives. At the first stage, young children usually attach negators either in the beginning or at the end of an utterance. At the second stage, negators are placed between the subject and the predicate. Negators at this stage include *don't* and *can't*, used as wholes (unanalysed), and negative commands appear possibly as a result of rote-learning. The final stage is more target-like in that the "auxiliary + not" rule has been acquired, and that *don't*, *can't*, etc. are now analyzed.

Why do children acquire English in such an order? There are two explanations. First of all, it might be possible that children are not yet cognitively ready for the complicated grammatical structures that they have to learn in order to develop full adult-like language competence. The second explanation, which is closely related to the first one, is that for children meaning is primary, but form is only secondary in communication. In the initial stage, they are unable to pay attention to both form and meaning.

12.5.3 Second Language Acquisition

The study of second language acquisition (SLA), as an independent field of inquiry, started in the late 1960s, and flourished in the 1970s and 1980s, perhaps as a result of the resurgence of interest in the internal mechanisms of the language teaching and learning process. It covers mainly the following areas: the role of L1 in L2 acquisition, developmental patterns of L2, and the role of input and output in L2 acquisition.

12.5.3.1 Role of L1 in L2 Acquisition

The influence of first language is generally manifested in two ways in terms of language transfer, that is, the influence of L1 habits on L2 acquisition. **Positive transfer** occurs when an L1 form is used in the production of an L2 utterance, and it is also a part of the L2 norm. That is, L1 facilitates the acquisition of L2. **Negative transfer** occurs when the L1 form in L2 production is not part of the L2 norm, and the resultant utterance is erroneous. That is, L1 interferes with the acquisition of L2.

The influence of L1 on L2 acquisition can be summarized in linguistic terms as follows: first, transfer is more conspicuous at the level of phonology than at the level of syntax. Secondly, transfer of L1 vocabulary is also prevalent. For example, the acquisition of L2 vocabulary seems to be facilitated if the L1 and the L2 are related languages. Thirdly, transfer is a major factor at the discourse level. For example, Chinese learners of L2 English use fewer passive sentences than English native speakers do owing to the fact that the two languages have quite different cohesive devices to keep a text coherent. Finally, transfer at the syntactic level is not so prominent possibly because learners have a more developed metalingual awareness of grammar (Ellis, 1994).

12.5.3.2 Learner Errors and Error Analysis

An "**error**" is a deviation in learner language that results from lack of knowledge of the correct rule. It is different from a "**mistake**" in that it can be overt (apparent in the surface form of the utterance) or covert (in the learner's meaning intention). In contrast, "mistake" is a deviation in learner language that occurs when the learner fails to perform according to his competence. It is a lapse that is caused by fatigue, inattention, etc. (Ellis, 1994). Errors may provide teachers with information about how much the learner has learnt (for pedagogic purposes), researchers with evidence of how language was learnt, and learners with devices by which they discovered the rules of the target language. Errors are studied by means of **Error Analysis** (EA), a procedure we follow to study learner language for practical and theoretical purposes (Ellis, 1994). It is different from **contrastive analysis** in that the latter is a procedure designed to find out the differences and similarities between languages in order to help teachers and learners to find out the difficulties of the second or foreign language being taught and learned.

12.5.3.3 Interlanguage and Developmental Patterns

Interlanguage is a term proposed by Selinker (1972) to refer to the systematic knowledge of an L2, which is independent of both the learner's L1 and the target language (Ellis, 1994; Odlin, 1989; See also Chapter 14). Learner language or interlanguage is generally characterized by being systematic and dynamic. It is systematic because learners behave "grammatically" in the sense that they draw on the rules they have internalized, and it is dynamic in the sense that the language learner's mental grammars are always in a state of change. Like L1 acquisition, the acquisition of the features of a second language occurs in stages. This is called the order of acquisition. The acquisition of a certain feature also occurs in stages. This is called the sequence of acquisition.

12.5.3.4 Fossilization

Most learners stop learning at certain stages in the acquisition process. This is referred to as **fossilization**. If, when fossilization occurs, the fossilized feature has assumed the same form as in the target language, then fossilization of correct form will occur; if the fossilized form is not the same as in the target language, the fossilization will manifest itself as error. Fossilized forms may sometimes seem to disappear but are always likely to reappear in productive language use, a phenomenon known as **backsliding**.

12.5.3.5 Role of Input in L2 Acquisition

Foreigner talk is a special register of language spoken by native speakers to L2 or foreign language learners who are not proficient in the language (Richards, Platt & Platt 2000; Ellis, 1994). It has many of the characteristics of caretaker talk we discussed previously. When native speakers communicate with non-native speakers, they modify their speech in two ways: one makes their speech more grammatical, and the other more ungrammatical. As a result, two types of foreigner talk are produced: ungrammatical and grammatical. Ungrammatical foreigner talk has the following characteristics: 1) omission of grammatical functors (such as copula, articles, conjunctions, subject pronouns, and inflectional morphology), 2) expansion (e.g. "you" is inserted before an imperative verb), 3) replacement/rearrangement (e.g. post-verbal negation is replaced by pre-verbal negative). In contrast, grammatical foreigner talk, which is the norm in most classrooms, has the following characteristics: 1) simplification, 2) regularization, and 3) elaboration. Simplification involves an attempt to simplify the language forms that are used, whereas regularization and elaboration are directed at simplifying the learners' task of processing the input and can, in fact, result in the use of language that is not always simple in itself.

Further Readings

Brown, H. D. 2001. *Principles of Language Learning and Teaching*. 北京:外语教学与研究出版社.

Carroll, D. W. 2000. *Psychology of Language*. 北京:外语教学与研究出版社.

Larsen-Freeman, D. & Long, M. H. 2000. *An Introduction to Second Language Acquisition Research*. 北京:外语教学与研究出版社.

Peccei, J. S. 2000. *Child Language*. 北京:外语教学与研究出版社.

Scovel, T. 1998/2000. *Psycholinguistics*. 上海:上海外语教育出版社.

桂诗春,2000,《新编心理语言学》。上海:上海外语教育出版社。

Questions and Exercises

1. Define the following terms.

psycholinguistics	lateralization	Broca's aphasia
Wernicke's aphasia	working memory	permanent memory
bottom-up processing	top-down processing	mental lexicon
schema	caregiver talk	positive transfer
negative transfer	interlanguage	fossilization
foreigner talk		

2. What is lateralization? What evidence do we have to support lateralization?
3. What is the composition of human information processing system?
4. What is bottom-up processing? What is top-down processing?
5. What is word knowledge? How is the mental lexicon organized?
6. What is caregiver talk? What functions does caregiver talk perform in the development of a child's language?
7. Explain the stages of first language acquisition. What patterns do children follow in the development of their first language (with English as a specific example)?
8. Can you tell the differences between first language and second or foreign language?
9. What are the differences between an error and a mistake?
10. What is interlanguage and how is it developed? What are the possible causes of fossilization?
11. What is foreigner talk? What are the differences and similarities between caregiver talk and foreigner talk?
12. Comment on the three models of sentence comprehension discussed in this chapter.
13. What insights have you gained from this chapter for language learning and teaching?
14. Do you think human beings are born with a language acquisition device (LAD) that helps native speakers of a language acquire their first language effortlessly and rapidly? Why (not)?
15. What characteristics does children's language have? What are the reasons for such characteristics?
16. What role does input play in first language and second language acquisition?

Chapter 12
Psycholinguistics: Language and Psychology

17. Observe carefully how a Chinese child develops his/her first language (Chinese) and try to find out some rules in terms of: a) vocabulary; b) syntax, and c) pronunciation.
18. Do you think second language and foreign language can be considered to be the same? Why (not)?
19. People often say that in order to learn a foreign language well you will have to forget your first language. Do you think this is possible and required for the success of foreign language learning? Why (not)?
20. The development of both first language and second language should follow certain orders and sequences. What implications can you draw from this fact for foreign language teaching?

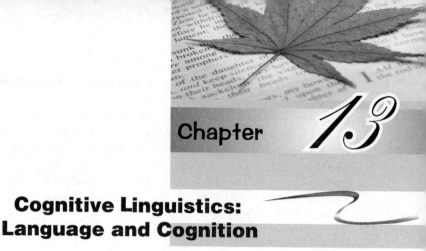

Chapter 13

Cognitive Linguistics: Language and Cognition

13.1 Introduction

Cognitive linguistics approaches language as an integrated part of human cognition which operates in interaction with and on the basis of the same principles as other cognitive faculties. It is therefore defined as the study of language in relation to such cognitive domains and faculties as bodily and mental experiences, image schemas, perception, attention, memory, viewing frames, categorization, abstract thought, emotion, reasoning, and inference.

Cognitive linguistics is a relatively new approach to the study of language and thought that has emerged within the modern interdisciplinary framework of cognitive science. Because it sees language as embedded in the overall cognitive capacities of mankind, topics of special interest for cognitive linguistics include the structural characteristics of natural language categorization, the functional principles of linguistic organization, the conceptual interface between syntax and semantics, the experiential and pragmatic background of language in use, and the relationship between language and thought.

The leading figures within cognitive linguistics are George Lakoff, Ronald Langacker and Leonard Talmy.

13.2 Categories and Categorization

The world consists of a variety of different phenomena. The most eye-catching among them are organisms and objects: people, animals, plants and all kinds of everyday artefacts such as books, tables, chairs, cars and houses. Usually we have no difficulty in identifying and classifying any of them, and in attributing class names to them. For example, colors can be classified into black, white, red, blue, green, yellow, etc. Chairs can be classified into deck chair, desk chair, armchair, barber chair, easy chair, folding chair, hall chair, high chair, invalid chair, lolling chair, lounge chair, office chair, rocking chair, shaving chair, shower chair, side chair, stacking chair, table chair, throne chair, wheelchair, writing chair, etc. This mental process of classification is commonly called **categorization**, and its products are the

Chapter 13
Cognitive Linguistics: Language and Cognition

categories, or **cognitive categories**.

The traditional view of categorization is shaped by the classical theory that goes back to Aristotle. According to this theory, a category is defined by a set of necessary conditions, which together are sufficient. For example, if we assume that the category BACHELOR is defined by the four conditions of being human, male, adult and unmarried, each one is necessary. If someone is not human, male, adult or unmarried, he is not a bachelor. On the other hand, the condition of being human, male, adult and unmarried is sufficient for membership in the category BACHELOR. It does not matter what other conditions someone or something may fulfill. Being a bachelor or not depends on these four conditions.

The classical theory of categorization can be characterized by the following points:

(i) Categorization depends on a fixed set of conditions of features.
(ii) Each condition is absolutely necessary.
(iii) The conditions are binary (yes-or-no).
(iv) Categories have clear boundaries.
(v) All members of a category are of equal status.

That categories have clear boundaries is a direct result of the fact that the defining conditions are binary. Everything either fulfils this set of conditions or it does not. If it does, it belongs to the category; otherwise it does not. As a result, categories have clear boundaries, and within their boundaries all members have the same status of full members.

The classical view is not totally wrong. We often do categorize things on that basis. But that is only a small part of the story. In fact, categorization is far more complex than that. A new theory, called **prototype theory**, has emerged. According to this theory, human categorization is based on principles that are far beyond those in the classical theory. When people categorize common objects, they do not expect them all to be on the equal status. They seem to have some idea of the characteristics of an ideal exemplar—a **prototype**. And they probably decide on the extent to which something else is a member of the same category by matching it against the features of the prototype. It does not have to match exactly; it just has to be sufficiently similar, though not necessarily visually similar. For example, in the category BIRD, there are various members such as robin, sparrow, dove, parrot, ostrich, and penguin. Robins are considered the best examples, i.e. prototypes, followed by doves, sparrows and canaries; owls, parrots, pheasants and toucans occupy a medium position, ducks and peacocks are considered even less good examples, while penguins and ostriches rank lowest.

Prototypes play an important role in what is called **default reasoning**, i.e.

reasoning in terms of assumptions which replace specific actual information as long as none is provided. For example, when Mary tells Peter,

(1) Look, there's a bird on the window sill.

Peter will think of a prototypical bird, not of an owl, a condor, an ostrich or a penguin. If someone mentions a "car", we will not think of a truck or a veteran car. It is therefore misleading to use the general terms for non-prototypical cases, misleading—but not semantically incorrect. Penguins *are* birds and we can refer to them as birds in appropriate contexts. For example, the following two sentences are perfectly acceptable:

(2) a. The only birds that live in the Antarctic are penguins.
　　b. Penguins come ashore to nest. The birds lay one to three eggs.

Prototype theory is useful for explaining how people deal with untypical examples of a category. This is how "unbirdy" birds such as pelicans and penguins can still be regarded as birds. They are sufficiently like the prototype, even though they do not share all its characteristics. But it has a further advantage: it can explain how people cope with damaged cases. Previously linguists had found it difficult to explain why anyone could still categorize a one-winged robin that couldn't fly as a bird, or a three-legged tiger as a quadruped. Now one just assumes that these get matched against the prototype in the same way as an untypical category member. A one-winged robin that is unable to fly can still be a bird, even though it is not such a typical one. Furthermore, the prototype effect seems to work for actions as well as objects or organisms. For example, people can, it appears, reliably make judgments that *murder* is a better example of killing than *execute* or *suicide*, and *stare* is a better example of looking than *peer* or *squint*.

13.3 Conceptual Metaphors

For most of us, metaphor is a figure of speech in which one thing is compared to another by saying that one is the other, as in *Achilles is a lion*. Here, we would probably say that the word *lion* is used metaphorically in order to achieve some artistic and rhetorical effect, since we speak and write metaphorically to communicate eloquently, to impress others with "beautiful", esthetically pleasing words, or to express some deep emotion. Perhaps we should also add that what makes the metaphorical identification of Achilles with a *lion* possible is that *Achilles* and *lions* have something in common, namely, their bravery and strength.

In the cognitive linguistic view, metaphor is defined as understanding one conceptual domain in terms of another conceptual domain. A convenient shorthand way of capturing this view of metaphor is the following:

Chapter 13
Cognitive Linguistics: Language and Cognition

CONCEPTUAL DOMAIN (A) IS CONCEPTUAL DOMAIN (B), which is what is called a **conceptual metaphor**. A conceptual metaphor consists of two conceptual domains, in which one domain (the **target domain**) is understood in terms of another (the **source domain**). A conceptual domain is any coherent organization of experience. For example, we have coherently organized knowledge about journeys that we rely on in understanding love, so we have the conceptual metaphor LOVE IS A JOURNEY.

Conceptual metaphors differ from metaphorical linguistic expressions or linguistic metaphors. The latter are words or other linguistic expressions that come from the language of the more concrete conceptual domain, i. e. the source domain. So all the linguistic expressions below that have to do with love and that come from the domain of journey are linguistic metaphorical expressions or linguistic metaphors, whereas the corresponding conceptual metaphor that they make manifest is LOVE IS A JOURNEY.

(3) LOVE IS A JOURNEY
　　Look *how far* we've *come*.
　　We're *at a crossroads*.
　　We'll just have to *go our separate ways*.
　　We can't *turn back* now.
　　I don't think this relationship is *going anywhere*.
　　Where are we?
　　We're *stuck*.
　　It's been a *long, bumpy road*.
　　This relationship is a *dead-end street*.
　　We're just *spinning our wheels*.
　　Our marriage is *on the rocks*.
　　We've *gotten off the track*.
　　This relationship is *foundering*.

In their widely read book *Metaphors We Live By*, Lakoff and Johnson (1980) point out the ubiquity of conceptual metaphors. Here are some other examples:

(4) ARGUMENT IS WAR
　　His claims are *indefensible*.
　　He *attacked every weak point* in my argument.
　　His criticisms were *right on target*.
　　I *demolished* his argument.
　　I've never *won* an argument with him.
　　You disagree? Okay, *shoot*!
　　If you use that *strategy*, he'll *wipe* you *out*.
　　He *shot down* all of my argument.

(5) IDEAS ARE FOOD
All this paper has in it are *raw* facts, *half-baked* ideas, and *warmed-over* theories.
There are too many facts here for me to *digest* them all.
I just can't *swallow* that claim.
Let me *stew* over that for a while.
That's *food* for thought.
She *devoured* the book.
Let's let that idea *simmer on the back burner* for a while.

This is just a small group of all the possible linguistic metaphors that speakers of English commonly and conventionally employ to talk about the target domains, such as "argument" and "idea". The nature of the relationship between the conceptual metaphors and the metaphorical linguistic expressions can be explained as follows: the linguistic metaphors (i.e. ways of talking) are the manifestations of the conceptual metaphors (i.e. ways of thinking). To put the same thing differently, it is the linguistic metaphors that reveal the existence of the conceptual metaphors.

An important generalization that comes from these conceptual metaphors is that conceptual metaphors typically employ a more abstract concept as the target and a more concrete concept as the source. Love, argument, idea are all more abstract concepts than journey, war, and food. This is why in most cases of everyday metaphors the source and target domains are not reversible. For example, we do not talk about food as ideas, or journey as love.

13.4 Conceptual Metonymies

Metaphor is not the only "figure of speech" that plays an important role in our cognitive activities. Another equally significant "trope" is metonymy. Metonymy is a cognitive phenomenon that is as fundamental as metaphor. The main claims made by cognitive linguists in the description of metaphor also apply to metonymy. Both metaphor and metonymy are conceptual in nature. They are means of extending the resources of a language and can be explained as mapping processes. The main difference between them is that while metaphor involves a mapping across different cognitive domains, metonymy is a mapping within one domain. The primary function of metaphor is understanding, whereas that of metonymy is referential. That is, metonymy allows us to use one conceptual entity to stand for another. Thus, **metonymy** can be defined as a cognitive process in which one conceptual entity provides mental access to another conceptual entity within the same domain. In other words, instead of mentioning an entity directly, we provide mental access to it through another entity. For example, we have the conceptual metonymy THE PRODUCER FOR THE PRODUCT (THE AUTHOR FOR THE WORK), and a number of metonymic linguistic expressions for it:

(6) THE PRODUCER FOR THE PRODUCT (THE AUTHOR FOR THE WORK)
I'm reading *Shakespeare*.
She loves *Picasso*.
Does he own any *Hemingway*?
He bought a *Ford*.

The following are some other conceptual metonymies and related metonymic linguistic expressions:

(7) THE PLACE FOR THE EVENT
America doesn't want another *Pear Harbor*.
Watergate changed our politics.
Let's not let Iraq become another *Vietnam*.

(8) THE PLACE FOR THE INSTITUTION
Washington is negotiating with *Moscow*.
The White House isn't saying anything.
Wall Street is in a panic.
Hollywood is putting out terrible movies.

(9) PART FOR WHOLE
We need some good *heads* on the project.
We need some new *faces* around here.

(10) WHOLE FOR PART
I'll fill up the *car*.
England scored just before half time.

(11) CONTAINER FOR CONTENT
Please drink a *cup* or two.
The *kettle* is boiling.

(12) INSTITUTION FOR PEOPLE RESPONSIBLE
You'll never get the *university* to agree to that.
I don't approve of the *government's* actions.

These conceptual metonymies are so common in our daily life that some people even say metonymies are more basic than metaphors.

13.5 Image Schemas

Image schemas are an important form of conceptual structure in cognitive linguistics. They are recurring structures of, or within, our cognitive processes, which establish patterns of understanding and reasoning. The basic idea is that because of our physical experience of being and acting in the world, we form basic conceptual structures which we then use to organize thought across a range of more abstract domains. These image schemas are proposed as a more primitive level of cognitive structure underlying metaphor and which provide a link between bodily experience and higher cognitive domains such as language. For example, the **container schema** derives from our experience of the human body itself as a container, from our experience of being physically located within bounded locations like rooms, beds, etc.; and also of putting objects into containers. The result is an abstract schema which can be represented by a very simple image like the following figure representing an entity within a bounded location.

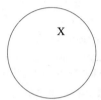

Figure 13.1: The container schema

Image schemas are dynamic embodied patterns—they take place in and through time. Moreover, they are multi-modal patterns of experience, not simply visual. For instance, consider how the dynamic nature of the container schema is reflected in the various spatial senses of the English word *out*. *Out* may be used in cases where a clearly defined **trajector** (TR) leaves a spatially bounded **landmark** (LM), as in:

(13) a. Peter went out of the classroom.
　　　b. Mary got out of her car.
　　　c. Spot jumped out of the pen.

In the most prototypical of such cases the landmark is a clearly defined container. However, *out* may also be used to indicate those cases where the trajector is a mass that spreads out, effectively expanding the area of the containing landmark:

(14) a. She poured out the beans.
　　　b. Roll out the carpet.
　　　c. Send out the troops.

Finally, *out* is also often used to describe motion along a linear path where the containing landmark is implied and not defined at all:

(15) The train started out for Beijing.

Experientially basic and primarily spatial image schemas such as the container schema may lend its logic to non-spatial situations. For example, one may metaphorically use the term *out* to describe non-spatial experiences:

(16) a. He's out of sight now. (visual field as a container)
   b. He's out of the race. (activities as containers)
   c. He's coming out of the coma now. (states as containers)

More abstract reasoning is shaped by such underlying spatial patterns. For example, the logic of containment is not just a matter of being in or out of the container. For example, if someone is in a deep depression, we know it is likely to be a long time before they are well. The deeper the trajector is in the container, the longer it will take for the trajector to get out of it.

Aside from the container schema, other important image schemas which have been proposed include the following: PART-WHOLE, PATH, BLOCKAGE, FULL-EMPATHY, BALANCE, LINK, COMPULSION, CENTRE-PERIPHERY, etc. These image schemas are not generally experienced in an isolated or self-contained fashion, but are instead interwoven and superimposed upon one another, and elaborated by the operation of conceptual metaphors at different levels. They are held to pervade not only the fabric of our experience, but also the fabric of our conscious understanding.

13.6 Iconicity

The notion of "**iconicity**" has become very popular in the last 25 years among functional and cognitive linguists. The intuition behind iconicity is that the structure of language reflects in some way the structure of experience. The structure of language is therefore explained by the structure of experience to the extent that the two match. The study of iconicity is a challenge to one of the design features of language, i.e. arbitrariness, which means that there is no resemblance between the signs of language and the thoughts they stand for.

The major types of iconicity in language which have been frequently studied are those of order, distance, and complexity which have played an important role in discussions of grammatical asymmetries.

13.6.1 Iconicity of Order

Iconicity of order refers to the similarity between temporal events and the linear arrangement of elements in a linguistic construction. Caesar's historic words *Veni, vidi, vici* (I came, I saw, I conquered) is a good case to prove this type of iconicity. Iconicity of order reflects the consistency of language with human cognition and the objective world. Let us consider the following two pairs of sentences:
(17) a. He opened the door and came into the classroom.
   b. * He came into the classroom, and opened the door.

(18) a. He jumped onto his horse and rode out into the sunset.
   b. * He rode out into the sunset and jumped onto his horse.

Obviously, in (17a) and (18a) the sequence of the clauses corresponds to the natural temporal order of events. In contrast, (17b) and (18b) are odd, to say the least, because they do not comply with this natural order. As far as the rules of syntax proper are concerned, nothing is wrong with (17b) and (18b). However, the sentences are unacceptable because the order in which the clauses are arranged violates the principle of order iconicity.

13.6.2 Iconicity of Distance

Iconicity of distance means that the linguistic distance between expressions corresponds to the conceptual distance between them. For example, lexical causatives (e.g. *kill*) tend to convey a more direct causation than periphrastic causatives (e.g. *cause to die*).

(19) a. He killed the chicken.
   b. He caused the chicken to die.

While (19a) emphasizes the happening of causing and dying at the same place and at the same time, (19b) does not necessarily mean that. (19a) can be represented as "One of whom caused the event in question, the other of whom died in that event"; and (19b) can be represented as "He caused something to come about, namely that the chicken died". Thus, we see that where cause and result are formally separated, conceptual distance is greater than they are not.

To cite another example, restrictive relative clauses are far more likely to form constituents with their heads than nonrestrictives and less likely to be set off by special pause or intonation.

(20) The boys who arrived late sat at the back of the class. (restrictive relative clause)
(21) The boy, whose name is John, is my brother. (nonrestrictive relative clause)

13.6.3 Iconicity of Complexity

Iconicity of complexity means that more complex meanings are expressed by more complex forms. For example, in English, the comparative and superlative of adjectives denote increasingly higher degrees and are coded by increasingly longer suffixes, such as *long*, *longer*, and *longest*. It is also demonstrated in such derivatives as *act* → *act-ive* → *act-iv-ate* → *act-iv-at-ion*.

This principle of iconicity can be used as well to explain why the description of a multi-event is longer than that of a single event. For example:

(22) a. He slept.
   b. He slept, then got up.

c. He slept, got up and took a shower.

13.7 Grammaticalization and Lexicalization

The term grammaticalization in the modern sense was coined by the French linguist Antoine Meillet in his *L'évolution des formes grammaticales* (1912). Meillet's definition was the attribution of grammatical character to an erstwhile autonomous word.

In historical linguistics and language change, **grammaticalization** is a process of language change by which words representing objects and actions (i. e. nouns and verbs) become grammatical markers (affixes, prepositions, etc.). Thus it creates new function words by a process other than deriving them from existing bound, inflectional constructions, instead of deriving them from content words. For example, the Old English verb *willan* (to want, to wish) has become the Modern English auxiliary verb *will*, which expresses intention or simply futurity.

For an understanding of this process, a distinction needs to be made between lexical items, or content words, which carry specific lexical meaning, and grammatical items, or function words, with little or no lexical meaning, which serve to express grammatical relationships between the different words in an utterance. Grammaticalization has been defined as the change whereby lexical items and constructions come in certain linguistic contexts to serve grammatical functions, and, once grammaticalized, continue to develop new grammatical functions. Simply said, grammaticalization is the process in which a lexical word or a word cluster loses some or all of its lexical meaning and starts to fulfill a more grammatical function. Where grammaticalization takes place, nouns and verbs which carry certain lexical meaning develop over time into grammatical items such as auxiliaries, case markers, inflections, and sentence connectives.

A well-known example of grammaticalization is that of the process in which the lexical cluster *let us*, for example in *let us eat*, is reduced to *let's* as in *let's you and me fight*. Here, the phrase has lost its lexical meaning of *allow us* and has become an auxiliary introducing a suggestion, the pronoun *us* reduced first to a suffix and then to an unanalyzed phoneme.

Another example of grammaticalization occurs in American English with *sure*, where it is used in routine phrases and as a response. It also features in many collocations, such as *sure do*, *sure can* and *sure is*.

Grammaticalization has been discussed and researched for a long time in both China and the West. The great number of studies on grammaticalization in the last decade show grammaticalization remains a popular item and is regarded as an important field within linguistic studies in general. Among recent publications there is a wide range of descriptive studies trying to come up with umbrella definitions and exhaustive lists, while others tend to focus more on its nature and significance, questioning the opportunities and boundaries of grammaticalization. An important and popular topic which is still debated is the question of unidirectionality.

Lexicalization is the process of making a word to express a concept. Here are some examples and observations from experts and other writers: *The Oxford English Dictionary* (1988) defines *lexicalize* as "to accept into the lexicon, or vocabulary, of a language", and lexicalization as "the action or process of lexicalizing". In this sense simple and complex words, native as well as loanwords can be lexicalized. Thus, Lyons (1995) says "that the relationship of the transitive (and causative) concept of 'to cause someone to die' is expressed by a separate word, to *kill* (*someone*)." Quirk et al. (1985) restrict lexicalization to words formed by word-formation processes, explaining it as the process of creating a new word (a complex lexical item) for a (new) thing or notion instead of describing this thing or notion in a sentence or with a paraphrase.

Lexicalization contrasts with grammaticalization, and the relationship between the two processes is subject to some debate. Grammaticalization and lexicalization may both refer to synchronic and diachronic processes, as well as to theoretical frameworks. Brinton & Traugot (2005) identifies the basic commonality between the two among most researchers as regarding "... the pairing of meaning and form, and the extent to which this pairing is systematic or idiosyncratic". Major stumbling blocks in further determining the relationship between grammaticalization and lexicalization (a necessary step in understanding the two types of changes) have been the recognition among most that grammar and lexicon are not mutually exclusive categories, that in a sense the lexicon arguably entails all words and certain word parts, regardless of their being more grammatical/systematic or more lexical/idiosyncratic, and that linguists have too often mixed lexicalization with degrammaticalization.

Further Readings

Lee, D. 2001. *Cognitive Linguistics: An Introduction*. Oxford: Oxford University Press.
Ungerer, F. & Schmid, H. J. 2008. *An Introduction to Cognitive Linguistics* (Second Edition). 北京:外语教学与研究出版社.
Croft, W. & Cruse, D. A. 2004. *Cognitive Linguistics*. Cambridge: Cambridge University Press.
Taylor, J. 2001. *Linguistic Categorization* (Second Edition). 北京:外语教学与研究出版社.

Chapter 13

Cognitive Linguistics: Language and Cognition

Questions and Exercises

1. Define the following terms.

cognitive linguistics	categorization	category
prototype theory	prototype	default reasoning
conceptual metaphor	conceptual metonymy	image schem
iconicity	grammaticalization	lexicalization

2. Illustrate the characteristics of the classical theory of categorization. Is prototype theory more useful than the classical theory? Why or why not?
3. Distinguish conceptual metaphor from linguistic metaphor.
4. What are the similarities and dissimilarities between conceptual metaphor and conceptual metonymy?
5. Illustrate the uses of the preposition *in* in English with reference to the container schema.
6. How can we use principles of iconicity to account for the structure of language?

Chapter

Applied Linguistics: Language Teaching and Learning

14.1 Introduction

Applied linguistics, as its name suggests, is "a branch of linguistics where the primary concern is the application of linguistic theories, methods and findings to the elucidation of language problems which has arisen in other areas of experience" (Crystal, 1991: 22). It is an umbrella term that covers a wide set of numerous areas of study connected by the focus on language.

The governing board of AILA (Association Internationale de Linguistique Appliquée, i. e. International Association of Applied Linguistics) describes applied linguistics as "an interdisciplinary field of research and practice dealing with practical problems of language and communication that can be identified, analyzed or solved by applying available theories, methods and results of linguistics or by developing new theoretical and methodological frameworks in linguistics to work on these problems". (AILA, 2008)

Today, the term applied linguistics can be used to refer to at least three uses: 1) the study of language teaching and learning; 2) the application of language study in any area of practical concern; 3) the application of the findings of theoretical linguistics. However, in general usage the term refers to the study of language teaching and learning (Richards et al., 1985). This chapter will mainly focus on language teaching and learning.

14.2 How is Language Learned?

As a foreign language learner or teacher, the first question to ask may be how to learn or teach language successfully. In order to answer this question, researchers have been devoting a lot of efforts to the study of language learning processes. In the following parts, some theories of language learning will be introduced briefly.

14.2.1 Behaviorism

Behaviorism is a predominantly American learning theory developed in the early twentieth century. It assumes that a learner is essentially passive, responding to environmental stimuli. The learner starts off as a blank slate (i.e. *tabula rasa*) and learning is viewed as the development of stimulus-response associations through habit formation, habits being developed by practice and reinforcement. A stimulus is that which produces a change or reaction in an individual or organism and a response is the behavior which is produced as a reaction to a stimulus. As a result, behaviorism is the learning theory which explains how an external event (a stimulus) causes a change in the behavior of an individual (a response).

According to behaviorism, all behaviors can be viewed as responses to stimuli and a behavior happens in an associative chain of stimulus-response (S-R). All learning is thus characterized as associative learning, or habit formation, brought about by the repeated association of a stimulus with a response.

Skinner (1957), the best known behaviorist, characterized language as a "sophisticated response system" that humans acquire through automatic conditioning processes (Wardhaugh, 1976: 142). Some patterns of language are reinforced and others are not. Only those patterns reinforced by the community of language users will persist. As the consequence of behavior, reinforcement is a stimulus which follows the occurrence of a response and affects the future frequency of that response. It is known as positive reinforcement when it increases the probability of a response or negative reinforcement if it decreases the probability of that response.

14.2.2 The Innateness Hypothesis: Universal Grammar

Chomsky (1959) challenged the behaviorist explanation for language learning in his review of Skinner's book *Verbal Behavior*. He argued that the behaviorist theory failed to account for "the logical problem of language acquisition"—the fact that children come to know more about the structure of their language than they could reasonably be expected to learn on the basis of the samples of language they hear. The language children are exposed to include false starts, incomplete sentences, and slips of the tongue, and yet they learn to distinguish between grammatical and ungrammatical sentences. Chomsky concluded that children's minds are not blank slates to be filled by imitating language they hear in the environment. This led to the **innateness hypothesis** which argues that children are born with an innate knowledge of at least some of the universal structural principles of human language. This knowledge is embodied in a mechanism called language acquisition device (LAD). Without postulating such a device Chomsky believes it would be impossible to account for many significant phenomena in child language acquisition. For instance, normal children can master their native language by an early age, which is very fast considering the complexity of language and the relative lack of intellectual maturity children bring to other tasks. The linguistic data to which children are exposed are full of irregularities and anomalies and also differ for each child. Yet they acquire the same underlying abstract system of their native language. Children differ markedly in their learning of other subjects, but the differences in the command of the underlying system of their native language are negligible. In consequence, Chomsky believes that children must be predisposed to learn any language as a native language and that the LAD must contain the principles that are universal to all human languages. This universal grammar prevents children from pursuing all sorts of wrong hypotheses about how language might work. If children are pre-equipped with universal grammar, then what they have to learn are the ways in which the language they are acquiring makes use of the principles in the universal grammar.

14.2.3 Interlanguage Theory

The concept of **interlanguage** has been highly influential in second language acquisition research since the 1960s. The term interlanguage was proposed by Selinker (1972) in order to draw attention to the possibility that the learner's language can be regarded as a distinct language variety or system with its own particular characteristics and rules. Interlanguage is a structured and interlocking system which the learner constructs at a given stage of learning a second language. A second or foreign language learner, at any particular moment in his learning sequence, is using a language system which is independent of both the target language and the learner's mother tongue. It is a third language, with its own grammar, its own lexicon and so on. The rules used by the learner are to be found in neither his own mother tongue, nor the target language.

According to interlanguage theory, learners do not suddenly become speakers of the target language. They go through a process of making and testing hypotheses about the target language, with or without the assistance of formal instruction. They begin with knowledge about language in general, gained from their native language, and move toward the target language. Bit by bit, they read just their mental model of the new language, improving their communicative competence in that language. Successful hypotheses become mental constructions that correspond to the rules of the new language. Unsuccessful hypotheses are revised or discarded. At any particular moment, the language produced by learners of the target language is located on an interlanguage continuum between the native language and the target language

(Selinker, 1972). Truly successful students make the journey to a high level of competence in the target language, while less successful students become fossilized somewhere along the interlanguage continuum (Brown, 1994).

Interlanguage theory changed many people's attitude toward the errors learners make. Errors can be viewed as evidence for the learners' gradual process of trial-and-error, and thus the study on them can shed light on the process learners go through in learning and using a language.

14.2.4 The Input Hypothesis

The **input hypothesis** was proposed by Stephen Krashen in the 1970s. There are three key elements to this hypothesis. First, language is acquired, not learned, by the learner receiving "comprehensible input"—language that contains structures that are "a little beyond" the learner's current level of mastery ($i+1$). Next, speech should be allowed to emerge on its own and the ability to produce language need not be taught directly. There is usually a silent period and "speech will come when the acquirer feels ready. The readiness state arrives at different times for different people" (Krashen, 1994: 55). Finally, the input should not deliberately contain grammatically programmed structures. "If input is understood, and there is enough of it, $i+1$ is automatically provided" (Krashen, 1994: 57)

14.2.5 The Output Hypothesis

The **output hypothesis** was proposed by Swain (1985) on the basis of her criticism of the input hypothesis. Swain holds that although comprehensible input may lead to understanding, it does not involve the development of syntactic plans which production processes require. For full grammatical competence to be developed, learners need to be pushed into the production of comprehensible output. Swain (2005) outlined three functions of output in second language learning:

1) The noticing/triggering function. While attempting to produce the target language, learners may notice that they do not know how to say (or write) precisely the meaning they wish to convey. In other words, the activity of producing the target language may prompt learners to recognize consciously some of their linguistic problems.

2) The hypothesis testing function. From the learners' perspective, output may be a "trial run" reflecting their hypothesis of how to express the meaning to convey. Following the output, learners will receive feedback, which either confirms or rejects their hypothesis, and they will modify their output in response to the feedback.

3) The metalinguistic (reflective) function. Output can serve the function

of using language to reflect on language produced by learners themselves or others so as to mediate language learning. Reflection on language may deepen the learners' awareness of forms, rules, and form-function relationships if the context of production is communicative in nature.

14.3　Individual Differences in Language Learning

Language learning theories may throw some light on the processes of learning a language common to all learners. However, there is no denying that different learners may have different characteristics, which may have effects on their learning processes and achievements. Many individual differences have been identified including language aptitude, learning style, motivation, anxiety, and learning strategies.

14.3.1　Language Aptitude

Language aptitude is the natural ability to learn a language. It is believed to predict how well, relative to other individuals, an individual can learn a foreign language in a given amount of time and under given conditions. "A person with high language aptitude can learn more quickly and easily than a person with low language aptitude, all other factors being equal" (Richards et al., 1985: 155). Carroll (1991) identified four aspects of language aptitude:
1) Phonemic coding ability: the ability to code foreign sounds in a way that they can be remembered later;
2) Grammatical sensitivity: the ability to recognize the grammatical functions of words in sentences;
3) Inductive learning ability: the ability to identify patterns of correspondence and relationships involving form and meaning;
4) Rote learning ability: the ability to form and remember associations between stimuli.

14.3.2　Learning Style

Learning style is also called cognitive style. It is a term used in cognitive psychology to describe the way individuals think, perceive and remember information, and hence their preferred ways of learning. Different learners may prefer different ways of learning. For example, some may want explanations for grammatical rules, while others may need more practice through which they can discover the underlying rules. Some like to write down words or sentences to help them remember, while others may need some kind of assisting materials, such as pictures, to help them remember better.

Chapter 14
Applied Linguistics: Language Teaching and Learning

Different learning styles have been identified and the distinction that has attracted the greatest attention is that between field dependence and field independence. **Field dependence** is a learning style in which a learner tends to see things holistically and thus has difficulty in identifying the parts that make up the whole. Field dependent learners are people-oriented and find social interaction easy and pleasurable, so they are sociable and work well in groups. **Field independence**, in contrast, is a learning style in which a learner tends to analyze information into its component parts, and to distinguish the essential from the inessential. Field independent learners see things more analytically and are more individualistic and less inclined to social interaction. They are portrayed as aloof, preferring to find solutions to problems for themselves. Both of the two learning styles can have advantages in language learning: field independent learners can link with a capacity to analyze linguistic materials, and perhaps learn systematically; field dependent learners can engage in communicative language use, and to "talk to learn".

Reid (1986) emphasized learners' sensory preferences and described three basic learning styles: **auditory learning** occurs through hearing the spoken word; **kinesthetic learning** occurs through doing and interacting; **visual learning** occurs through looking at images, mind-maps, demonstrations and body language. It is no good to say which learning style is better than another, with each having its advantages and disadvantages.

14.3.3 Motivation

Motivation is usually defined as a "psychological trait which leads to achieve some goal. In language learning, that goal may be mastery of the language or achievement of some lesser aim" (Johnson & Johnson, 1999: 219—220). It is widely believed that high motivation is one of the essential factors for the success of language learning.

There are different types of motivation. One popular distinction was made by Gardner and Lambert (1972) between **instrumental motivation** and **integrative motivation**. The former refers to learning a language as an instrument to achieve practical goals, such as obtaining a job, reading foreign language books or newspapers, passing an examination. The latter refers to learning a language out of interest in, or desire to identify with, the target culture. **Intrinsic motivation** and **extrinsic motivation** form another pair of commonly accepted distinction. The former aims at achieving pleasure and satisfaction from the language learning process, whereas the latter emphasizes language learning as a means to achieve certain goals. Intrinsic and extrinsic motivations may inhibit each other (Brown, 1994). The above two pairs of concepts are considered well matched. "Integrative motivation" is to a large extent "intrinsic", and "instrumental motivation" is "extrinsic" (Chambers, 1999). Compared with instrumental or extrinsic motivation, integrative or intrinsic motivation is believed to be related to better learning outcome (Brown, 1994).

14.3.4 Anxiety

Anxiety for language learners refers to the feelings of worry, nervousness, and stress that many learners experience when learning a language. For a long time, researchers thought of anxiety as a permanent feature of a learner's personality. However, more recent research on learner anxiety acknowledges that anxiety is more likely to be dynamic and dependent on particular situations (Lightbrown & Spada, 2006). A student may feel anxious when giving an oral presentation in front of the whole class but feel relaxed when interacting with peers in group-work. In whatever the context, anxiety can play a negative role in language learning if it interferes with the learning process. It is believed that anxious students do not learn as efficiently as relaxed students since anxious students have to focus on both the task at hand and their reactions to it. Of course, not all anxiety is bad and a certain amount of tension can have a positive effect and even facilitate learning. For instance, in some learning environments, a certain amount of anxiety can urge students to work hard towards a desired goal.

14.3.5 Learning Strategies

Learning strategies are the techniques used by learners for remembering and organizing samples of the target language (Johnson & Johnson, 1999). There are four main classes of learning strategy (Dornyei & Skehan, 2003):
1) Cognitive strategies, involving the manipulation or transformation of the learning materials (e.g. repetition, summarizing, using images);
2) Metacognitive strategies, involving higher-order strategies aimed at analyzing, monitoring, evaluating, planning, and organizing one's own learning processes;
3) Social strategies, involving interpersonal behaviors aimed at increasing the amount of the target language communication and practice the learner undertakes (e.g. initiating interaction with native speakers, cooperating with peers);
4) Affective strategies, involving taking control of the emotional conditions and experiences that shape one's subjective involvement in learning.

In the field of language learning strategy, one of the most attractive questions is what could be learned from the "good language learner"; that is,

Chapter 14

Applied Linguistics: Language Teaching and Learning

what characteristics make some learners more successful than others in learning a language. Stern (1975) found that good language learners tend to use the following ten learning strategies:

1) Planning strategy (I) (cognitive): Good learners have sufficient self-knowledge to know what style they should adopt to be successful.
2) Planning strategy (II) (affective): Good learners are not passive but take an active independent role in learning.
3) Empathic strategy: Good learners adopt a tolerant and outgoing approach to the target language and have empathy with its speakers. Integrative motivation is crucial, as is lack of inhibition about learning a new language.
4) Formal strategy: Good learners are aware of the form of language and consciously try to get to know the target language.
5) Experimental strategy: Good learners make guesses about the target language systematically and are prepared to change them.
6) Semantic strategy: Good learners look for meaning in what they hear.
7) Practice strategy: Good learners seize every opportunity for practice.
8) Communication strategy: Good learners seek out occasions to use the language in real-life situations.
9) Monitoring strategy: Good learners check their output continuously and learn from their mistakes.
10) Internalizationstrategy: Good learners deliberately cut themselves off from their first language.

14.4 Approaches and Methods in Foreign Language Teaching

Foreign language teaching started more than 150 years ago. From then on there have been many teaching approaches and methods, inclusive of the Grammar-Translation Method, the Direct Method, the Audiolingual Method, the Communicative Approach and the Task-based Approach.

14.4.1 The Grammar-Translation Method

Grammar Translation is the teaching method prevailing in the eighteenth, nineteenth and early twentieth centuries and is still used in foreign language teaching today. It is derived from the classical method of teaching Greek and Latin and is based on the following assumptions: language is primarily graphic; the main purpose of language learning is to build knowledge of the structure of the language either as a tool for literary research and translation or for the development of the learner's logical powers; the process of foreign language learning must be deductive, requires effort, and must be carried out with constant reference to the learner's native language.

In a class of the Grammar-Translation Method, teaching is conducted in the native language. A chapter in a typical textbook of this method would begin with a massive bilingual vocabulary list. Grammar points would come directly from the texts and be presented contextually in the textbook, to be explained elaborately by the instructor. Grammar thus provides the rules for assembling words into sentences. Tedious translation and grammar drills would be used to exercise and strengthen the knowledge without much attention to content. Very little attention is placed on pronunciation or any communicative aspects of the target language. The skill exercised is reading, and then only in the context of translation.

Because the Grammar-Translation Method emphasizes reading rather than the ability to communicate in a language, it has been under attack for ignoring the spoken language, for encouraging false notions of equivalence between the native and target languages, and for presenting isolated sentences rather than connected texts.

14.4.2　The Direct Method

The Direct Method emerged in the late nineteenth century and enjoyed popularity in Europe up to the 1920s. The Direct Method was once quite successful in private language schools in the early nineteenth century and we still can find its influence on language teaching today. The basic premise of the Direct Method is that foreign language learning should be more like first language learning. Its advocates believe that a foreign language could be taught without translation or the use of the learners' native language if meaning is conveyed directly through demonstration and action. The main characteristics of the Direct Method can be summarized as follows:

1) Only everyday vocabulary and sentences are taught;
2) Grammar is taught inductively, by situation and through visual presentation;
3) Classroom instruction is conducted exclusively in the target language;
4) Concrete vocabulary is taught through demonstration, objects, pictures and abstract vocabulary is taught through association of ideas;
5) Both speech and listening comprehension are taught and extensive listening and imitation practice should be done until forms become automatic;
6) Oral communication skills are built up in a carefully graded progression organized around question-and-answer exchanges between teachers and students in small intensive classes;
7) Correct pronunciation is emphasized with the first few weeks devoted to pronunciation;

Chapter 14
Applied Linguistics: Language Teaching and Learning

8) All reading matter is first presented orally.

14.4.3 The Audiolingual Method

The Audiolingual Method was very popular from the 1940s through the 1960s. The theory of language underlying it is derived from structural linguistics. Language is viewed as a system of structurally related elements for the encoding of meanings, the elements being phonemes, morphemes, words, structures, and sentence types. Learning a language is assumed to entail mastering the elements or building blocks of the language and learning the rules by which these elements are combined. Another important tenet of structural linguistics is that the primary medium of language is oral: speech is language. The Audiolingual Method is also based on behaviorism, in which learning is viewed as a process of habit formation.

Dialogues and drills form the basis of audiolingual classroom practices. Dialogues provide the means of contextualizing key structures and illustrate situations in which structures might be used as well as some aspects of the target language culture. Dialogues are used for repetition and memorization. Correct pronunciation, stress, rhythm, and intonation are emphasized. After a dialogue has been presented and memorized, specific grammatical patterns in the dialogue are selected and become the focus of various kinds of drill and pattern-practice exercises.

The Audiolingual Method reached its period of most widespread use in the 1960s, but then came criticism on two fronts. One the one hand, its theoretical foundations were attacked as being unsound in terms of both language theory and learning theory. On the other hand, the Audiolingual Method did not live up to the claims made for it, at least, at school levels. Students were often found to be unable to transfer skills acquired to real communication outside the classroom, and many found the experience of studying through audiolingual procedures to be boring and unsatisfying.

14.4.4 The Communicative Approach

The Communicative Approach to language teaching was developed by British applied linguists as a reaction against grammar-based approaches in the 1970s. It started from a theory regarding language as communication, whose main characteristics are summarized as follows (Richards & Rodgers, 1986):

1) Language is a system for the expression of meaning;
2) The primary function of language is for interaction and communication;
3) The structure of language reflects its functional and communicative uses;
4) The primary units of language are not merely its grammatical and

structural features, but categories of functional and communicative meaning as exemplified in discourse.

The goal of language teaching is to develop what Hymes (1972) referred to as "communicative competence". Hymes used this term in order to contrast a communicative view of language and Chomsky's theory of competence. **Communicative competence** is the knowledge which enables someone to use a language effectively and the ability to use this knowledge for communication. Hymes (1972) proposed four sectors of communicative competence:

1) Whether (and to what degree) something is formally possible: This includes not only linguistic grammaticality but also non-verbal and cultural grammaticality (i.e. conformity to meaningful rules of behavior). It is dependent both upon knowledge and use.

2) Whether (and to what degree) something is feasible. This refers to psycholinguistic factors, such as memory limitation and perceptual devices. For example, an extremely long or complicated sentence that is grammatical may not be feasibly processed or understood.

3) Whether (and to what degree) something is appropriate. Appropriateness concerns the relation of language to context. Particular attention has been given to cultural appropriateness, to the way in which an utterance or sequence of utterances may be grammatical and feasible but inappropriate in a given context.

4) Whether (and to what degree) something is in fact done. Language users should have some knowledge of which forms actually occur, and of the probability of that occurrence. That is, the language produced is supposed to be native-like, authentic and conventional.

The concept of communicative competence was further developed by Canale and Swain (1980), who identified four dimensions of communicative competence:

1) **Grammatical competence**: the knowledge of lexical items and of rules of morphology, syntax, sentence-grammar semantics, and phonology;

2) **Sociolinguistic competence**: the knowledge of the relation of language use to its social-cultural context, including role relationships, the shared information of the participants, and the communicative purpose.

3) **Discourse competence**: the knowledge of rules governing cohesion and coherence, that is, knowledge of rules for "the combination of utterances and communicative functions" to form the entire text or discourse.

4) **Strategic competence**: the verbal and non-verbal communication strategies that may be called into action to initiate, terminate,

maintain communication and compensate for break-downs in communication.

The range of exercise types and activities compatible with the Communicative Approach is unlimited, provided that such exercises and activities enable learners to attain the communicative objectives, engage learners in communication, and require the use of such communicative processes as information sharing, negotiation of meaning, and interaction (Richards & Rodgers, 1986: 76).

14.4.5 The Task-based Approach

The Task-based Approach has gained popularity in the field of language teaching since the 1990s. "Learning by doing" is the basic notion of this approach, whose advocates believe that significant learning can only take place through the learner's active participation in the construction of knowledge, in formulating their own personal understanding of the various information and sensory experiences that they are presented with. Tasks, therefore, form a significant part of the learning process and integration of new concepts/skills and prior knowledge for the accomplishment of an open-ended task is the main learning goal of this approach. Nunan (2006) defines task as "a piece of classroom work that involves learners in comprehending, manipulating, producing or interacting in the target language while their attention is focused on mobilizing their grammatical knowledge in order to express meaning, and in which the intention is to convey meaning rather than to manipulate form. The task should also have a sense of completeness, being able to stand alone as a communicative act in its own right with a beginning, a middle and an end." In task-based language teaching, students are required to internalize key specific concepts of a subject domain and other necessary skills for the accomplishment of the tasks, so students are allowed to develop their creativity. The teachers' role is to design tasks according to the specific knowledge or skills which they expect the students to learn. Students play the role of active learners, while the teacher plays the role of a facilitator.

14.5 Language Testing

Language testing plays an important role in language teaching. It is a natural extension of classroom work, providing teachers and students with useful information that can serve as a basis for the improvement of teaching and learning. The effect of testing on teaching and learning is known as **"backwash"**, which can be positive or negative. If too much importance is attached to a test, then preparation for it can come to dominate all teaching and learning activities. And if the test content and testing techniques are different from the objectives of the course, then there is likely to be negative backwash. In contrast, if the test is supportive of good teaching and, where necessary, exert a corrective influence on bad teaching, there will be positive backwash.

14.5.1 Types of Test

There are different classifications of language testing based on different criteria. According to the purposes for which language testing is carried out, there are four types of test:

1) **Proficiency test**. It is designed to assess the student's ability in a language regardless of any training they may have had in that language. This type of test is not usually related to any particular course of instruction, but measures the student's general level of language mastery. Many tests familiar to us including TOEFL (Test of English as a Foreign Language), TOEIC (Test of English for International Communication), and IELTS (International English Language Testing System) belong to this type.

2) **Achievement test**. It is designed to assess how much of a language a student has learned with reference to a particular course of study or program of instruction. For example, the mid- and final-term examinations are usually based on what have been taught and are designed to see whether the students have achieved the expected teaching objectives, so they are achievement tests.

3) **Diagnostic test**. It is designed to show what skills or knowledge a learner acquires and does not acquire. It is used, for example, at the end of a unit in the course-book or following a lesson designed to teach one particular point and it will give immediate feedback to the student. If the student's learning has been successful, the results will give a considerable lift to the student's morale and he is likely to approach the next learning task with fresh enthusiasm. If he finds he has not mastered the point at issue, the test should give him clear indications of how he falls short, so that he can do some useful revision.

4) **Placement test**. It is designed to sort new students into teaching groups, so that they can start a course at approximately the same level as other students in the class.

Based on the methods of scoring, there is the distinction between **subjective** and **objective testing**. If no judgment is required on the part of the scorer, then the scoring is objective. A multiple choice test is a good example of objective test. In contrast, if judgment is needed, the scoring is said to be subjective. A writing test is a good example of subjective test, since the scoring of the candidates' compositions needs to be judged subjectively by the scorer.

The difference in the interpretation of the testing results leads to the distinction between **criterion-referenced** and **norm-referenced testing**. The former refers to the test which measures students' performance according to a particular standard or criterion which has been agreed upon. The student must reach this level of performance to pass the test, and a student's score is therefore interpreted with reference to the criterion score, rather than to the scores of other students. Criterion referenced tests are concerned about what a student can actually do in the language, not how his performance compares with that of others. In contrast, a norm-referenced test is designed to measure how the performance of a particular student or group of students compares with the performance of another student or group of students whose scores are given as the norm. A student's score is therefore interpreted with reference to the scores of other students or group of students, rather than to an agreed criterion score.

14.5.2 Qualities of a Good Test

The three most important characteristics of a good test are reliability, validity and practicality.

1) **Reliability**. Reliability of a test is its consistency of measurement. A good test should be consistent in its measurement. A test is said to be reliable if it gives the same results when it is given on different occasions or when it is used by different people.

2) **Validity**. A test is valid if it measures what it is supposed to measure, or if it does what it is supposed to do. There are three kinds of validity vital for language testing. **Content validity** is concerned with what goes into the test. The content of a test should be decided by considering the purpose of the assessment, and the test should adequately and sufficiently measure the particular skills it sets out to measure. **Construct validity** is concerned with whether the items in a test reflect the essential aspects of the theory on which the test is based. For example, it can be argued that a speed reading test based on a short comprehension passage is an inadequate measure of reading ability (and thus has low construct validity) unless it is believed that speed reading of short passages relate closely to the ability of reading a book quickly and efficiently and is a proven factor in reading ability. **Face validity** is concerned with what teachers and students think of the test. One way to judge face validity is to ask the teachers and students concerned for their opinions, either formally by means of a questionnaire or informally by discussion in class or staff rooms.

3) **Practicality.** The main questions of practicality are administrative. How long will the test take? What special arrangements have to be made? Is there any equipment needed? How long will it take to get the marking done, and how many people will be involved? In brief, tests should be as economical as possible in time (preparation, sitting, and marking) and in cost (materials and hidden cost of time spent).

Further Readings

Johnson, K. 2001. *An Introduction to Foreign Language Learning and Teaching*. 北京:外语教学与研究出版社.

Richards, J. C. & Rodgers, T. S. 1986/2008. *Approaches and Methods in Language Teaching* (Second Edition). 北京:外语教学与研究出版社.

Ur, P. 2001. *A Course in Language Teaching: Practice and Theory*. 北京:外语教学与研究出版社.

崔刚,罗立胜,2006,《英语教学理论与实践》。北京:对外经济贸易大学出版社。

桂诗春,1988,《应用语言学》。长沙:湖南教育出版社。

刘润清,韩宝成,2004,《语言测试和它的方法》。北京:外语教学与研究出版社。

Questions and Exercises

1. Define the following terms.

behaviourism	innateness hypothesis	interlanguage
input hypothesis	output hypothesis	language aptitude
learning style	motivation	anxiety
learning strategy	Grammar-Translation Method	Direct Method
Audiolingual Method	Communicative Approach	communicative competence
Task-based Approach	proficiency test	achievement test
diagnostic test	placement test	criterion-referenced testing
norm-referenced testing		

2. What are the major research areas of applied linguistics?
3. What are the main points of the behaviorist view of language learning?
4. What are the main points of universal grammar theory about language learning?
5. What are the differences between Chomsky's ideas and behaviorism?
6. According to the interlanguage theory, what are the major causes for learners' errors?
7. According to the output hypothesis, what are the main functions of output?
8. What are the characteristics of the Grammar-Translation Method?
9. What are the characteristics of the Direct Method?
10. What are the principles of the Audiolingual Method?
11. What are the characteristics of the Communicative Approach?
12. What are the characteristics of the Task-based Approach?
13. What are the major types of language test?
14. How can we design a good test?
15. Based on the individual differences in language learning in this chapter, can you evaluate your own characteristics to see in what aspects you are advantageous or disadvantageous in language learning?

Chapter 14
Applied Linguistics: Language Teaching and Learning

16. What kind of learning strategies do you prefer? Compare your learning strategies with those of the good language learners as described by Stern (1975), and say how far you are from the good language learners in terms of learning strategies.
17. Comment on the language teaching methods and approaches. What do you think is the best way to teach a foreign language?

References

Adams, V. 1973. *An Introduction to Modern English Word-Formation*. London: Longman.
AILA, 2008. What is AILA? Retrieved from http://www.aila.info/about/index.htm.
Aitchison, J. 1992. *Teach Yourself Linguistics*. London: Hodder & Stoughton.
Aitchison, J. 2000. The *Articulate Mammals: An Introduction to Psycholinguistics*. 北京:外语教学与研究出版社.
Austin J. L. 1962. *How to Do Things with Words*. Oxford: Oxford University Press.
Baldick, C. 1991. *The Concise Oxford Dictionary of Literary Terms*. Oxford: Oxford University Press.
Barna, L. 1994. Stumbling blocks in intercultural communication. In Samovar, L. & Porter, R. (eds.) *Intercultural Communication: A Reader* (Seventh Edition). Belmont, CA: Wadsworth.
Bauer, L. 1988. *Introducing Linguistic Morphology*. Edinburgh: Edinburgh University Press.
Baugh, A. C. & Cable, T. 2001. *A History of the English Language* (Fourth Edition). 北京:外语教学与研究出版社.
Bell, R. 1976. *Sociolinguistics: Goals, Approaches and Problems*, London: Batsford.
Benedict, R. 1935. *Patterns of Culture*. London: Routledge.
Bernstein, B. 1972. Social Class, Language and Socialization. In Giglioli, P. O. (ed.) *Language and Social Context*. Baltimore, Md.: Penguin Books.
Bloch, B. & Trager, G. L. 1942. *Outline of Linguistic Analysis*. Baltimore: Linguistics Societyof America/Waverly Press.
Bloom, P. 2000. *How do Children Learn the Meanings of Words*. Cambridge, MA.: MIT Press.
Bloomfield, L. 1933/2002. *Language*. 北京:外语教学与研究出版社.
Bloor, T. & Bloor, M. 2001/2007. *The Functional Analysis of English: A Hallidayan Approach*. 北京:外语教学与研究出版社.
Brinton, L. J. & Traugot, E. C. 2005. *Lexicalization and Language Change*. Cambridge: Cambridge University Press.
Brown, G. & Yule, G. 1983/2000. *Discourse Analysis*. 北京:外语教学与研究出版社.
Brown, H. D. 1994. *Teaching by Principles: An Interactive Approach to Language Pedagogy*. New Jersey: Prentice Hall.
Brown, H. D. 1994/2002. *Principles of Language Learning and Teaching*. 北京:外语教学与研究出版社.
Burnett, A. 1981. *Milton's Style*. London and New York: Longman.
Burnley, J. D. 1992. *The History of the English Language: A Source Book*. London: Macmillan.
Canale, M. & Swain, M. 1980. Theoretical bases of communicative approaches to second language teaching and testing. *Applied Linguistics*, 1/1, 1—47.
Carroll, J. 1991. Cognitive abilities in foreign language aptitude: Then and now. In Parry, T. & Stansfield, C. (eds.) *Language Aptitude Reconsidered*. Englewood Cliffs, NJ: Prentice-Hall.
Carroll, D. W. 2000. *Psychology of Language*. 北京:外语教学与研究出版社.
Carstairs-McCarthy, A. 1992. *Current Morphology*. London: Routledge.
Carstairs-McCarthy, A. 2002. *An Introduction to English Morphology: Words and Their Structure*. Edinburgh: Edinburgh University Press.

Chambers, G. N. 1999. *Motivating Language Learners*. Clevedon: Multilingual Matters.
Chomsky, N. 1957. *Syntactic Structures*. The Hague: Mouton.
Chomsky, N. 1959. Review of Verbal Behavior by B. F. Skinner. *Language* 35, 26—58.
Chomsky, N. 1965. *Aspects of the Theory of Syntax*. Cambridge, Mass.: MIT Press.
Chomsky, N. 1986. *Barriers*. Cambridge, Mass.: MIT Press.
Chomsky, N. 1995. *The Minimalist Program*. Cambridge, Mass.: MIT Press.
Clark, J. & Yallop, C. 2000. *An Introduction to Phonetics and Phonology*. 北京:外语教学与研究出版社.
Cook, V. & Newson, M. 2000. *Chomsky's Universal Grammar: An introduction*. 北京:外语教学与研究出版社.
Corder, S. P. 1973. *Introducing Applied Linguistics*. Harmondsworth: Penguin Books.
Coulthard, M. 1985. *An Introduction to Discourse Analysis*. London: Longman.
Croft, W. & Cruse, D. A. 2004. *Cognitive Linguistics*. Cambridge: Cambridge University Press.
Crystal, D. 1985/1991. *A Dictionary of Linguistics and Phonetics*. Oxford: Blackwell.
Crystal, D. 1997/2002. *The Cambridge Encyclopedia of Language* (Second Edition). 北京:外语教学与研究出版社.
Culpeper, J. 2001. *Language and Characterisation: People in Plays and Other Texts*. London: Longman.
Culpeper, J. & Haugh, M. 2014. *Pragmatics and the English Language*. Basingstoke: Palgrave MacMillan.
Daneš, F. 1974. Functional sentence perspective and the organization of the text. In Daneš, F. (ed.) *Papers on Functional Sentence Perspective*. Prague: Academia.
Davies, A. 1990. *Principles of Language Testing*. Oxford: Basil Blackwell
Davis, S. 1991. *Pragmatics: A Reader*. Oxford: Oxford University Press.
Denison, N. 1971. some observations on language variety and plurilingualism. In Ardener, E. (ed.) *Social Anthropology and Language*. London: Tavistock.
Dension, D. 1993. *English Syntax: Verbal Construction*. New York: Longman Publishing.
Derewianka, B. 1990. *Exploring How Text Works*. Sydney: Primary English Teaching Association.
Dodd, C. H. 2006. *Dynamics of Intercultural Communication* (Fifth Edition). Shanghai: Shanghai Foreign Language Education Press
Dornyei, Z. & Skehan, P. 2003. Individual differences in second language learning. In Doughty, C. J. & Long, M. H. (eds) *Handbook of Second Language Acquisition*. Malden, MA: Blackwell
Ducrot, O. & Todorov, T. 1979. Trans. by Porter, Catherine. *Encyclopedic Dictionary of the Sciences of Language*. Baltimore and London: The John Hopkins University Press.
Eggins, S. 1994. *An Introduction to Systemic Functional Linguistics*. London: Pinter.
Ellis, R. 1994. *The Study of Second Language Acquisition*. Oxford: Oxford University Press.
Fasold, R. 2001. *The Sociolinguistics of Language*. 北京:外语教学与研究出版社.
Fauconnier, G. 1997. *Mappings in Thought and Language*. Cambridge: Cambridge University Press.
Fennell, B. A. 2005. *A History of English: A Sociolinguistic Approach*. 北京:外语教学与研究出版社.
Firth, J. R. 1957. *Papers in Linguistics*, 1934-1951. London: Oxford University Press.

Fodor, J. A., Bever, T. G. & Garrett, M. F. 1974. *The Psychology of Language: An Introduction to Psycholinguistics and Generative Grammar*. New York: McGraw-Hill.

Freeborn, D. 2000. *From Old English to Standard English* (Second Edition). 北京: 外语教学与研究出版社.

Fries, P. 1981. On the status of Theme in English: arguments from discourse. *Forum Linguisticum* 6(1), 1—38.

Fries, P. 1995. Themes, methods of development, and texts. In Hasan, R. & Fries, P. (eds.) *On Subject and Theme*. Amsterdam: Benjamins.

Fromkin, V. & Rodman, R. 1983. *An Introduction to Language* (Third Edition). New York: Holt, Rinehart & Winston.

Gardner, R. C. & Lambert, W. E. 1972. *Attitudes and Motivation in Second Language Learning*. Rowley, Mass.: Newbury House.

Giglioli, P. O. (ed.) 1972. *Language and Social Context*. Baltimore, Md.: Penguin Books.

Gimson, A. C. & Arnold, E. 2000. *An Introduction to Phonetics and Phonology*. 北京: 外语教学与研究出版社.

Gleason, J. B. 1997. *The Development of Language*. Boston, MA.: Allyn and Bacon.

Goodman, K. S. et al. 1987. *Language and Thinking in School: A Whole-language Curriculum* (Third Edition). New York: Richard C. Owen Publishers, Inc.

Green, G. 1989. *Pragmatics and Natural Language Understanding*. New Jersey: LEA Publishers.

Grice, H. P. 1967. Logic and Conversation. In Grice, P. (ed.) 1989/2002. *Studies in the Way of Words*. 北京: 外语教学与研究出版社.

Grundy, P. 1995. *Doing Pragmatics*. London: Edward Arnold.

Gu, Y. 1993. The impasse of perlocution. *Journal of Pragmatics* 20, 405—432.

Haberlandt, K. 1994. *Cognitive Psychology*. Boston, MA.: Allyn and Bacon.

Haiman, J. (ed.) 1985. *Iconicity in Syntax*. Amsterdam: John Benjamins.

Hall, E. T. 1959. *The Silent Language*. New York: Doubleday.

Hall, R. A. 1968. *An Essay on Language*. Philadelphia & New York: Chilton Books.

Halliday, M. A. K. 1978/2001. *Language as Social Semiotics: The Social Interpretation of Language and Meaning*. 北京: 外语教学与研究出版社.

Halliday, M. A. K. 1985/1994/2008. *An Introduction to Functional Grammar*. 北京: 外语教学与研究出版社.

Halliday, M. A. K. & Hasan, R. 1976/2001. *Cohesion in English*. 北京: 外语教学与研究出版社.

Halliday, M. A. K. & Hasan, R. 1989. *Language, Context, and Text*. Oxford: Oxford University Press.

Hands, P. 1996/1998. *Chambers English Dictionary of Idioms*. Chambers Harrap Publishers Ltd.

Haynes, J. 1995. *Style*. London & New York: Routledge.

Heine, B. 1997. *Cognitive Foundation of Grammar*. Oxford: Oxford University Press.

Hockett, C. F. 1958. *A Course in Modern Linguistics*. New York: Macmillan.

Hoey, M. 1983. *On the Surface of Discourse*. London: George Allen and Unwin.

Hofstede, G. 2001. *Culture's Consequences: Comparing Values, Behaviors, Institutions, and Organizations Across Nations* (Second Edition). Thousand Oaks, CA: SAGE Publications.

Hopper, P. J. & Traugott, E. C. 2001. *Grammaticalization*. 北京: 外语教学与研究出版社.

Huang, Yan 2007. *Pragmatics*. Oxford: Oxford University Press.

Hudson, R. A. 1980/2000. *Siociolinguistics*. 北京: 外语教学与研究出版社.

Hudson, R. A. 1984. *Invitation to Linguistics*. Oxford: Blackwell.
Hymes, D. 1972. On communicative competence. In Pride, J. B. & Holmes, J. (eds.) *Sociolinguistics*. Harmondsworth: Penguin.
Jakobson, R. 1960. Linguistics andpoetics. In Sebeok, T. A. (ed.) *Style and Language*. Cambridge: MIT Press.
Jespersen, O. 1922. *Language: Its Nature, Development and Origin*. London: Allen & Unwin.
Johnson, M. 1987. *The Body in the Mind*. Chicago: The University of Chicago Press.
Johnson, K. & Johnson, H. 1999. *Encyclopedic Dictionary of Applied Linguistics: A Handbook for Language Teaching*. Oxford: Blackwell.
Kádár, D. & Haugh, M. 2013. *Understanding Politeness*. Cambridge: Cambridge University Press.
Katamba, F. 1989. *An Introduction to Phonology*. London and New York: Longman.
Kaye, J. 1989. *Phonology: A Cognitive View*. Hillsdale, New Jersey: Lawrence Erlbaum.
Kempson, R. M. 1977. *Semantic Theory*. Cambridge: Cambridge University Press.
Kohls, R. 1979. *Survival Kit for Overseas Living*. Chicago, IL: Intercultural Press.
Kövecses, Z. 2002. *Metaphor: A Practical Introduction*. Oxford: Oxford University Press.
Kramsch, C. 1998/2000. *Language and Culture*. 上海:上海外语教育出版社.
Krashen, S. 1981. *Second Language Acquisition and Second Language Learning*. Oxford: Pergamon.
Krashen, S. 1994. Bilingual education and second language acquisition theory. In Bilingual Education Office (ed.) *Schooling and Language-minority Students: A Theoretical Framework* (Second Edition). Los Angeles: Evaluation Dissemination and Assessment Center, California State University.
Labov, W. 1973. Some features of English of Black American. In Bailey, R. & Robinson, J. L. (eds.) *Varieties of Present-Day English*. New York: Macmillan.
Lakoff, G. 1987. *Women, Fire and Dangerous Things*. Chicago: University of Chicago Press.
Lakoff, G. & Johnson, M. 1980. *Metaphors We Live By*. Chicago: University of Chicago Press.
Lakoff, G. & Johnson, M. 1999. *Philosophy in the Flesh: The Embodied Mind and its Challenge to Western Thought*. New York, NY: Basic Books.
Langacker, R. W. 1987. *Foundations of Cognitive Grammar Vol. I: Theoretical Prerequisites*. Stanford: Stanford University Press.
Langacker, R. W. 1991. *Foundations of Cognitive Grammar Vol. II: Descriptive Application*. Stanford: Stanford University Press.
Larsen-Freeman, D. & Long, M. H. 2000. *An Introduction to Second Language Acquisition Research*. 北京:外语教学与研究出版社.
Lee, D. 2001. *Cognitive Linguistics: An Introduction*. Oxford: Oxford University Press.
Leech G. 1969. *A Linguistic Guide to English Poetry*. London: Longman.
Leech, G. 1981. *Semantics* (Second Edition). Harmondsworth: Penguin Books.
Leech, G. 1983. *Principles of Pragmatics*. London: Longman.
Leech, G. & Short, M. H. 1981/2001. *Style in Fiction*. 北京:外语教学与研究出版社.
Lehmann, W. P. 2002. *Historical Linguistics: An Introduction*. 北京:外语教学与研究出版社.
Leith, D. 1997. *A Social History of English*. London: Routledge.
Levinson, S. C. 1983. *Pragmatics*. Cambridge, England: Cambridge University.
Lightbrown, P. M. & Spada, N. 2006. *How Languages Are Learned*. New York: Oxford University Press

Lyons, J. 1968. *Introduction to Theoretical Linguistics*. Cambridge: Cambridge University Press.
Lyons, J. 1970. *New Horizons in Linguistics*. Harmondsworth: Penguin.
Lyons, J. 1977. *Semantics*. 2 vols. Cambridge: Cambridge University Press.
Lyons, J. 1981. *Language and Linguistics*. Cambridge: Cambridge University Press.
Lyons, J. 1995/2000. *Linguistic Semantics: An Introduction*. 北京:外语教学与研究出版社.
Martin, J. R. 1992. *English Text: System and Structure*. Amsterdam: Benjamins.
Martin, J. R. & Rose, D. 2003/2007. *Working with Discourse: Meaning Beyond the Clause*. 北京:北京大学出版社.
Mathesius, V. 1939. On so-called functional sentence perspective. *Slovo a Slovesnost* 5, 171—174.
Matthews, P. H. 1981. *Syntax*. Cambridge: Cambridge University Press.
Matthews, P. H. 1997. *Oxford Concise Dictionary of Linguistics*. Oxford University Press.
Matthews, P. H. 2000. *Morphology* (Second Edition). 北京:外语教学与研究出版社.
Matthews, P. H. 2001. *A Short History of Structural Linguistics*. Cambridge University Press.
McArthur, T. 1992. *The Oxford Companion to the English Language*. Oxford: Oxford University Press.
McCarthy, M. 1991. *Discourse Analysis for Language Teachers*. Cambridge: Cambridge University Press.
McGalliard, J. C. 1970. *Aspects of the History of English*. New York: Holt, Rinehart and Winston, Inc.
Mey, J. 1991/2001. *Pragmatics: An Introduction*. 北京:外语教学与研究出版社.
Miller, G. & Chomsky, N. 1963. Finitary models of language users. In Bush, R., Galanter, E. & Luce, R. (eds.) *Handbook of Mathematical Psychology*. New York: Wiley & Sons.
Miller, G. A. 1956. The magic number seven plus or minus two: Some limits on our capacity for processing information. *Psychological Review* 63, 81—97.
Morris, C. W. 1938. *Foundations of the Theory of Signs*. Chicago, IL: University of Chicago Press.
Nietzsche, F. 1873. On truth and lies in a non-moral sense. In Kaufmann, W. (ed.) 1976. *The Portable Nietzsche*. London: Penguin.
Nunan, D. 2005. *Task-based Language Teaching*. Cambridge: Cambridge University Press
Nunan, D. 2006. Task-based language teaching in the Asia context: Defining "task". *Asian EFL Journal* 3(8).
Odlin, T. 1989. *Language Transfer*. Cambridge: Cambridge University Press.
Ogden, C. K. & Richards, I. A. 1923. *The Meaning of Meaning*. London: Routledge & Kegan Paul.
Ouhalla, J. 2001. *Introducing Transformational Grammar: From Principles and Parameters to Minimalism*. 北京:外语教学与研究出版社.
Palmer, F. R. 1981. *Semantics* (Second Edition). Cambridge: Cambridge University Press.
Paltridge, B. 2006. *Discourse Analysis*. London: Continuum.
Peccei, J. S. 2000. *Child Language*. 北京:外语教学与研究出版社.
Pinker, S. 1994. *The Language Instinct*. Penguin Books Ltd.
Poole, S. C. 2000. *An Introduction to Linguistics*. 北京:外语教学与研究出版社.
Quirk, R., Greenbaum, S., Leech, G. & Svartvik, J. 1985. A Comprehensive Grammar of the English Language. London: Longman.
Radden, G. & Dirven, R. 2007. *Cognitive English Grammar*. Amsterdam: John Benjamins.

Radford, A. 2000. *Syntax: A Minimalist Introduction*. 北京:外语教学与研究出版社.
Radford, A. 2002. *Syntactic Theory and the Structure of English: A Minimalist Approach*. 北京:北京大学出版社.
Radford, A. et al. 2000. *Linguistics: An Introduction*. 北京:外语教学与研究出版社.
Reid, J. M. 1986. Learning style preferences of EFL students. *TESOL Quarterly* 20, 87—111.
Richards, J. C. et al. 2002. *Longman Dictionary of Language Teaching and Applied Linguistics* (Third Edition). London: Pearson.
Richards, J. C., Platt, J. & Platt, H. 1992/2000. *Longman Dictionary of Language Teaching and Applied Linguistics*. 北京:外语教学与研究出版社.
Richards, J. C., Platt, J. & Weber, H. 1985. *Longman Dictionary of Applied Linguistics*. Harlow: Longman.
Richards, J. C. & Rodgers, T. S. 1986/2008. *Approaches and Methods in Language Teaching* (Second Edition). 北京:外语教学与研究出版社.
Richardson, J. E. 2007. *Analysing Newspapers: An Approach From Critical Discourse Analysis*. Basingstoke: Palgrave MacMillan.
Roach, P. 2000. *English Phonetics and Phonology: A Practical Course*. 北京:外语教学与研究出版社.
Roach, P. 2001/2003. *Phonetics*. 上海:上海外语教育出版社.
Robins, R. H. 2000. *General Linguistics* (Fourth Edition). 北京:外语教学与研究出版社.
Saeed, J. I. 2009. *Semantics* (Third Edition). 北京:外语教学与研究出版社.
Salkie, R. 1995. *Text and Discourse Analysis*. London: Routledge.
Samovar, L. A., Porter, R. E. & Stefani, L. A. 1981/2000. *Communication Between Cultures*. 北京:外语教学与研究出版社.
Sapir, E. 1921/2002. *Language*. 北京:外语教学与研究出版社.
Saussure, F. D. 2002. *Course in General Linguistics*. 北京:外语教学与研究出版社.
Schendl, H. 2001/2003. *Historical Linguistics*. 上海:上海外语教育出版社.
Schiffrin, D. 1994. *Approaches to Discourse*. Oxford: Blackwell.
Scollon, R. & Scollon, S. W. 2000. *Intercultural Communication: A Discourse Approach*. 北京:外语教学与研究出版社.
Scovel, T. 1998/2000. *Psycholinguistics*. 上海:上海外语教育出版社.
Searle, J. 1969. *Speech Acts: An Essay in the Philosophy of Language*. Cambridge: Cambridge University Press.
Searle, J. 1979. *Expression and Meaning: Studies in the Theory of Speech Acts*. Cambridge: Cambridge University Press.
Selinker, L. 1972/1974. Interlanguage. In Richards, J. C. (ed.) *Error Analysis: Perspectives on Second Language Acquisition*. London: Longman.
Selinker, L. 1992. *Rediscovering Interlanguage*. London: Longman.
Shore, C. M. 1995. *Individual Differences in Language Development*. Thousand Oaks: Sage Publications.
Short, M. H. 1996. *Exploring the Language of Poems, Plays and Prose*. London: Longman.
Simpson, J. M. Y. 1984. *A First Course in Linguistics*. Edinburgh: Edinburgh University Press.
Simpson, P. 1997. *Language Through Literature: An Introduction*. London: Routledge.
Sinclair, J. & Coulthard, R. M. 1975. *Towards an Analysis of Discourse*. Oxford: Oxford University Press.
Skinner, B. F. 1957. *Verbal Behavior*. New York: Appleton Century.

Spencer, A. 1991. *Morphological Theory*. Oxford: Blackwell.
Spencer, A. 2001. Morphology. In Aronoff, M. & Rees-Miller, J. (ed.) *The Handbook of Linguistics*. 北京:外语教学与研究出版社.
Stern, H. H. 1975. What can we learn from the good language learner? *Canadian Modern Language Review*, 31, 304—18.
Stockwell, R. & Minkova, D. 2001. *English Words: History and structure*. Cambridge: Cambridge University Press.
Stork, F. C. & Widdowson, J. D. A. 1974. *Learning about Linguistics: An Introductory Workbook*. London: Hutchinson.
Stubbs, M. 1983. *Discourse Analysis*. Oxford: Blackwell.
Swain, M. 1985. Communicative competence: Some roles of comprehensible input and comprehensible output in its development. In Gass, S. & Madden, C. (eds.) *Input in Second Language Acquisition*. New York: Newbury House.
Swain, M. 2005. The output hypothesis: theory and research. In Hinkel, E. (ed.) *Handbook of Research in Second Language Teaching and Learning*. Mahwah, NJ: Lawrence Erlbaum.
Talmy, L. 2000. *Toward a Cognitive Semantics*. Cambridge, Mass.: The MIT Press.
Taylor, J. 2001. *Linguistic Categorization* (Second Edition). 北京:外语教学与研究出版社.
Thomas, J. 1995. *Meaning in Interaction: An Introduction to Pragmatics*. London: Longman.
Thompson, G. 1996/2008. *Introducing Functional Grammar* (Second Edition). 北京:外语教学与研究出版社.
Thornborrow, J. & Wareing, S. 2000. *Patterns in Language: Stylistics for Students of Language and Literature*. 北京:外语教学与研究出版社.
Toolan, M. 1996. *Language in Literature: An Introduction to Stylistics*. London: Arnold.
Townsend, D. J. & Bever, T. G. 2001. *Sentence Comprehension: The Integration of Habits and Rules*. Cambridge, MA: MIT Press.
Trask, R. L. 2000. *Historical Linguistics*. 北京:外语教学与研究出版社.
Traugott, E. C. & Pratt, M. L. 1980. *Linguistics for Students of Literature*. New York: Harcourt Brace Jovanovich, INC.
Trudgill, P. 1974. *Sociolinguistics: An Introduction to Language and Society*. Harmondsworth: Penguin.
Ungerer, F. & Schmid, H. J. 2008. *An Introduction to Cognitive Linguistics* (Second Edition). 北京:外语教学与研究出版社.
Verschueren, J. 1999. *Understanding Pragmatics*. London: Arnold.
Wardhaugh, R. 1976. *The Contexts of Language*. Rowley, MA: Newbury House.
Wardhaugh, R. 1986/2000. *An Introduction to Sociolinguistics*. 北京:外语教学与研究出版社.
Widdowson, H. G. 1975. *Stylistics and the Teaching of Literature*. London: Longman.
Widdowson, H. G. 1992. *Practical Stylistics*. Oxford: Oxford University Press.
Widdowson, H. G. 1999. *Teaching Language as Communication*. 上海:上海外语教育出版社.
Willis, D. & Willis, J. 2007. *Doing Task-based Teaching*. Oxford: Oxford University Press.
Wittgenstein, L. 1953. *Philosophical Investigations*. Oxford: Blackwell.
Wright, L. & Hope, J. 2000. *Stylistics: A Practical Coursebook*. 北京:外语教学与研究出版社.
Yule, G. 1996/2000. *Pragmatics*. 上海:上海外语教育出版社.
Yule, G. 2000. *The Study of Language* (Second Edition). 北京:外语教学与研究出版社.
Yule, G. 2006. *The Study of Language* (Third Edition). Cambridge: Cambridge University Press.

陈原,1983,《社会语言学》。上海:学林出版社。
程雨民,2004,《英语语体学》(修订本)。上海:上海外语教育出版社。
戴炜栋,2005,《新编简明语言学教程》。上海:上海外语教育出版社。
董启明,2008,《新编英语文体学教程》。北京:外语教学与研究出版社。
杜瑞清、田德新、李本现,2004,《跨文化交际学选读》。西安:西安交通大学出版社。
何自然、陈新仁,2004,《当代语用学》。北京:外语教学与研究出版社。
胡壮麟,1994,《语篇的衔接与连贯》。上海:上海外语教育出版社。
胡壮麟,2000,《理论文体学》。北京:外语教学与研究出版社。
胡壮麟,2001,《语言学教程》。北京:北京大学出版社。
胡壮麟、姜望琪,2002. *Linguistics: An Advanced Course Book*. 北京:北京大学出版社。
胡壮麟、朱永生、张德禄、李战子,2005,《系统功能语言学概论》。北京:北京大学出版社。
黄国文,2001,《语篇分析的理论与实践——广告语篇研究》。上海:上海外语教育出版社。
计道宏,2006,《语言学教程自学纲要》。天津:南开大学出版社。
贾玉新,1997,《跨文化交际学》。上海:上海外语教育出版社。
李赋宁,1991,《英语史》。北京:商务印书馆。
李延福,1988,《英语语言学基础读本》。济南:山东大学出版社。
刘世生,1998,《西方文体学论纲》。济南:山东教育出版社。
刘振前、时小英,2002,隐喻的文化本质与外语教学.《外语与外语教学》第2期,17—20。
秦秀白,1986,《文体学概论》。长沙:湖南教育出版社。
石定栩,2002,《乔姆斯基的形式句法》。北京:北京语言大学出版社。
童庆炳,1994,《文体与文体的创造》。昆明:云南人民出版社。
王守元,2000,《英语文体学要略》。济南:山东大学出版社。
王玉龙,1996,《英语修辞与写作》。青岛:青岛出版社。
王佐良、丁往道(主编),1987,《英语文体学引论》。北京:外语教学与研究出版社。
文秋芳,1995,《英语语言学导论》。南京:江苏教育出版社。
徐通锵,1991,《历史语言学》。北京:商务印书馆。
徐有志,1992,《现代英语文体学》。开封:河南大学出版社。
许力生,2004,《跨文化交际英语教程》。上海:上海外语教育出版社
赵艳芳,2001,《认知语言学概论》。上海:上海外语教育出版社。
朱永生、严世清、苗兴伟,2004,《功能语言学导论》。上海:上海外语教育出版社。
祝畹瑾,1992,《社会语言学概论》。长沙:湖南教育出版社。

Glossary

A

abbreviation 缩写;缩略法
absolute synonym 绝对同义词
accent 口音;重音
accusative (case) 受格;宾格
achievement test 成绩测试
acoustic phonetics 声学语音学
acquisition 习得
acronym 首字母缩写词
acronymy 首字母缩略法
active 主动的
actor 动作者
address form 称谓形式
addressee 受话者
addresser 发话者
adjacency pair 相邻话对
adjective 形容词
adjective phrase 形容词短语
adverb 副词
adverbial phrase 副词短语
affective meaning 情感意义
affective strategy 情感策略
affix 词缀
affixation 词缀法
affricate 塞擦音
agreement 一致
Agreement Maxim 一致准则
alliteration 头韵
allomorph 语素变体
allophone 音位变体
alveolar 齿龈;齿龈音
ambiguity 歧义
American structuralism 美国结构主义
analogical creation 类推造词
analytic language 分析型语言
anapaest 抑抑扬格
anaphor 回指词
anaphoric reference 回指照应
antecedent 先行词
anthropological linguistics 人类语言学
anticipatory co-articulation 先期协同发音
anticlimax 突降法;渐降法
antithesis 对偶
antonym 反义词
antonymy 反义现象;反义关系
anxiety 焦虑
aphasia 失语症
applied linguistics 应用语言学
appreciatory meaning 褒义
Approbation Maxim 赞誉准则
appropriateness condition 适宜条件;得体条件
arbitrariness 任意性
argument 论元;谓项;主目
articulatory phonetics 发音语音学
aspirated 送气的
assimilation 同化
associative meaning 联想意义
assonance 准押韵;半谐音
Audiolingual Method 视听法
auditory learning 听觉学习
auditory phonetics 听觉语音学
auxiliary 助词

B

baby-talk 儿语;娃娃腔
backformation 逆构词法;逆成法
backsliding 回滑现象
backwash 反拨
balanced sentence 平衡句
base 词基
behaviorism 行为论;行为主义
behaviouristic 行为论的
bilabial 双唇音
bilingualism 双语现象
Binary Principle 二分原则
Binding Theory 约束理论
Black English 黑人英语
Black English Vernacular 黑人英语方言
blend 混成词
blending 混成法
borrowed word 借词;外来词

bottom-up processing 自下而上加工
bound morpheme 粘着语素
bow-wow theory 摹声说
broad transcription 宽式音标
broadening(语义)扩大
Broca's aphasia 布罗卡失语症
Broca's area 布罗卡区

C

caregiver talk (同 caretaker talk)照看语
caretaker talk 保姆式语言
case 格
Case Grammar 格语法
Case Theory 格理论
cataphoric reference 下指照应
categorization 范畴化
category 范畴
causative 使役的；使役动词
c-command c-统制
child-directed language 儿向言语
chunking 组块；语块
classical rhetoric 古典修辞学
Classical Theory 古典理论
clausal ellipsis 小句省略
clausal substitution 小句替代
clause 小句
climax 高潮
climax repetition 高潮重复
clipping 截短法
closed-class word 封闭性词类
co-articulation 协同发音
co-articulation effect 协同发音效应
coda 音节尾
code 语码
code model 语码模式
code switching 语码转换
cognitive category 认知范畴
Cognitive Grammar 认知语法
cognitive linguistics 认知语言学
cognitive meaning 认知意义
cognitive strategy 认知策略
coherence 连贯
cohesion 衔接
co-hyponyms 共下义词
collocation 搭配
collocative meaning 搭配意义

color term 色彩词
co-meronyms 共"部分"词
command 命令；指令
commissive 承诺类
communication strategy 交际策略
Communicative Approach 交际法
communicative competence 交际能力
communicative dynamism 交际动态
comparative 比较级
comparative reference 比较照应
competence 能力
complement 补语；补足语成分
complementaries 互补反义词
complementary distribution 互补分布
complementary terms 互补反义词
complementizer 补语化成分
complementizer phrase 补语化短语
complete synonym 完全同义词
complex sentence 复合句
complex word 复合词
componential analysis 成分分析
compound 合成词
compound sentence 合成句
compound word 合成词
compounding 合成法
computational linguistics 计算语言学
conative function 意动功能
conceptual domain 概念域
conceptual meaning 概念意义
conceptual metaphor 概念隐喻
conceptual metonymy 概念转喻
conceptualism 概念论
concord 一致
conjunction 连接；连接词
connotation 内涵[义]
connotative meaning 内涵意义
consonance 辅音韵；和声
consonant 辅音
consonant cluster 辅音丛
constative 表述句
constituent 成分
constituent command 成分统制
construct validity 结构效度
construction 构式；结构
contact 接触

contact language 接触语;交际语
container schema 容器图式
content validity 内容效度
content word 实词
context 语境
contextual meaning 语境意义
contextual theory 语境观
contradiction 矛盾关系
contradictory terms 矛盾词
contraries 对立反义词
contrary terms 对立反义词
contrastive analysis 对比分析
conversation analysis 会话分析
conversational implicature 会话含义
conversational maxim 会话准则
converse terms 反向反义词
conversion 转化法;转类法
conversives 反向反义词
Cooperative Principle 合作原则
coordinate clause 并列小句
coordinate construction 并列结构
Copenhagen School 哥本哈根学派
creativity 创造性
creole 克里奥尔语;混合语
creolization 克里奥尔语化
criterion-referenced testing 标准参照测试
critical discourse analysis 批评话语分析
cultural transmission 文化传承
culturally-loaded word 文化负载词
culture 文化
culture-loaded word 文化负载词

D

dactyl 扬抑抑格
dative (case) 与格
deception 欺骗;佯骗
declaration 宣告类
declarative 陈述的;陈述句
deep structure 底层结构
default reasoning 默认推理;却省推理
degradation (语义) 降格
deixis 指示现象;指示词
demonstrative reference 指示照应
denotation 外延[义];所指
denotative function 指称功能
dental 齿;齿音

derivation 派生
derivational morpheme 派生语素
derivational morphology 派生形态学
derogatory meaning 贬义
descriptive 描写的
descriptive linguistics 描写语言学
design features 设计特征
determiner 限定词
determiner phrase 限定词短语
developmental order 发展顺序
deviance 偏离;变异
deviation 偏离;变异
diachronic linguistics 历时语言学
diagnostic test 诊断测试
dialect 方言
dialect continuum 方言连续体
dialectal variety 方言变体
diaphragm 隔膜
diatypic variety 功能变体
dichotomy 对分;二分法
diglossia 双语制;双言现象
dimeter 二音步诗行
ding-dong theory 先天反射说
diphthong 双元音
Direct Method 直接法
direct object 直接宾语
directive 指令类
discourse 语篇;话语
discourse analysis 语篇分析;话语分析
discourse competence 语篇能力
Discourse Grammar 语篇语法
displacement 移位性
dispreferred 非优选(语列)
distinctive feature 区别特征
divine-origin theory 神授起源说
dominance 统辖
downgraded predication 降格述谓结构
duality 二层性

E

economy principle 经济原则
elaborated code 复杂代码;完备代码
elevation (语义) 升格
elision 省音
ellipsis 省略
emotive function 情感功能

empathic strategy 移情策略
empty word 虚词
endocentric construction 向心结构
endophoric reference 内指照应
entailment 蕴涵
episodic memory 情节记忆
error 错误
error analysis 错误分析
essential condition 基本条件
ethnic group 族群
ethnography of communication 交际民族学
etymology 词源学
euphemism 委婉语
euphemistic expression 委婉表达
evolution theory 进化说
exclamatory 感叹的
exocentric construction 离心结构
exophoric reference 外指照应
experiential function 经验功能
experimental strategy 试验策略
expressive function 表达功能
expressive 表情类
Extended Standard Theory 扩展的标准理论
extrinsic motivation 外在动机

F

face validity 卷面效度;表面效度
felicity condition 适切条件;合适条件
feminine rhyme 阴韵
field dependence 场依赖型
field independence 场独立型
field of discourse 话语范围
figurative 修辞的;辞格的
figure of speech 修辞格
finite 限定成分
first language 第一语言
first language acquisition 一语习得
first pair part 第一话对成分
foot 音步
foregrounding 突出;前景化
foreign language 外语
foreigner talk 外国式语言
forensic linguistics 法律语言学
form word 形式词
formal strategy 形式策略
formalism 形式主义

fossilization 僵化;石化
free morpheme 自由语素
fricative 摩擦音
full (or perfect) homonym 同音同形异义词
function word 功能词
functional linguistics 功能语言学
functional sentence perspective 功能句法观

G

garden path sentence 花园路径句
gender 性;性别
general linguistics 普通语言学
generalized conversational implicature 一般会话含义
generative grammar 生成语法
generative linguistics 生成语言学
Generosity Maxim 慷慨准则
genitive (case) 所有格
Given 旧信息;已知信息
glide 滑音
Glossematics 语符学
glottal 声门音
goal 目标
Government and Binding Theory 管约论
grammar 语法
Grammar Translation 语法翻译法
grammatical category 语法范畴
grammatical cohesion 语法衔接
grammatical competence 语法能力
grammatical device 语法手段
grammatical meaning 语法义
grammatical word 语法词
grammaticalization 语法化
graphology 语相学;字系学
Great Vowel Shift 元音大迁移

H

head 中心语;中心词
head movement 中心语移位
headed construction 中心结构
hierarchical network model 层级网络模型
hierarchical structure 等级结构;层次结构
high variety 高变体
high-context culture 高语境文化
historical linguistics 历史语言学
holonym 表"整体"的词;整体词

holophrase 独词语
homograph 同形异义词
homonym 同音/形异义词
homonymy 同音/形异义现象;同音/形异义关系
homophone 同音异义词
honest deception 佯骗
hyperbole 夸张
hyponym 下义词
hyponymy 上下义关系

I

iamb 抑扬格
iconicity 象似性
iconicity of complexity 复杂象似性
iconicity of distance 距离象似性
iconicity of order 顺序象似性
idiolect 个人语言
illocution 言外行为;行事行为
image schema 意象图式
immediate constituent analysis 直接成分分析
imperative 祈使的;祈使句
implicature 含义
inconsistency 自相矛盾
indexical 指示词
indirect object 间接宾语
indirect speech act 间接言语行为
inference 推理
inflection phrase 屈折短语
inflectional morpheme 屈折语素
inflectional morphology 屈折形态学
information structure 信息结构
initialism 首字母拼音词
innateness hypothesis 天赋论
input 输入
input hypothesis 输入假设
insertion sequence 插入语列
instrumental motivation 工具性动机
integrative motivation 融合性动机;整合型动机
interactive theory 互动论
intercultural communication 跨文化交际
interdental 双齿音
interjection 感叹词
interlanguage 中介语
interlanguage theory 中介语理论

internalization strategy 内化策略
International Phonetic Alphabet 国际音标
interpersonal function 人际功能
interrogative 疑问的;疑问句
interrogative operator 疑问操作词
intonation 语调
intonation contour 语调升降曲线;语调模式
intonation pattern 语调模式
intrinsic motivation 内在动机
invention theory 发明说
irony 反讽

J

jargon 行话;黑话

K

kinesthetic learning 动觉学习;体验学习
kinship term 亲属词

L

labial 唇;唇音
labiodental 唇齿音
la-la theory 浪漫说
landmark 界标
language 语言
language acquisition 语言习得
language acquisition device 语言习得机制
language aptitude 语言学能
language comprehension 语言理解
language contact 语言接触
language faculty 语言机能
language production 语言产生
langue 语言
larynx 喉
late assignment of syntax theory 后句法指派理论
late closure strategy 后闭合策略
lateral 边音;边音的
lateralization 大脑功能偏侧化
learning 学习
learning strategy 学习焦虑
learning style 学习风格
lenition 辅音弱化
lexeme 词位
lexical cohesion 词汇衔接
lexical device 词汇手段
lexical meaning 词汇义

lexical semantics 词汇语义学
lexicalization 词汇化
lexicon 词库;词典
lexis 词汇
linear structure 线性结构
lingua franca 通用语
linguistic community 语言社团
linguistic determinism 语言决定论
linguistic relativism 语言相对论
linguistics 语言学
liquid 流音
literal meaning 本义;字面义
litotes 曲言法
loan word 借词;外来词
local structure 局部结构
locution 言说行为;发话行为
London School 伦敦学派
long-term memory 长期记忆
long vowel 长元音
loose sentence 松散句
low variety 低变体
low-context culture 低语境文化

M

macrolinguistics 宏观语言学
macrostructure 宏观结构
main clause 主句
main stress 主重音
Manner Maxim 方式准则
manner of articulation 发音方式
marked 有标记的
masculine rhyme 阳韵
meaning 意义
meaning shift 词义转移
mechanistic 机械论的
meiosis 弱陈法
mental lexicon 大脑词库
merge 合并
merging operation 合并操作
meronym 表"部分"的词;部分词
meronymy 部分与整体关系
message 信息
metacognitive strategy 元认知策略
metafunctions 元功能;纯理功能
metalingual function 元语言功能
metanalysis 元分析;再分化

metaphor 隐喻
metaphoric competence 隐喻能力
metaphorical code-switching 喻意型语码转换
metathesis 语音易位
meter 格律
metonymy 转喻
metrical pattern 格律模式
microstructure 微观结构
Middle English 中古英语
minimal attachment strategy 最小附加策略
minimal pair 最小对比对
minimal set 最小对比集合
Minimalist Program 最简方案
mistake 差错
mixed sentence 混合句
mode of discourse 话语方式
Modern English 现代英语
Modesty Maxim 谦虚准则
modifier 修饰语;修饰成分
modular theory 模块理论
monitoring strategy 监控策略
monometer 单音步诗行
monophthong 单元音
monosyllabic 单音节的
mood 语气
morph 形素;语素形式
morpheme 语素;词素;形素
morphology 形态学
motherese 妈妈语
motivation 动机
Move α α 移位
movement 移位
Movement Theory 移位理论
multilingualism 多语现象
multimodal discourse analysis 多模态话语分析

N

naming view 命名观
narrow transcription 窄式音标
narrowing (语义)缩小
nasal 鼻音
nasal cavity 鼻腔
native word 本族语词
negative 否定的;否定结构
negation 否定句;否定结构

negative transfer 负迁移
neo-Firthian school 新弗斯学派
neologism 新词
neo-Saussurean linguistics 新索绪尔语言学
New 新信息
node 节点
nominal ellipsis 名词省略
nominal substitution 名词替代
nominative (case) 主格
nonrestrictive relative clause 非限定性关系从句
non-standard dialect 非标准方言
nonterminal node 非终极节点
no-place predicate 空元谓词
norm-referenced testing 常模参照测试
noun 名词
noun 名词短语
nucleus 核心；音节核
number 数

O

object 宾语
objective testing 客观测试
Old English 古英语
one-place predicate 一元谓词
onomatopoeia 象声词；拟声法
onset 节首
opaque word 隐性词
open-class word 开放词类
operator movement 操作词移位
operator phrase 操作词短语
oral cavity 口腔
oral-gesture theory 口头手势说
output 输出
output hypothesis 输出假设
over-lexicalization 过度词汇化
overregularity 过度规则；超规则现象
overstatement 夸张；夸大其词
oxymoron 矛盾修饰法

P

palatal 硬腭；硬腭音
paradigm 范式；词形变化表
paradigm analysis 词形变化分析
paradigmatic relation 聚合关系
paradox 悖论；似是而非的隽语

parallel model 平行模式
parallelism 排比；平行结构
paraphrase 解释；同义句
parole 言语
parsing 句法分析；切分
part of speech 词类；词性
participle 分词
particularized conversational implicature 特殊会话含义
passive 被动的
pejorative meaning 贬义
pentameter 五音步诗行
performance 运用
performative 施为句
periodic sentence 圆周句
perlocution 言后行为；取效行为
permanent memory 永久记忆；长期记忆
perseverative assimilation 后滞同化
person 人称
personal pronoun 人称代词
personal reference 人称照应
pharyngeal cavity 咽腔
pharynx 咽
phatic communion 寒暄语；寒暄交谈
phatic function 寒暄功能
phone 音子
phoneme 音位
phonetic notation 语音注音法
phonetic transcription 语音转写
phonetics 语音学
phonology 音位学
phonotactics 音位配列学
phrase structure 短语
phrase structure rule 短语结构规则
phrase-marker 短语标记
pidgin 洋泾浜语
pitch 音高；声调高低
place of articulation 发音部位
placement test 分班测试
planning strategy 计划策略
plosive 爆破音；爆发音
plural 复数
poetic function 诗性功能
Politeness Principle 礼貌原则
polyglot 通晓多种语言的人

polysemic word 多义词
polysemy 一词多义现象
polysyllabic 多音节的
pooh-pooh theory 感叹说
positive transfer 正迁移
possessive pronoun 属格代词
possessive determiner 属格限定词
practicality 实用性
practice strategy 操练策略
pragmatics 语用学
Prague School 布拉格学派
pre-announcement 宣布前语列
predicate 谓词;谓语
predication 述谓结构
predication analysis 述谓分析
predicator 谓语
preference organization 优选结构
preferred 优选(语列)
prefix 前缀
prefixation 前缀法
pre-invitation 邀请前语列
preparatory condition 准备条件
preposition 介词
preposition phrase 介词短语
pre-request 请求前语列
prescriptive 规定的
pre-sequence 预示语列;前语列
presupposition 预设;前提
presupposition trigger 预设触发语
primary stress 主重音
principles and parameters theory 原则与参数理论
process 过程
productivity 能产性
proficiency test 水平测试
progressive assimilation 顺同化
pronominal 代词
pronoun 代词
proposition 命题
propositional content condition 命题内容条件
prosodic feature 韵律特征
prototype 原型
prototype theory 原型理论
psycholinguistics 心理语言学
pun 双关
purr word 褒词

Q
Quality Maxim 质准则
Quantity Maxim 量准则

R
reanalysis 再分析;重新分析
Received Pronunciation 标准发音
recursive 递归的
reference 指称;照应
referential function 指称功能
reflected meaning 反射意义
reflexive 反身代词
regional dialect 地区性方言
register 语域
regressive assimilation 逆同化
reiteration 重述
Relation Maxim 关系准则
relative terms 关系词
reliability 信度
repetition 重复
representation 表征;表达式
representative 阐述类
restricted code 局限性代码
restrictive relative clause 限定性关系从句
Rheme 述位
rhetoric 修辞学
rhyme 韵;押韵
rhyme-scheme 押韵格式
rhyming pattern 押韵模式
rhythmic pattern 韵律模式;节奏模式
Role and Reference Grammar 角色与指称语法
root 词根

S
Sapir-Whorf hypothesis 萨丕尔—沃尔夫假说
schema 图式
second language 第二语言
second language acquisition 二语习得
second pair part 第二话对成分
secondary stress 次重音
segment 音段
semantic analysis 语义分析

semantic anomaly 语义异常
semantic feature 语义特征
semantic field 语义场
semantic memory 语义记忆
semantic network 语义网络
semantic strategy 语义策略
semantics 语义学
semiotic triangle 符号三角;语义三角
semiotics 符号学
semi-vowel 半元音
sense 意义
sense relation 语义关系
sensory store 感觉储存
sentence 句子
sentence meaning 句义
sentence structure 句子结构
sequence of development 发展序列
serial model 序列模式
shortening 缩短法
short-term memory 短时记忆
signifiant/signifier 能指
signifié/signified 所指
silent period 沉默期
simple sentence 简单句
simple word 简单词
sincerity condition 真诚条件
singular 单数
situational code-switching 情景型语码转换
snarlword 贬词
social dialect 社会方言
social meaning 社会意义
social strategy 社会策略
sociolect 社会方言
sociolinguistic competence 社会语言能力
sociolinguistics 社会语言学
source domain 源域
sound symbolism 语音象征
speaker meaning 说话者意义
specifier 标志语;标句词
speech act 言语行为
Speech Act Theory 言语行为理论
speech community 言语社团
speech organ 发音器官
speech sound 语音
speech variety 言语变体

spreading activation model 扩散激活模型
standard dialect 标准方言
Standard Theory 标准理论
statement 陈述句
stem 词干
stop 塞音
story grammar 故事语法
strategic competence 策略能力
Stratificational Grammar 层次语法
stress 重音
structural approach 结构法
structural word 结构词
structure word 结构词
style 文体;风格
stylistic analysis 文体分析
stylistic meaning 文体意义
stylistics 文体学
subject 主语
subjective testing 主观测试
subordinate clause 从句
subordinate construction 从属结构
substitution 替代
suffix 后缀
suffixation 后缀法
superlative 最高级
superordinate 上义词
suprasegmental 超音段
suprasegmental feature 超音段特征
surface structure 表层结构
syllable 音节
Sympathy Maxim 同情准则
synchronic linguistics 共时语言学
synecdoche 提喻
synonym 同义词
synonymy 同义现象;同义关系
syntactic structure 句法结构
syntagmatic relation 组合关系
synthetic language 综合型语言
syntax 句法;句法学
system 系统
systemic functional linguistics 系统功能言学

T

taboo 禁忌语
Tact Maxim 得体准则
Tagmemics 法位学

tag question 附加疑问句
target domain 目标域
Task-based Approach 任务教学法
tautology 同义反复；冗辞
telegraphic speech 电报式言语
temporal dialect 时间方言；历时变体
tenor of discourse 话语基调
tense 时态
terminal node 终极节点
tetrameter 四音步诗行
text 语篇；篇章
text linguistics 篇章语言学
textual function 语篇功能
textual pattern 语篇模式
texture 织体；语篇特征
thematic meaning 主位意义
thematic progression 主位推进
thematic structure 主位结构
Theme 主位
theoretical linguistics 理论语言学
θ-Theory 题元理论
tone 声调；音调
tone group 调群
top-down processing 自上而下加工
trace 虚迹
trachea 气管
traditional grammar 传统语法
trajector 轨迹
transference 转义
transferred epithet 移就；移位修饰
transformational rule 转换规则
transformational-generative（TG）grammar 转换生成语法
transition relevance place 转换关联位置
transitivity 及物性
transparent word 透明词
tree diagram 树形图
trimeter 三音步诗行
triphthong 三合元音
trochee 扬抑格
turn-taking 话轮转换
two-place predicate 二元谓词

U

unaspirated 不送气的
underlying structure 底层结构

understatement 低调陈述；含蓄表达
universal grammar 普遍语法
unmarked 无标记的
utterance 语段；话语
uvula 小舌；小舌音

V

validity 效度
value dimension 价值维度
variety 变体
velar 软腭音
velum 软腭
verb 动词
verb phrase 动词短语
verbal ellipsis 动词省略
verbal or linguistic repertoire 语言知识库；全部语言变体
verbal substitution 动词替代
vernacular 本土语；本地话；方言
visual learning 视觉学习
vocabulary 词汇
vocal cords 声带
vocal folds 声带
voice 语态
voiced (sound) 浊音
voiceless (sound) 清音
vowel 元音

W

Wernicke's aphasia 韦尼克失语症
Wernicke's area 韦尼克区
wh-movement wh-移位
wh-operator wh-操作词
wh-question 特殊疑问句
word 词；单词
wordclass 词类
word formation 构词
word meaning 词义
word order 词序
working memory 工作记忆

X

X-bar X-语杠
X-Bar Theory X-语杠理论

Y

yes-no question 一般疑问句
yo-he-ho theory 杭育声说

《语言学基础教程(第二版)》相关图书推荐
"十二五"普通高等教育本科国家级规划教材

北京高等教育精品教材;北京大学优秀教材;北京大学规划教材
《语言学教程(第五版)》胡壮麟主编,姜望琪、钱军副主编

《语言学教程》自1988年首次出版以来,改版五次,印刷九十余次,发行量达二百五十万册。目前已被国内高等院校普遍作为英语专业本科、硕士语言学方向必修教材以及考研必读教材,并吸引了大量对语言学感兴趣的非英语专业读者。使用本书为教材的老师可以免费申请配套课件!

《语言学教程(第五版)》配套练习册
《语言学教程(第五版)练习册》

胡壮麟 主编,姜望琪、钱军副 主编

配合教程第五版调整练习内容,力求和《语言学教程》完全配套;
增加参考阅读,方便学有余力的读者自学;
以 QUESTIONS AND EXERCISES 的形式,提炼学生学习、考研需关注的主要知识点。

若您想更深入、更系统地进行语言学研究,请参照
《语言学高级教程(第二版)》

胡壮麟、姜望琪 主编

为我国英语专业研究生,特别国外语言学与应用语言学专业的研究生编写的语言学教材;
内部语言学与外部语言学并重,理论语言学与应用语言学兼顾;
作者均为国内知名语言学家,各章节脉络清晰,相互渗透。

其他相关推荐

《系统功能语言学概论(第三版)》	胡壮麟 等
《语篇语言学研究》	姜望琪
《对比语言学导论(英文版)》	柯 平
《英语词汇学教程》	夏 洋
《认知隐喻学(第二版)》	胡壮麟
《语言符号学》	王铭玉
《语言哲学研究》(上、下)	王 寅
《语言与文体》(上、下) D. McIntyre and B. Busse	申 丹 导读
《批评话语分析方法》 Ruth Wodak and Michael Meyer	李战子 导读
《语篇研究——跨越小句的意义》 J.R. Martin and David Rose	王振华 导读
《(批评)话语分析的新议程—理论.方法与跨学科究》 Ruth Wodak and Paul Chilton	苗兴伟 导读
《论辩话语中的策略操控—语用论辩学拓展》 Frans van Eemeren	毛浩然,吴 鹏 导读
《交际中的人际关系仪式—群内仪式互动研究》 Daniel Z. Kadar	陈新仁 导读
《语言学与应用语言学百科全书》	梅德明
《基于语料库的当代美国政治语篇的架构隐喻模式分析： 以布什与奥巴马的演讲为例》	汪少华,梁婧玉
《英语数字素养评价研究》	张 薇
《日汉对比认知语言学——基于中国日语学习者偏误的分析》	王 忻
《语言与社会》	朱 跃
《中西法律语言与文化对比研究》	张法连
《计量文体学导论》	施建军

即将出版

《认知翻译学》	文 旭、肖开容
《认知翻译学—— 基于体认语言学的思考》	王 寅
《意识与翻译》	岳 峰
《国家语言能力理论体系构建研究》	文秋芳、张天伟
《高校外语教师专业学习共同体建设的理论研究》	文秋芳、任庆梅

《语言学基础教程》(第二版)

尊敬的老师:

　　您好!

　　为了方便您更好地使用本教材,获得最佳教学效果,我们特向使用该书作为教材的教师赠送本教材配套课件资料。如有需要,请完整填写"教师联系表"并加盖所在单位系(院)公章,免费向出版社索取。

北京大学出版社

教 师 联 系 表

教材名称	《语言学基础教程》(第二版)			
姓名:	性别:	职务:		职称:
E-mail:		联系电话:	邮政编码:	
供职学校:		所在院系:		
				(章)
学校地址:				
教学科目与年级:			班级人数:	
通信地址:				

　　填写完毕后,请将此表邮寄给我们,我们将为您免费寄送本教材配套资料,谢谢!

北京市海淀区成府路205号
北京大学出版社外语编辑部　刘文静　　　　外语编辑部电话:010-62754382
邮政编码:100871　　　　　　　　　　　　邮 购 部 电 话:010-62534449
电子邮箱:liuwenjing008@163.com　　　　　市场营销部电话:010-62750672